The Ji Hong Taiji System

EVOLUTIONARY THEORY   APPLICATION   METHODOLOGY

HONG YUAN LUO AND JENNIFER GU

Ji Hong International Studies Services Limited

I. Taiji I. Title
© 2005, 2004, 1988 by the Ji Hong Tai Chi College
First published in China in 1988 by the Guangdong Higher Education Press
Second printing 2004
Third printing 2005
All rights reserved 10 9 8 7 6 5 4 3 2 1
Printed in China
Published by the Ji Hong International Studies Services Limited
Edmonton, Alberta, CANADA
Luo, Hong Yuan and Gu, Jennifer.

       The Ji Hong Taiji System:

       Evolutionary Theory, Application and Methodology— 3rd ed. p. cm.

       Includes bibliographical references and index.

       ISBN: 0-9736786-0-7

Note to Reader:
The author, translators and publisher of this text shall not be held responsible for any injury or loss suffered in any way or manner by any reader or user of this text. Any application of the techniques, ideas and suggestions in this text shall be at the sole risk of the reader or user of this text. The physical and psychological exercises described in this text may be too strenuous for some readers. Before engaing in any physical exercises contained in this text, the reader shall consult his or her physician for advice. The readers, their successors and assigns, hereby absolutely and forever release any claims that they may or might have as against the author, translators and publisher of this text for any injury or loss including death from the use or application of this text.

LUO HONG YUAN[羅紅元] is the third son of renowned Taijiquan master and scholar Luo Ji Hong[羅基宏]. He began his martial arts training under the instruction of his father at the age of 6. He subsequently trained under other Taiji masters, most notably Gu Liu Xin[顧留馨] and Lei Mu Ni[雷慕尼]. In 1982, Hong Yuan graduated from the Guangzhou Physical Education Institute having specialized in Wushu. He became an instructor and lecturer of Wushu at the South China Teachers University. In 1984 he won a gold medal in Taijiquan form at the Wu Han[武漢] International Taijiquan and Sword Performance and Tournament Conference. It was also during this period that Hong Yuan published a number of articles and dissertations including A Simple Analysis of Taijiquan Internal Energy and Theory which won awards at the First National Conference on Taijiquan Dissertation and the First National Wushu Study Conference.

In 1988, Hong Yuan accepted an invitation from Newberry College in the United States to hold a series of seminars on Qigong and Taijiquan. That same year he conducted a Taijiquan workshop in the city of Calgary in Canada. In 1991, he and his wife Gu Dai Juan[古岱娟] established the Ji Hong Tai Chi College in Edmonton, Canada. Since then, Hong Yuan has continued to study and analyse Taijiquan. He has maintained the traditional concepts of Taiji while developing modern scientific methods to explain them. His efforts have produced a large number of students who have won numerous awards in national and International Taijiquan Forms and Push Hands competitions.

In his efforts to promote Chinese Wushu, Luo Hong Yuan was elected President of both the Canadian Chinese Kuo Shu Federation (CCKSF) and the United Wushu Federation in 1997. He was elected First Vice-President of the Confederation of Canadian Wushu Organizations and named Head Coach of Wushu Team Canada. That year, he led the team to the World Wushu Championships in Rome, Italy. In 1999 he was selected to be Team Manager of Sanshou Team Canada and took the national team to the World Wushu Championships in Hong Kong, China. He has received an Outstanding Achievement Award from the Mayor of the City of Edmonton. In 2004, Luo Hong Yuan passed the international qualification exams and has been recognized by the International Wushu Federation in Beijing as a Level A International Wushu Adjudicator and a 7th Duan [七段](grade) holder in Wushu.

GU DAI JUAN [古岱娟] began her martial arts training at the age of 8, followed by instruction in Taijiquan by Masters Luo Ji Hong, Gu Liu Xin and Lei Mu Ni. She graduated in 1985 from the Guangzhou Physical Education Institute with a specialization in Wushu and obtained a teaching position at the South China Normal University.

In 1983 she began her competition career by winning the gold medal in the mixed male/female Taijiquan category at the Guangdong[廣東] Provincial Games. Dai Juan was the gold medalist in Women's Taijiquan at the National Institute of Physical Education Invitational Tournament in 1984. That same year, she won the gold medal in Women's Traditional Taijiquan at the Wuhan International Taijiquan and Sword Competition. In 1986 she won the silver medal in Women's Taijiquan at the Guangdong provincial Games. In 1988 she was the gold medal finalist in Female Taijiquan and Taiji Weapons at the Guangzhou Taijiquan and Sword Selection Competition.

That year she was invited to hold a series of instructional seminars in Taijiquan and modern Wushu in Calgary, Canada. In 1991 she helped her husband, Luo Hong Yuan establish the Ji Hong Tai Chi College in Edmonton, Canada and has been dedicated to the training of hundreds of students in Taijiquan and modern Wushu. As a result, her pupils have filled more than 26 positions on Wushu Team Canada in recent years and have competed in many Pan American and World Wushu Championships. She was recognized for Outstanding Accomplishment in Sport by the City of Edmonton in 1995 and 1996 the Mayor of the City of Edmonton presented her with an Outstanding Achievement Award. She was also elected Vice-President of the United Wushu Federation of Canada. She currently serves as the Chairperson (Western Region) of the Confederation of Canadian Wushu Organizations. In 2005, Master Gu was recognized by the International Wushu Federation in Beijing as an International Wushu Adjudicator. Also in 2005, Gu Dai Juan was named Head Coach of Wushu Team Canada and led the national team to the World Wushu Championships in December of that year.

PREFACE TO THE 1ST EDITION

During the latter part of the 1950's, while I was busy with organizing and promoting Wushu at the Shanghai [上海] Sports Centre, I was also preparing articles and papers on Taijiquan to be published in the local newspaper Wen Hui Bao [文匯報]. I received correspondence from a Mr. Luo Ji Hong from the city of Jie Yang [揭陽], Province of Guangdong soliciting my views and opinions on Taijiquan. Mr. Luo was at one time in poor health. However, after he began practising Taijiquan, his condition seemed to have remarkably improved. In 1963 I invited Mr. Luo to visit me in Shanghai whereupon I introduced him to the study of Wu [武] (Hao) style Taijiquan under the direction of Master Hao Shao Ru [郝少如].

Mr. Luo began a serious study of Wu (Hao) style, both in theory and in the application of push-hands. For a period of three months he practised the art with other students, exchanging his experiences and views with them. After he left Shanghai, Mr. Luo maintained contact with me through regular correspondence in which he applied modern scientific methods to explain the principles of Taijiquan.

In 1964, Mr. Luo participated in the open discussion of "About Spiral Force in Taiji" in a special column of *Study of Sport* in the Sports Journal. He and I exchanged our views regularly and Mr. Luo eventually published a number of articles entitled *Comment on "About Spiral Force in Taiji"* and *My Thoughts on Spiral Force in Taiji* and *Taiji Silk Reeling Power*. Mr. Luo's views on these topics were quite unique and were generally well-received.

In February 1975 I was asked by the Chief Editorial Board of the People's Publication Press to edit and publish a review of the five traditional styles of Taijiquan. I invited Mr. Luo to draft the section on the Wu (Hao) style of Taiji. Unfortunately, publication of the book was halted and the original draft was lost in the intervening years.

In April of 1984, at the Wuhan International Taiji Performance Competition, Mr. Luo attended, bringing his son Hong Yuan and his student Gu Dai Juan. Both Hong Yuan and Dai Juan won gold medals in the competition. As they were all staying in the designated hotel near the competition site, I was able to meet with Mr. Luo again after a separation of 20 years. We talked about our experiences in Taijiquan over the years and practiced push hands well into the night on many occasions.

On May 22, 1984, Mr. Luo left Wuhan and came to Shanghai where he continued to intensely study and practice Taijiquan with numerous practitioners. He later returned to his hometown of Jie Yang to resume his teaching. Unfortunately, his sustained, intense efforts resulted in the collapse of his health and he died. Mr. Luo was truly dedicated to the study of Taijiquan. His views on Taiji were unique and he has set an everlasting example for all students of Taijiquan.

Today, Luo Hong Yuan has published a book on Taijiquan and has held seminars on Taiji in several foreign countries. Such accomplishments are the result of his upbringing under the careful guidance of his father, Luo Ji Hong. Unfortunately, Ji Hong died too soon and did not witness the success of his son. The success of Luo Hong Yuan, however, in continuing his father's life-long passion of the study of Taiji will remain a comfort to my dear friend Luo Ji Hong.

Gu Liu Xin,
Shanghai
July 1, 1988

PREFACE TO THE 2nd EDITION

The first edition of this book was published over 17 years ago and sold out almost immediately. Over the years we have had many requests for a second printing. Consequently, we have decided to revise and supplement the first edition with our expanded knowledge of Taiji which we have accumulated these seventeen years through our teaching experience of Taiji in Canada and the application of our theories in many international competitions. We hope to share the results of our research with our readers who we hope will, in turn, enlighten us with their comments.

In this 2nd edition we have included two new chapters in Section I: first, *The Light of Taiji*; and second, *The Memoirs, Correspondence and Excerpts of Master Luo Ji Hong*. These two chapters illustrate the training experience of Master Luo Ji Hong and his views on Taiji. Recently, thanks to the generosity of the descendants of Master Gu Liu Xin, we received the bulk of twenty years of correspondence between Master Luo Ji Hong and Master Gu. This correspondence reveals the profound knowledge and insight of both Taiji masters. Copies of some of these letters are included in this revised edition. In addition, we have expanded the chapter detailing the training of Luo Ji Hong's son, Luo Hong Yuan (one of the co-authors of this book). It is hoped that through the description of the experiences of these two generations of the Luo family, the reader can have a better appreciation and understanding of the evolution of Taiji.

This revised edition retains the original sections on "Theory" and "Training" with minor changes in the chapter on "Taiji and the Theory of Yin and Yang". However, the updated chapter on "The Technique of Self-Control in Taijiquan" discusses for the first time the newly developed theories on "Air Bag-Like Elasticity (ABLE)" [氣囊式彈性体], "Taiji Qi Shi" [太極氣勢] and Taiji's "Readiness State" [太極預應狀態]. The resultant condition upon successful accomplishment of such training, and the quality and substance of Taijiquan are also discussed in print for the first time. In the chapter on "The Techniques of Control", the authors discuss the various techniques, based on Taiji Readiness State, to control the opponent. These techniques employ of a number of skills and tactics, including psychological preparation. Section III on "Training and Exercises" contains some of the practical exercises corresponding to the theoretical framework.

This 2nd edition attempts to discuss the concepts and theories of Taiji in a progressive manner. It is intended to be used as a reference book for practice and discussion. We have used some of the content of this book in our DVDs as training aids.

When the first edition of this book was published in 1988, we thanked Master Gu Liu Xin who wrote the Preface, and Master Hong Jun Sheng [洪均生] who wrote the Introduction. Today, we express our gratitude to all our friends, associates, and volunteers who assisted in translating, editing, proofing and preparing this 2nd edition for printing. Our wonderful team of volunteer translators who gave up much of their spare time to translate the Chinese edition into English:

Laurence Huang (Chicago, U.S.A.)	Chapters One and Three
Josie Tong (Edmonton, Canada)	Chapter Two
Jim Liang, Queenie Lam (Toronto, Canada)	Chapter Four
Bosco Yiu (Edmonton, Canada)	Chapters Five, Six and most of the introductory material
Paul Wan (Calgary, Canada)	Chapter Seven
Jim Liang, Michael Eng (Toronto, Canada)	Chapter Eight

Our assistant editors who helped bring the various chapters together into a cohesive and smooth flowing book:

Mark Hardes (Toronto, Canada)
Nicole Carriere (Edmonton, Canada)
David Chung (Calgary, Canada)

Our photographers whose photos in Chapters Five through Eight make a memorable visual impact:

David Ching (Calgary, Canada)
Stephen Lau (Calgary, Canada)

Our cover design is due to the artistry of:

Chen Zhi Hui (China)
Richard Anderson Omura (Edmonton, Canada)
Mark Yiu (Edmonton, Canada)

Our interior book design is by:

Mark Hardes (Toronto, Canada)

Our special thanks go to our Project Coordinator who had to wear many hats during this lengthy and time consuming process:

David Ward (Edmonton, Canada)

whom we remind of one of Master Luo Ji Hong's favourite sayings:

Time is valuable. Hurry up and practise.

Luo Hong Yuan and Gu Dai Juan
Edmonton, Canada
October 2005

太極拳技理与训练

顾留馨题

Calligraphy by Gu Liu Xin
"Taijiquan Theory and Training"

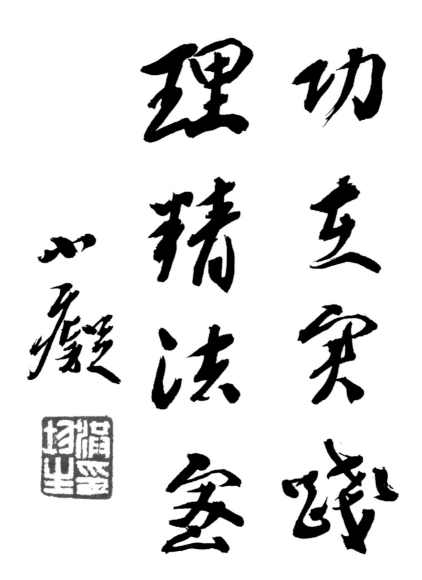

Dedication by Hong Jun Sheng
"Accurate in Theory, Profound in Principle"

6月16日来信收到。

所想意见，情辞恳恳，善于采纳，如此……！你说"致之实践，空谈无济，确似无法之水，无本之木"言简意赅，极当中肯！太极拳纵精体微密，若空言，终无所得！吾浸淫斯艺，垂二十年，良师指拨，益友切磋，日就月将，未敢稍懈；似觉有获，然诸种奥理，层出不穷，究其堂奥，殊非易易！有生之日，孜孜以求，锲而不舍，精益求精。冀此古老艺苑之花，吉绚……于世界之百花园中，蓬勃绽放，方吾志也！

小变枝节，实拳术，尤需认真探究，循规蹈矩，脚踏实地，野狐掸禅，必无有功，且有柔性疑模，无法学习也。学拳如此，窃以为然！望诸位后学共同研习，他山之石，可以攻玉，互砺共进，庶几有成，时光不再，愿其勉之！

太极拳诸项，首重眼眼功夫，吾项承忘人以虚领顶劲，主张中正安舒为第一要义，言之极为恰切，当此以为根基！又当眼眼探索，动作必与关节……之要求，刘作一致始佳。此中曲折，只有躬身实践

"Luo Ji Hong's letter to his students" June 21, 1977

Excerpt:
"If you wish to know how to get down the mountain, you will need to seek the advice of those who went down before you. "

"If one thinks this is only a simple step and practices blindly without seeking advice from the masters, it is like boiling an empty pot; till one is old, one would still be as confused as ever."

"Daily practice is a must in order to achieve success".

Master Jennifer Gu and Master Luo at Lake Luise, Alberta
in Yang Style "Golden Rooster Stands on one Leg" Posture (2003)

The Ji Hong Taiji System

EVOLUTIONARY THEORY   APPLICATION   METHODOLOGY

Table of Contents

INTRODUCTION

PRINCIPLES AND THEORIES

TRAINING AND EXERCISES

Master Jennifer Gu and Master Luo in Yang Style "Play the Pipa" Posture (1998)

The Ji Hong Taiji System

EVOLUTIONARY THEORY   APPLICATION   METHODOLOGY

INTRODUCTION

太極之光

慈思堂 翟子書賀

"The Light Of Taiji"

CHAPTER 1

The Light of Taiji
A Reminiscence of My Father's Taiji Journey

My father, Luo Ji Hong, was born August 12, 1920, in the small village of Xingning [興寧], Guangdong Province, in Southern China. His family belonged to the Ke Jia [客家] tribe (visitors) who had migrated from Central to Southern China over 100 years before. When my father was three years old, my grandfather passed away while on a business trip, leaving behind my grandmother and my father in poor and miserable circumstances. Xingning was one of the poorest areas in South China. From generation to generation, the Kejianese struggled for the basic necessities of life. However, they paid very serious attention to the education of their children, hoping that their offspring would be successful in their pursuit of academic studies, and thus be able to improve their lives. Though my grandmother barely had enough food for her family, she managed to send my father to a private traditional school and then to a standard school.

My grandfather's death and the family's poor situation made my father grow up very smart and determined. Playtime with other kids was sacrificed for diligent and devoted studies. Born with an overwhelming desire for knowledge, he was always at the top of the school's honour roll. He received a scholarship from the Sociology Department at the prestigious Zhong Shan [中山] University in 1947.

In 1958, my father suffered from kidney problems. He had three surgeries. Right after his left kidney was removed, his right kidney was found to be deteriorating. At that time, my father was very weak and his body weight fell from 65 to 45 kilograms. Neither oriental nor western medicine promised any hope for a cure, and he was deemed to have only six months left to live.

Because of the bleeding from his remaining kidney, doctors prescribed complete bed rest during his treatment. While accepting the medical treatment, my father also searched through a variety of medical books for alternative treatments. When he found that Taiji was known to be successful in treating certain chronic diseases and extending life with better results than medication, my father decided to go against the doctor's advice and went to practise Taiji in a nearby park. Different from all the other beginners and showing his innate optimistic attitude, my father was very focused during his Taiji study. Not only did he intend to master Taiji's external movements, but also its internal properties. During his training practice, he questioned everything, and when his first teacher could not provide any more answers, he attempted to find them in Taiji books.

A miracle happened after several months of Taiji practice. My father's terminal disease went into remission, which left even his doctors surprised. When they learned what was going on, they encouraged my father to practise Taiji with his teacher in his hospital room. Father invited Zhao

Zhi Lin [趙芝麟], the most famous teacher in the area, to become his Enlightenment Teacher[1]. From that day forward, my father and Taiji had developed a special bond. Well on his way to recovery, my father was soon discharged from the hospital.

As he began to regain his health, my father progressed in Taiji. He was deeply charmed by this splendid national treasure. The profound Taiji theory, its subtle philosophical substance, agile movements and beautiful postures, and especially the accurate and secretive internal content of Taiji's martial art, greatly inspired Father to study Taiji. During his recovery, and ignoring the advice of others, he rented an attic in a house close to Master Zhao Zhi Lin in Shantou [汕頭], many miles from home, to continue his study of Taiji. Early every morning, my father practised Taiji in the park. After breakfast, he continued his practice, studied theory or exchanged his learning experience with other Taiji students. (Illustration. 1-1-1)

Luo Ji Hong's early Taiji training
(Illustration 1-1-1)

Taiji push-hands, or *tuishou* [推手], is a physically demanding training exercise. Initially, most of his fellow students, who were in better physical condition and had years of experience, were reluctant to push hands with my recovering father, fearful of hurting him. At his insistence, however, they eventually, although hesitantly, agreed to practise *tuishou* with my father.

---

[1] Enlightenment Teacher: the term usually given to the instructor who initiates a student into the wonders of Taiji.

At that time, the most popular and most basic principles of push-hands were *using intent but not force, four ounces to overcome a thousand pounds, yield at the same rate as your opponent advances* and *total softness*. Following Master Zhao's admonition to *loosen the hips* and *sit down on the rear leg*, time and again, my father made a great effort to practise these basic requirements. His legs were so sore and painful that he could hardly walk up and down the stairs, yet practising this way did not bring apparent progress and when doing push-hands with fellow students, he did not experience *the wonder of the weak overcoming the strong*. Time and again he would be thrown to the ground. However, he would just get up, dust off his pants and continue to push hands. Such persistence and undaunted spirit inspired great admiration from Master Zhao and his students.

Later on, whenever my father mentioned that experience, he would say: *Determination and spirit are the most important 'organs' for dealing with difficulty. These 'organs' will activate all other systems and parts of the human body to unite and win over difficulties and diseases. Then and there, while practising push-hands, I was pushed and fell down time and again, and it looked like I was weak and a loser. However, during the practice, I forgot that I was suffering from a severe illness. With this determination and spirit I was strong, a winner, and this helped my recovery a great deal.* This was one of the major reasons that my father achieved a miraculous recovery from his terminal disease.

My father's pursuit of the Taiji truth could almost be described as obsessive, however his devotion was touching. At any given moment, he would be thinking about Taiji, even in a vehicle or on a boat. In his Taiji diary, (that we fortunately recovered) he would write lines such as: *Riding to some place in a vehicle, all of a sudden I realized . . .* When he had an inspiration, he would pick up any piece of paper, even a handy telegram, and write his discovery on it.

When my father started to learn Taiji, his teacher and several articles admonished him to *lift up the crown of his head.* Consequently, he put a bowl full of water on top of his head for a day, which resulted in a very stiff neck the next morning. To practise *sink the shoulder and lower the elbow,* he would hold an umbrella under his arm regardless of the weather. My mother was too embarrassed to go out with him. To improve the elasticity of his back and legs, he would never sit down during a bus ride, but practised body adjustments to absorb the impact of bumps.

In another incident, he stood at the edge of a pier, watching the waves and their rhythms for two hours. He then tried to incorporate the same harmony of folding and flowing into his *internal power*. Passers-by thought he was going to commit suicide and called the police.

Besides practising forms and push-hands with masters and other students, my father made use of various available materials to create special training methods. For example, he used the trunk of a tree, as thick as the diameter of a rice bowl, to practise *fa jing*[2] [發勁]. The intensity of his *fa jing* was measured by the frequency of the shaking tree trunk. A tree trunk with a shoulder-width diameter was used to practise *buffalo strength*[3], to feel the effect of *pulling power* and *submitting power.* Sugar canes helped him to practise the art of *hiding internal movements from others.* Reaching out, his hand would barely touch the leaf of a sugar cane while he moved his whole body into different postures. The requirement was that he had to maintain contact with

---

[2] *fa jing*: emission of "explosive" power or trigger force.
[3] *buffalo strength*: the intense, continuous internal pressure that appears similar to the slow, methodical power of a buffalo when pulling a plough or pushing a grindstone.

the leaf at all times but not cause it to move.

Not satisfied with his progress in Taiji, my father turned to study traditional Taiji theories. He sought help from the people around him to buy, rent or borrow books about Taiji theory. At that time, my father had to support a family of nine with his disability pay. It was the beginning of the 1960s, a time when China had economic difficulties. In spite of all that, he still saved enough money to purchase many Taiji books from traditional and used bookstores all over the nation.

Once, he asked to borrow the works of Chen Xin [陳鑫] from Gu Liu Xin, as he could not find a set to add to his collection. On receiving the books, he wrote to Master Gu: *I was waiting for your Chen books as if longing for the first letter from a new love! Today, I received those four books with another document of information and your letter. It is very hard to express how happy I feel!* This statement demonstrates my father's strong desire for knowledge. Each time he received a new book, he would treasure it, study its content, chew on it word by word, make copious notes and incorporate it into his practice.

He had developed his own methodology for studying. When researching a subject, he would select a subject from Taiji theory and write it on a blackboard. He told me humorously: *To solve and explain a topic in Taiji theory, I would assemble a research team with myself as the team leader and Wang Zong Yue [王宗岳], Wu Yu Xiang [武禹襄], Chen Xin and all the other authors of Taiji theory books as team members. When announcing the topic, I would invite each team member to make a speech and to represent his own point of view. Finally, as the team leader, I would review all the points and come to a conclusion.* This was my father's method of *active reading*. From several diverse points of view, he was able to see the whole picture.

He also believed that Taiji is a physical exercise and should include the study of human biology, dynamic movement and mathematics. To learn more about these subjects and to lay down a theoretical foundation for revealing the secrets of Taiji, he studied textbooks from institutes for physical education and medical schools.

After a period of in-depth theoretical and practical studies, my father realized that the essence of Taiji was the implementation of yin and yang, but not *softness throughout*. Taiji push-hands should have internal power as its material basis, but that power should behave like a spiral in any point of a movement, to control and resolve external force.

He then explored the relationship between body alignment in Taiji and the adjustment of the *ming men*[4] [命門], which is centred on the lower back, to generate spiral movements combined with enormous flexibility and elastic power while pushing hands.

In less than half a year, my father greatly advanced his push-hands practice, surpassing all his fellow students. One day after class, Master Zhao asked my father to stay and push-hands with him. My father won the friendly exchange with ease. This shocked Master Zhao, who had many years experience in Taiji practice and teaching. The next morning, he invited my father back to his house. Upon my father's arrival, Master Zhao announced: *I have studied Taiji for 30 years and have taught for over 20. Yet, with less than two years training you have defeated me! As my*

---

[4] *ming men*: literally "Gate of Life". On the lower back, below the spinous process of the second lumbar vertebra (L2), just beneath the two kidneys directly behind the navel.

student, I am proud of your achievement but, how is this possible? (Illustration.1-1-2)

Luo Ji Hong (L) pushing hands with Zhao Zhi Lin
(Illustration 1-1-2)

My father explained the conclusions he had reached from studying a portion of the Taiji classics. He expressed his regret that he did not have access to more books and offered to share whatever he had learned with Master Zhao and his fellow students. At that, Master Zhao summoned all his senior students and demanded they turn over all their books on Taiji to my father. As my father was fortunate enough to be one of the few educated students in the school, and probably the only one who could translate the classical Chinese literature, they were only too happy to oblige. Later, my father also did push-hands with various masters of different Taiji styles in Shantou and other areas. He successfully defeated them all, which shocked the Taiji community in the area. Only one and half years after starting Taiji, my father had presented another miracle.

In a letter to master Gu, he stated: *After reading* Dynamics of Athletic Biology *by the Russian author D.D. Donski, I was greatly inspired. Analyzing Taiji push-hands using some of the concepts of the dynamics of movement made it quite straightforward and understandable. Melted in heart, cast in hands[5], the progress I made recently in push-hands surprised even me. Teachers and*

---

[5] *Melted in heart, cast in hands:* absorb and understand the theory, then put it into physical practice.

fellow students are also very interested in my methodology of studying Taiji. Chen Xin said, 'One needs to understand the theory before learning martial arts.' In certain aspects, Chen Xin's saying is correct. Though 'it is an empty theory without practice, it is a blind practice without theory.' (Joseph Stalin). It is practice that builds the body in martial arts. Empty talk and exaggerated papers do not help. One must act according to the words 'Practice, study, practice again, study again, until infinity' (Mao Ze Dong [毛澤東]). However, one's direct experience is limited, so one must learn from the experience collected by others. Study is one example of this kind of learning. This section of the letter sufficiently expresses Father's persistent pursuit of knowledge and the truth. It also embodies the true meaning of turning knowledge to power. Thus, Father took great pleasure in practising Taiji. He ate simple meals and became healthier by the day. His head, bald from the medication he had taken for his kidney disease, started to grow new, dense hair. A new life had begun.

At about this time, Master Gu published his new book titled *Simplified Taijiquan*. My father rushed to borrow this book from a friend and read through the book without pause. To his astonishment, it described concepts such as *internal power* and *spiral force*, which he had explored and experienced through his own practice. Still excited by the content of the book, he wrote a long letter to both the publisher and Master Gu, reviewing Master Gu's book. With the determination of a person actively pursuing knowledge, Father expressed his views and admiration for the book. Master Gu immediately replied with generous humility and understanding: *July 28th, The publisher forwarded your long letter, with comments on my book 'Simplified Taijiquan'. Thank you for your compliments. The level of the topics you raised in your letter is not easy to attain without correct research and study. Many practitioners never attain this understanding. Your progress shows that your way of study is valid.* Master Gu went on in his letter: *Today, it is especially important to study the training methods of various styles of Taiji. The old masters in the past did not reveal all their secrets and were not good at analysis, so there are a lot of unanswered questions. I will work with you to explore the essence of Taiji and prove it with scientific reasoning. We can utilize the Taiji properties of prolonging life, enhancing health and strengthening the body to serve our socialist construction and for international cultural exchange in Chinese medicine.*

After that day, my father corresponded regularly with Master Gu and formed a serious teacher-student relationship. Their correspondence comprised over 100 letters, full of their devotion to Taiji, which discussed the results of their research on Taiji. In his first letter to Master Gu, my father stated: *Fortunately, while I am not able to summarize the experiences and conclusions of years of study, you describe them so accurately, thoroughly and legibly. You dialectically analyze the experiences of old masters and put them in words so simply and so vividly. I really admire your deep skills and your profound insights.* Thus, my father made Master Gu his teacher. Master Gu in return regarded my father as part of the new generation of Taiji theorists and researchers. In another letter to my father, he wrote: *First, congratulations on your enrolment in medical school in order to get a solid foundation to systematically analyze and develop Taiji. Enlightenment Teachers like Tang Hao [唐豪] and I never had such an opportunity. If Master Tang Hao were alive, he would also be delighted with the appearance and progress of our successors.*

During his study of Taiji, my father concluded that the level of quality in Taiji practice was declining from one generation to the other. Rather than developing their art, certain individuals within Taiji circles sought to be recognized as the *true heir* to Taiji. A backward, corrupt, closed and conceited heritage system, in combination with the lack of guidance from scientific theory, seriously stood in the way of Taiji moving to a higher level.

In an emotional letter to Master Gu, my father pointed out the pathetic current situation of the art: *It is never easy to put all the principles of various styles into one melting pot. They all originated from the same source and the principles should be the same, yet each style differs from the others, and each has its unique doctrines. Some have different names for the same concept; some are partially similar and partially different, and some are completely opposite, like fire and water. Some masters care only for their own style. Attempting to be different, they mystify their style's principles. Some have limited knowledge, cheating themselves as well as others. Some are even worse, actively deifying past masters and changing historical facts. For a long period of time this was one of feudal society's methods of ruling. This pattern was adopted by all levels of the society, but especially the martial arts!* He wrote further: *Taiji theories from older generations discussed abstract concepts. The authors, who were experienced in the martial arts, had profound insights, but could not express their ideas in words. Very often they could describe the result, but could not explain its cause. We are in a different era now, armed with various scientific tools. Inheriting is for developing. Inheriting is the means, and development is the goal.* Father explicitly stated: *The only way for Taiji to survive is to modernize. We need contemporary people with a contemporary viewpoint; people with knowledge as well as the scientific ability to analyze Taiji theory. Finally, we need a contemporary training and tournament system.*

He realized that Taiji was a profound and vast science. The study of its fundamental theories should include traditional Chinese philosophy, especially the dialectics of yin and yang as well as biology, natural sciences and Chinese medicine. During his recovery he educated himself in mathematics, body dynamics, physics and biology. He attended courses in athletic theory at the Physical Education Institute and studied anatomy and physiology at Shantou Medical College, where he enrolled as an auditing student. My father would lose all track of time in the autopsy room. He studied so intensely that he often skipped meals and forgot to sleep. Even during holidays, he would put up a human skeleton sample at home to study. Finally, he harvested the fruit of all his hard work, passing all his course examinations with top scores.

The study of modern natural sciences, especially physiology, elevated my father's understanding of Taiji to new heights. Using modern scientific methods, he was determined to pursue a three-to-five-year comprehensive research program of Taiji. Commenting on my father's plan, Master Gu wrote with great enthusiasm a note of encouragement. *In regard to research in Taiji theory, there are no complete works right now. You are determined to take three to five years to do it. I believe you are qualified for this research. I hope you can start work immediately. Persist, advance accordingly, absorb more, consider more and experiment more. In three to five years, there will be results. I want to congratulate with the couplet: 'Classic knowledge—consider plus analyze; new knowledge—cultivate turn profound.'*

My father was highly educated and had a liberal mind. He was against blindly following the old ways. In one of his publications he pointed out: *Our task should not be the translation of the classic works. Rather we should reveal their essence, observe their internal organic system, illustrate issues and guide our practice.* Because of his education, my father was better equipped than many previous students of Taiji.

He always made new discoveries when studying the Taiji theory. For example, a basic Taiji tenet stresses *four ounces overcome a thousand pounds*. Also, Taiji masters always avoided the term *force*. Based on his years of practice, however, my father pointed out that *to push a thousand pounds with four ounces, one needs to train to have a thousand-pound force*. This clarified the adage of *four ounces push a thousand pounds* and rebutted the old misunderstanding by many people that Taiji did not have to use force to defeat opponents. Further, he stated that in Taiji push-hands, matching of forces and internal power was not the absolute purpose. Instead, push-hands becomes a contest of wits by the use of one's advantage over an opponent's disadvantage. Humorously, he compared *locking collar bones* and locking the *ming men* to pulling on a ring in a buffalo's nose. In more detail, the whole body and its internal power (a thousand pounds) should be focused on pulling the opponent's *ming men* (four ounces), with the effect that the opponent loses control and stops resisting. This accurately explains the concept of *four ounces overcome a thousand pounds* used as a method to control an opponent and is the essence of Taiji as a martial art.

My father also conducted extensive research on Taiji's internal power. He believed that internal power is generated through body adjustment. Each joint is set by lengthening the muscles and forming a whole, flexible entity in the mode of the *five bows*. Additionally, by adjusting the *yi* [意] (intent) and *qi* [氣] (internal energy), the body becomes an integrated entity in which internal and external are capable of generating a prevailing elasticity that allows an individual to move quickly and efficiently. We call this state "Taiji Readiness State or Condition".

When applying Taiji in competition, my father compared the concept of *stillness over movement* to the processing of materials in a factory. In a complete embodiment of Taiji tactics, one would first set oneself to become like a processing plant that is ready for processing material; the "Taiji Readiness State". Then he would take the opponent's power as material, using tactics such as *voluntarily supplying of material, forcing to supply material* and *inducing to supply material,* thus completely embodying the Taiji theory.

In 1963, Gu Liu Xin invited my father to attend the National Martial Arts Performance Conference in Shanghai. Finally, my father was given the opportunity to meet Master Gu in person, the man with whom he had corresponded only by mail for over a year. Master Gu honoured my father by meeting him at the railroad station. When he saw the revered Master Gu the first time, he was moved beyond words. Master Gu told my father: *While you are in Shanghai, you must seriously study Wu [武] (Hao) style Taiji from Master Hao Shao Ru [郝少如]. Only the inheritor, Master Hao, can explain the principles of the Wu (Hao) style. It is excellent material for us to study, absorb, review and develop.* Master Gu took my father straightaway to meet Master Hao Shao Ru. Master Gu asked Master Hao to teach my father intensively during his short visit.

During his three months in Shanghai, Father received extra attention from Master Hao, who maintained his strict requirements about learning the profound content of the Hao system. Soon after starting to study, my father had a serious problem. Since he had studied Yang [楊] and Wu [吳] styles, he had a different body alignment than that required for Wu (Hao) style. At first he could not command the method of Wu (Hao) style to *uphold the hip and hang up the inner legs*, and *tailbone rolled up to hold up the dan tian*[6] [丹田]. Master Hao's teaching method would not permit a student to go on to the next movement unless he had mastered the previous one. Days passed by, and my father was still struggling with the initial movement. Eventually, under the careful guidance of Master Hao and other senior students, he finally mastered the body alignment of Wu (Hao) style.

My father's diligence, as well as his serious study of Taiji theory, helped him to progress

---

[6] *dan tian*: a spherical space inside the abdominal cavity approximately three inches below the navel where qi is said to be collected and stored.

10

by leaps and bounds. His learning experience gained through studies and practice was appreciated and won the respect of Hao Shao Ru. Master Hao said later: *During my many years of teaching, I have seldom seen a student as diligent and intelligent as Mr. Luo Ji Hong.* After his visit to Shanghai my father wrote to Master Gu: *The Wu (Hao) style training methodology still keeps the traditional essence, which is especially worthy of admiration. Master Hao's teaching is extremely strict. His examples are vivid and live, beyond any books. In Taiji, it is very important to obtain teaching by words and the heart.* (Illustration 1-1-3).

(L-R) Hao Shao Ru, Luo Ji Hong, Gu Liu Xin (Shanghai 1963)
(Illustration 1-1-3)

While in Shanghai, my father had the opportunity to *push hands* with Master Gu. After several bouts, my father asked Gu if he was using Xing Yi[7] [形意] instead of Taiji. Gu exclusively used a quick, straight-line attack. This was my father's first experience with the short-range offensive style of *tuishou*. Gu explained that there were three traditional ways of pushing hands: 1) Long Range or Large Spiral; 2) Medium Range or Subtle Spiral; and 3) Short Range or Invisible Spiral. Gu was a proponent of the Short Range style and explained that one must have very strong internal pressure or the Invisible Spiral method would be ineffective. His push hands was almost entirely offence, using short, quick, tightly spiralled movements. Master Gu used tremendously strong internal power with small but effective movements, causing opponents to fly at the first touch. Since my father's previous push-hands training used large circles, he could not easily adjust to Master Gu's push-hands technique.

Over the course of the next three months, my father would often push hands with Master Gu. From this practice, he learned to build up his internal pressure and to redirect an opponent's force back on him using sudden, smaller movements. My father incorporated this teaching of the *small circle spiral* and *cold power*[8] with the Large Spiral long-range techniques that he learned from his Yang style training. This made my father realize how deep and profound Taiji is.

When my father was in Shanghai, Master Gu was the director of the Shanghai Sports Stadium. To develop Taiji further, he invited representative masters of the five major Taiji styles to teach in the stadium. This made studying Taiji very convenient for my father. Besides learning

---

[7] *Xing Yi*: Mind-Form Boxing. an internal style known for its linear movements and explosive power
[8] *cold power*: the ability to instantly emit a powerful force, seemingly from nowhere

Wu (Hao) style from Master Hao, he also had the opportunity to study Wu style form from Master Wu Ying Hua [吳英華], Wu style push-hands from Master Ma Yueh Liang [馬岳梁], and Yang style form and push-hands from Master Fu Zhong Wen [傅鍾文]. When leaving the stadium one night after a push-hands class held by Master Hao, he shook hands with a very skinny and weak-looking student who had a disabled right leg. Because he was still in the push-hands state of mind, my father twisted his opponent's hand without realizing it. The fellow exclaimed: *Good move! Why not push forward?* Father realized he had just met a "kindred spirit" who was as addicted to Taiji as he was. His only regret was meeting him so late. It turned out his name was Shao Pin Gen [邵品根], and he was a senior student of Master Zhao Shou Cun [趙壽邨], who was one of Wu Jian Quan's [吳鑒泉] best students. Master Shao also studied other styles of Taiji and martial arts. For the next 20 years, Master Shao and my father shared a bond of Taiji. After my father pushed hands with Master Shao, he was deeply impressed with his skill of *understanding power*. As soon as they touched hands, Master Shao would be like the wind and shadow where the opponent could not attach to his power. Thus he had developed the Taiji skill of *the weak beats the strong* to an extreme. When my father did *push-hands* with Hao Shao Ru, Master Hao would be like a highly pressurized huge air bag. As soon as you pushed, he would rebound and throw you out. The harder you pushed, the harder you rebounded. In Master Gu's style, it was the powerful internal strength that in combination with small circular twists of the joints as well as straight and sideways sweeps that made him unstoppable. My father also studied Yang style from Master Wang Shou Xian [王守先].

Father's schedule was full every day and, busy as a bee, he was learning from one master after another. To comprehend and master the essence of a movement, my father would spend a sleepless night in the dorm practising alone. Each day after class, my father would make entries in two journals: one to record a master's teaching, the other to write down his own understanding and experience. It is a great pity that both journals were burned during the Cultural Revolution.

During his studies, my father followed four steps: collection, digestion, absorption and development. While studying any move or principle, he wanted first to understand the *why*, and second to understand *how* to do it well. Only these two points of understanding made it possible for him to reduce blind acceptance and enhance the efficiency of his studies.

The trip to Shanghai created in my father an *open view* and gave him a good *view of the great world of Taiji*. Father realized that *this marvellous national treasure of Taiji could last so long because it really had its unique value and its profound charm* (his correspondence). Taking the huge leap of jumping from Taiji theory to Taiji practice reinforced his determination in pursuit of the profound essence of Taiji.

Prior to his departure for Shanghai, my father obtained a letter of introduction from Xu Zhi Yi [徐致一], a famous Wu Jian Quan Style teacher in Beijing, to Master Zhang Da Quan [張達泉]. Zhang was a classmate of Wu Jian Quan himself and Father considered him to be the greatest living exponent of Wu style Taiji. Master Zhang invited my father into his home. After a brief discussion, they cleared the furniture out of the main room. Master Zhang blindfolded himself and proceeded to *push hands* with my father. Zhang demonstrated an incredible mastery of *dong jing*[9] [懂勁] or understanding energy. No matter which direction my father moved, Master Zhang could locate his centre of gravity and direct my father

---

[9] *dong jing*: the advanced ability to sense your opponent's energy, to "read" his intentions and consequently to be able to anticipate and control his movements while maintaining control of your energy flow

off balance. At the same time, he was able to control my father's force using Large Circle movements. Not only was Master Zhang blindfolded, he was also 84 years old at the time!

My father began training under Master Zhang and was constantly amazed at the master's skill in *tuishou*. One time, while practising in a park, my father observed Zhang pushing hands with a number of students. My father noticed that Zhang would often rock back on his heels while pushing. He had discovered Zhang's weakness! When it came to my father's turn to push against the Master, he faced a dilemma. Should he exploit the apparent error in Zhang's technique or should he allow the old master to save face by letting him win? My father chose not to take advantage and, consequently, was easily pushed by Master Zhang. Soon afterwards, one of Zhang's senior students came up to my father and said: *I noticed you thought you had the Master at a disadvantage, but you refrained from pressing. It was fortunate for you that you did. Watch!* At that moment, another new student, one with a strong background in the external martial arts, who had come to the same conclusion as my father, was pushing against Zhang and obviously concentrating on the master's heels.

Without any apparent effort, Zhang sent him flying a considerable distance into a puddle. My father suddenly realized that, instead of being off-balance when rocking back on his heels, Zhang Da Quan was actually narrowing his central axis. Thus, a small movement from the axis resulted in a large, powerful movement farther away from his body. My father studied this concept diligently and credited Zhang Da Quan with teaching him how to narrow his own central axis and control an opponent's focal point. He felt that this resulted in greater flexibility in his movements and a faster reaction time. One of Master Zhang's students was a three-time national Taiji champion. It was this student who encouraged my father to study anatomy and physiology in order to advance his understanding of Taiji principles.

On June 1, 1964, an unprecedented historical event occurred in the Taiji world. Its originator was the Wu style Master Xu Zhi Yi who published the essay "About Spiral Force in Taiji" in the magazine *Sports Journal*. The article disputed the view that spiral force was common to all Taiji styles. This aroused a strong reaction in the Taiji world. On July 24, my father led the response to this essay with his article "Comment on 'About Spiral Force in Taiji'." Unfortunately the editors misspelled his name as Luo Hong JI. He followed up with two more articles titled, "My Thoughts on Spiral Force in Taiji," which was published on November 11, and "What is Spiral Force in Taiji," which remained unpublished owing to a sudden stop of the debate by the *Sports Journal*. My father's comments revealed the nature of spiral force in Taiji. Using examples from classical Taiji theory, modern philosophy, physiology and physics, he clearly pointed out that *spiral force was vortex force* and nothing else. It had an axis force, tangent force and centre force. Therefore, the force had directions and at the same time it had no directions. When pushed by an external force, spiral force showed the agile and variable spring action as required by the Taiji principles to *follow the opponent's change*. This further proved that spiral force objectively existed as a common property of Taiji as a whole and not as an individual property for a specific Taiji style. Without this common property, Taiji would not be a unique national martial art and athletic sport. Father's keen point was applauded by Taiji professionals both inside and outside China, and he became a celebrity in the Taiji world. At the beginning of 1966, my father became a special columnist with *Martial Arts Magazine*. He was hired by Shen Jia Zhen [沈家楨], the famous Taiji Master and chief editor of the magazine, which was sponsored by the Martial Arts Association of the province of Zhejiang [浙江] (the magazine was later shut down during the Great Cultural Revolution). In February 1975, Master Gu was commissioned by the "People's Publication Editors Department" to organize a five-volume compilation of the five traditional styles of Taiji. Approved by Master Hao, Master Gu invited my father to compile the volume about Wu (Hao) Style Taiji. However, owing to the political situation at the time, the five books were not published, though fortunately, the drafts survived. My father was thus highly regarded by the top masters of their generation.

In 1965, my father's health had recovered to such an extent that he returned to work full time. He was appointed supervisor at a mine 60 miles from home. There he worked all day and taught Taiji to an ever-growing number of students in the evenings.

In 1966, one of the most turbulent episodes in China's history began. The Great Cultural Revolution started a period of chaos and destruction whose effects are still felt today. Because he had once taught English, had been friends with a foreign priest in his youth and had received his education before the 1949 revolution, my father was branded an "enemy of the people." The Red Guard showed up at the mine site one day, seized my father and tied him to a tree. They kept him there all day under the burning sun, berating him for his "crimes" and demanding to know who his "accomplices" were. One of his Taiji students risked his life to bring my father some water. My father asked him to hurry to our home and warn us. He begged the student to hide his Taiji books and journals. The man and another student rushed to our hometown and warned my family of what had occurred. One student took all my father's textbooks and hid them at his home, while the other student hid my father's personal journals. Unfortunately, the second student was also harassed by the Red Guard. They found my father's journals and notebooks and destroyed them.

My father was eventually found "guilty" and sentenced to a concentration camp for "re-education." There, he was forbidden to practise Taiji. He managed, however, to maintain his studies in various ways. At night in bed he would practise Qigong[10] and *Sitting Taiji*. He would practise Taiji movements in the shower when the guards were not looking.

The guards could be brutal in the camp. One incident involved a particularly vicious guard who liked to have the prisoners kneel in a line with their hands behind their backs during the evening "indoctrination" sessions. He would then walk behind them, shout out an accusation and kick them forward so they would fall face-first into the ground. On occasion, he would scatter sharp stones in front of the kneeling prisoners so they would cut themselves as they fell. Because of my father's reputation as a Taiji master, they would make him kneel on a brick ledge more than a foot off the ground so he had farther to fall. One day, as the guard was going down the line screaming at the prisoners and kicking them, he came up behind my father. Using the strong internal pressure he had developed from Hao style, my father resisted the guard's kicks. No matter how hard he tried, the guard could not budge my father! Finally, in a terrible rage, the guard took a run and lashed out viciously at my father's back. My father slightly turned his body deflecting the kick and causing the guard to stumble forward onto the ground. In order to disguise what he had done, my father then fell forward on his shoulder, making it look as if the guard had succeeded. After that, the guards began to treat my father with a wary respect.

My father later told me that Taiji saved his life in the camp. In one incident, a guard tried to beat him with a shovel. My father deflected the blow and applied *fa jing* to the deflection, causing the shovel to fly out of the guard's hands. As my father calmly picked up the shovel, the guard, fearing for his life, ran off screaming. My father simply returned the implement to its

---

[10] *Qigong*: exercises (moving and/or stationary) to develop and enhance the collection and storage of *qi* in the body.

storage place. After that, my father was always escorted by several guards wherever he went. The guards, however, were instructed not to come within two metres of my father as he was considered "dangerous."

In 1965, my father was "paroled" to work in an agricultural commune. There he had a bit more freedom and began to cautiously teach Qigong and simplified Taiji to his fellow inmates in the evenings.

In 1972, he was allowed to return to the mine as a labourer and he tried to pick up the threads of his life. He resumed his correspondence with old friends and colleagues, discovering that many of them, like Gu Liu Xin and Hao Shao Ru, had shared similar fates to his own. As soon as the political situation relaxed, Father resumed his old habits, happily enjoying research and writing on Taiji theory (Illustrations. 1-1-4, 1-1-5)

Luo Ji Hong in a Yang style pose
(Illustration 1-1-4)

Luo Ji Hong demonstrating Yang style punch
(Illustration 1-1-5)

The Great Cultural Revolution had a serious impact on Father's golden days of Taiji studies. During these critical times, my father was concerned about the collection of Taiji books that he had gathered with difficulty. Among the collection was his correspondence with Master Gu discussing years of Taiji study results. Regrettably, his Taiji journals as well as the correspondence with Master Gu were discovered and burned[11].

While my father was researching Taiji theory, he did a lot of teaching to popularize Taiji. In one of his letters to Master Gu, he wrote: *I am still on disability leave for my recovery. My teaching has kept me so busy that I had to provide more chairs for the crowd who came to see me. They are mostly chronically ill patients who have lost their faith in medication and hope to find a substitute form of treatment. I am the example. Someone joked, 'Director Luo's room is a clinic for Qigong and therapy without a clinic sign.' It is true I had the confidence to set this 'clinic' up. Soon I will have three to four clubs to teach, and will recruit more students. Some say, when more people attend the class, the expenses of the medical clinic will be reduced. This is*

---

[11] In 1991, Master Gu's descendants found Gu Liu Xin's copies of the correspondence when sorting through his effects and gave those to me.

my hope. My Father's profound studies in Taiji theory, his moral integrity, his warm personality and friendliness—these characteristics attracted people to him from all over. My father would sincerely welcome anyone who had a desire to learn Taiji, teach them enthusiastically and never be concerned about his own troubles. My strongest impression of him is that whenever a student came, he would often say, *Time is valuable. Hurry up and practise.* My father was also very selective about his students, and he would only teach people of good character. He often advised students that they should first learn how to be a man before they learn Taiji.

Taijiquan is not only a high-level martial art but also a profound art. Father compared his Taiji journey with the example of the other side of the river where hundreds of flowers are blooming in the brilliant sunshine. He took it as his responsibility to seek a shortcut and to lead the latecomers to the other side of the river. He used his knowledge from philosophy, physiology, body dynamics and so forth to create vivid illustrations that would turn the mysterious Taiji theory into clear and charming simple words. Through his years of teaching practice, my father divided Taiji training into two components: self-control and control of the opponent. My father pointed out that one had to control oneself in order to control the opponent.

He designed a complete training system for Taiji, which included body adjustment, control of *yi* (intent), development of *qi*, use of *jing* (internal strength) and athletic strength, control techniques, tactics and psychological training. My father also explored how specific parts of the body could be isolated and trained. This resulted in the creation of training methods that would address specific points, gradually progressing from internal to external.

For example, he used a rubber band to train the requirement of pulling and opposing as illustrated in the Taiji principle: *When one intends to advance forward, one must have a contrary tendency (backward); when one intends to ease upward, one must have a contrary tendency (downward).* This demonstrates how training equipment can be used to put an abstract concept to practical use. My father often required students to perform *fa jing* at will to check the state of stored power. He also used the concept of *buffalo strength* in push-hands to check the quality of internal strength. He used *question and answer push-hands* to check responsiveness. Thus my father devised, under the guidance of Taiji principles, a system of training that includes training goals, content, methods and the means of evaluating the results.

Father proved the effectiveness of his training system. Under his intensive training, Gu Dai Juan (Jennifer) and I represented Guangzhou in 1984 at the Wuhan International Taiji Performance Competition. We each won the gold medal in the Traditional Taiji Forms competition in the Women's and Men's Divisions respectively.

Later, we used my father's training system to train our own students, and in a very short period of time, we achieved a remarkable record of success. We have been successfully training Taiji's new generation, which is a direct reflection of my father's efforts to generalize and popularize Taiji. (Illustration 1-1-6).

(L-R) Luo Hong Yuan, Luo Ji Hong, Sun Jian Yun, Gu Dai Juan (Wuhan 1984)
(Illustration 1-1-6)

My father often told us that he was the explorer, tour guide and teacher of Taiji. In a letter to me he wrote: *My research and exploration of Taiji will be significant if my years of research results in a bridge that enables your generation of Taiji practitioners to have a straight path to a higher level, such as you would only need five years to get to the level that I achieved by spending ten years. Only through one generation's progress will the younger generation surpass the older.* My father foresaw that the only way to reverse Taiji's decline was to develop scientific methods to modernize Taiji.

After the Wuhan International Taiji Performance Competition, Father returned in April 1984 to Shanghai. It had been 20 years, and many good teachers and friends had passed away. While he continued to study Taiji with new and old friends, he felt an urgent need to sum up and document the valuable experience and theories of the senior masters while their generation was still alive. He wanted to preserve their knowledge and pass it on to the next generation.

Shortly before my father passed away, he wrote to me, though he did not mail the letter: *This visit of 45 days opened my eyes and enriched my knowledge—especially in those 26 days in Shanghai. I made many friends and gained a lot, particularly from Shao Pin Gen. His Taiji push-hands level is quite high, like a magician, very charming with an artistic quality. I focused on studying and summarizing his valuable experience of many years. When I came home, I digested it and started to feel its benefits, as if coming from the 'Necessary State.' I can do it at will, absorb and dissolve naturally. It added to my collection of Taiji, and it takes me to a new level.*

At that time, Father had been retired for two years and his health was excellent. His Taiji had greatly progressed and he returned from his latest visit to Shanghai like a tiger with wings. There was a sense of excitement in him. Father purchased the *Four Study Treasures*,[12] ready to

---

[12] *Four Study Treasures*: brush pen, ink, paper and ink grinder

start writing. At the same time, he was busy meeting one group of students after another, teaching Taiji, push-hands and *fa jing*. Every day he met over 10 groups of students. He often travelled to Chaozhou [潮州] and other areas to teach.

On June 14, 1984, upon returning from a teaching trip, Father met and practised with several groups of students despite his lack of rest. Unfortunately, he became sick from too much stress. Lacking access to even the most basic healthcare facilities, he passed away at the age of 65. Our family and the students he taught over the years without consideration of compensation were shocked, shaken and heartbroken. When he heard the bad news from one of my father's students, Master Gu emotionally wrote:

> *Comrade Ji Hong*
> *Eternity*
> *Twenty years and more, devoted to Taiji studies*
> *Much correspondence with debate*
> *Soul mate*
> *Friends over the ocean.*
> *April and May.*
> *Wu Han and Shanghai, reunion and exchange of thoughts.*
> *Sudden loss, but memories remain.*

This letter deeply expressed his close friendship with my father over decades of Taiji studies.

Over half of my father's life was devoted to studying Taijiquan theory and techniques. He adopted the best features from many styles and schools, proving to be a gifted and talented Taiji master and theorist. Though he was not born into a famous martial arts family and lived in the remote countryside, he was able to achieve a high level of Taiji skill, thanks to his talent, his intelligence and his persistent efforts.

Before my father was able to finish his compilation of everything he had researched and learned, he passed away. Yet his efforts and contribution to the development and modernization of Taiji are like a light tower, brightening our road to the future, an everlasting accomplishment, from generation to generation, shining forever! (Illustration. 1-1-7)

Luo Hong Yuan
Edmonton, Alberta
October 2005

18

Luo Ji Hong on the cover of New Martial Hero magazine (Hong Kong 1984)
(Illustration 1-1-7)

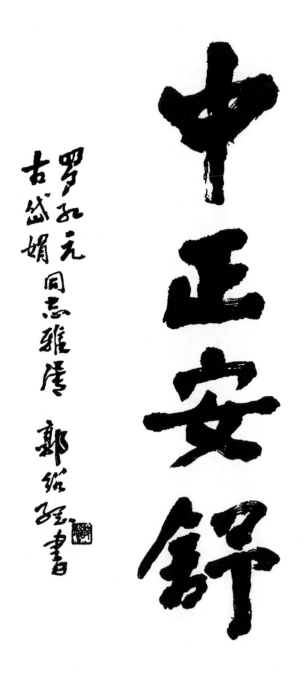

To: Mr. Hong Yuan Luo and Ms. Dai Juan Gu
"Centered and Balanced; Relaxed and At Ease"
From: Shao Gang Guo
(Mr. Guo is the President of Guang Zhou Fine Arts Institute)

CHAPTER 2

The Memoirs, Correspondence and Excerpts of Master Luo Ji Hong

SECTION 1: *The Guiding Principles of Taiji Training*

It is my belief that learning Taijiquan is no different from learning other skills. It is important to avoid empty discussion of theories and fast tracking. Practice - understand - practice more - understand more… It is a huge leap from body precept to cognitive reasoning and discussion of empty theories alone will not lead to success. *Admiring the fishes when upon a stream, it is best to retreat and knit a net. Walking miles makes one insignificant; climbing a high mountain makes one humble.* One sure and steady step will lead to the right path; however fast tracking without real effort will lead nowhere.

The foundation of Taijiquan lies in the work of the waist and legs. For posture in various moves, it is important to *relax the neck and lift the crown of your head*, while keeping the torso erect, centered and poised. This is, of course, easier said then done. For example, the basic movement of lifting leg and changing step may appear simple, yet to master this correctly requires much practice. The complexity of this seemingly simple movement can only be appreciated by those who have succeeded through diligent practice, serious reflection and persistence. It has been said, *If you wish to know the way down the mountain, ask those who have gone down before.* If, on the other hand, one thinks this is only a very simple movement, and practices blindly without seeking advice from the masters, it would be like *boiling an empty pot, till one is old. One would still be as confused as ever.*

To learn Taijiquan, begin with external forms, and then proceed to internal practice. As one begins to understand the application of *jing*[1] the internal and external will integrate and unite. It is at this stage that one feels the continuous buoyant flow of *qi* in the body, and every Taiji movement becomes second nature. *Five bows become one bow.* All parts of the body are as one, responding to one's command. To arrive at this stage one must understand *the three internal alignments* and *the three external alignments*. Without this knowledge, it would be like *building castles in the air, and seeking fish in the woods*, and one would not compare favourably to other Taiji practitioners. Daily practice is essential in order to achieve success. Many before us gave up because of a lack of diligent practice. Learning push-hands together with the forms will enhance the use of *jing* in Taiji. The essence of Taiji lies in concentration. *The body is a vessel and the mind is the lord.* The mind is in control of the circulation of *qi*, dissolving, inducing, grasping and exerting. The *three internal alignments* are the mind, *qi*, and *jing*.

---

[1] *jing* (literal meaning) swift power.

Taijiquan is a study of motion and intention. Both external (forms) and internal (intent) are of equal importance, and are not independent of each other.

The fundamental principle of push-hands is to develop control of one's body. With control of one's self through proper internal adjustments comes the ability to control others. Self control can be achieved through diligent daily practice of both the forms and push-hands. In practicing the forms, the goal is to develop a natural body posture of centering and roundness. During push-hands, this correct body posture is automatically maintained when encountering external force.

Mastery of the forms is a result of exercising the body and practice; understanding of the theories is a result of in-depth analysis using the mind. The concrete practice and abstract reasoning complement each other, leading to integration, enhancement and further improvement.

When teaching Taijiquan to students, explain both the internal and external. Individualize your instruction depending on the level of your students.

The forms are the external representation of Taijiquan. Intent represents the internal understanding of Taijiquan theories. In order to advance and improve on Taijiquan, one must appreciate the unity of internal intent and the external motion.

Recently I attempted a small experiment. I selected several young students and taught them Taijiquan forms and push-hands concurrently. I compared their advancement to those students who learned only forms. Although I cannot say this is scientific evidence, it was apparent that the group practicing both forms and push-hands was more advanced.

It is important to learn Taijiquan systematically, step by step, methodically. By following the masters before us, building upon their expertise and experience, we can move forward to achieve a new understanding and add to the knowledge base of Taijiquan. Here is how I perceive the proper way of learning Taijiquan: try to understand, practice, understand more, and practice more, and so on. Reading a few books will not make you an expert and practicing on your own without the benefit of masters will not work either. Adult students would appreciate knowing the theories of Taijiquan and learning from the experience of others. Through diligent practice and careful consideration of the underlying principles of each form and move, knowledge and skills will eventually take root.

Taijiquan is not easy to master and is well recognized as complex. Like training for any sport, a scientific approach and a well developed instruction program is necessary to make learning easier. It is also important to seek out good teachers and learn from well known masters. Without the guidance of excellent Taijiquan practitioners, it is difficult to succeed.

SECTION 2: *Principles of Body Adjustments in Taiji Training*

- Essential concepts regarding Taijiquan body adjustments:

    1. Drawing in chest: This body adjustment depends mainly on the collar bone. Maintaining a stable but relaxed collar bone will allow the chest to become hollow or concave, i.e.

to draw inward. The key is to relax the neck and to lift the head, with the collar bone maintaining stability at the same time. Drawing in chest is directly related to the elasticity of the body motion; especially important to the spine's (the main bow) capability to release *jing*. By drawing the chest inward, *qi* is built up and stored in the lower *dan tian* region, thus giving the sensation of an *empty chest and solid abdomen*.

2. Loose waist: The straightening of the spine requires the muscles around and below the waist to be relaxed or loose. A loose waist will result in the spine being straightened and pulled up, and is directly connected to drawing in the chest and lifting head. This body adjustment is essential to the process of *qi* sinking to the *dan tian* region. Without a loose waist, the legs will not be able to gather the *jing* and will become unsteady. When the waist is loose, the elbows will close in, resulting in *jing* moving forward.

3. Lifting the crotch: The adjustment of the pelvis area requires lightly contracting the muscles around the perineum and tilting the pelvis forward slightly, thus raising the *dan tian* and centering the body. Avoid sticking out or twisting the buttocks. Lifting the crotch and lifting the head belong to muscle work (subtle and quiet). Lifting the crotch and lifting the head work in concert with each other to stabilize and center the main axis of the body during movement. Body motion and muscle movement complement each other during action.

4. Wrapping the crotch: The strength of both knees is so strong that the knees feel as if they are rotating inward (a torque from outside each heel up to each knee, rotating the knees in, as if in the action wrapping the knees in).

- Body posture: Body centering is not to be confused with stopping in the center. While the body is centered, *qi* potential is near and close to the center. The body is like a pillar of *qi*, advancing and flowing, non-stop.

- *Use the body to guide the hands, use the hands to lead the body*: The first phrase means that the body motion precedes the movement of the hands; the second phrase means that the body moves relative to the leading position of the hands (as a stable point). The body motion and the guiding hands complement each other.

- Force released from the spine: In his book, *Thirteen Exercise Concepts and Analyses*, Master Wu Yu Xiang explained the precept of *force released from the spine*. In this principle, force means internal *jing* or power. How can the spine release *jing*? *Jing* is released as a result of various body adjustments working in concert with each other: the lifting (the crown) of the head, drawing in the chest and loosening the waist work together to enable the build up of *jing*, with the spine acting as the main bow. The release of *jing* is controlled by *qi* in the *dan tian* area.

When inhaling (the process of building up and storing *qi* in the *dan tian* region), the neck forms a front bow, the chest forms a back bow, and the waist forms another front bow. All three bows together with the spine form a large main bow. When exhaling, the bow is reversed and *jing* is released from the spine. *Qi* is gathered at the *dan tian*. Upon the release of *jing*, the abdomen feels open and loose while the Dai Mai Vessel [2][带脉] feels solid.

- *Smooth the neck and lift the head*: Smoothing the neck curve is a result of the action of lifting

---

[2] Dai Mai: (Girdle Vessel) A *qi* vessel that encircles the waist passing through both the *dan tian* and the *ming men*.

the crown of the head. This body adjustment acts like a balance beam for the rest of the body. Lifting the head enables *heaven and earth balance in the middle*. The head is perpendicular to the body's center of gravity. Lifting the head allows the body to center during movement, whether using empty steps or solid steps. The adjustment of the neck curve is in fact the adjustment of the head and the body, causing each section of the spine to move according to the principle of empty and solid, resulting in the release of *jing* as required.

Protecting the stomach: This means to relax the stomach. This body adjustment directly applies to the principles of *use the mind to move qi, use qi to exercise the body; follow the yi; dan tian leading jing*. Master Hao Shao Ru said, *Stabilize the center* which does not mean stop at the center. When this concept is finally understood and correctly applied, the feeling is like walking on water, and like a floating balloon. The attention to detail and minute movements of Wu (Hao) style is to be appreciated. In practicing, the tailbone feels as if it is curving upward, the upper and lower body align in one straight line, combining forces with each section of the legs. The knees are strong, the thighs are firm and use the knee joint as a pivot. Responding to forces from the ground up, the front of the thigh is rising up so that it is not totally solid but buoyant. When one finally understands and grasps the subtle and delicate exercise of the Wu (Hao) style, one cannot help but marvel at the wisdom of the giants before us.

Taijiquan is difficult to explain. In discussing the concept of *protecting the stomach* above, it appears to be out of context, but is not meant to be so.

Wu style appears to bend away from center. In the bow step the upper body is bent forward but in fact the body is centered while bent. While the form appears different, the essence remains the same. In Hao style the body appears more straight and centered. Using the hip joint as the horizontal axis, bend the hip at a slight angle, eyes look forward, the *bai hui* [百會] acupuncture point[3] pulls upward, with *qi* flowing throughout. Both feet point forward with the muscles of the back of the lower leg pulling upward. The heel of the rear leg and the *dai zhui* [大椎] acupuncture point[4] are aligned in a diagonal line. Although the physical alignments of Wu style are different from Hao style, the essence of their requirements is the same. Sinking one hip will result in the lifting (tilting up) of the other hip. People often misunderstand the body requirements of Wu style, resulting in incorrect postures.

SECTION 3: *Internal Energy (nei jing) and Transfer of Internal Energy*

The *qi engine* is the starter of all internal movements. Without the *qi* engine, internal exercise is no different from external exercise; it's like seeking the end without knowing the means. As such, the movements of open and close, buoyancy, internal and external are all the same.

Touch lightly to form a circle involves both *attach* and *detach. Attach is detach, detach is attach; yin is inseparable from yang, yang is inseparable from yin*. Touch lightly to form a circle consists of both offence and defence. *Offence is defence, and defence is offence*. The key secret of *Luan Huan Jue*[5] [亂環訣] lies in the phrase *touching lightly to form a circle*; endless

---

[3] *bai hui* accupuncture point: at the crown of the head.
[4] *dai zhui* accupuncture point: a point on the spinal column between the two shoulder blades.
[5] *Luan Huan Jue*: (Spontaneous Circular Technique) the ability to instantaneously determine which application will be best to counter your opponent's skills.

circle after circle, each part of the body is like a moving round bead. *A light touch forms a circle* results in *round and empty to effect magic*; *circle is empty, empty is circle*. Observe the application of emptiness inside the circle; emptiness means capacity. Observe the application of solidity outside the circle, which is round, swift and active, responding effectively, transforming into line and point at ease, turning and circling.

The shoulder joints, elbow joints and wrist joints, together directed by the body, form a lever system that is extremely agile and swift. Similar to the levers that propel the wheels of a train engine, our upper limbs can turn and move in a very efficient manner. However, unlike the unidirectional levers of a train's wheels, our arm can turn and rotate in different directions. The same applies to the wrist and hand. Each upper limb in fact forms a complex lever system that enables various actions and multiple changes at will. Indeed the design of such a complex lever system would challenge the best mechanical engineer.

Bend and extend and *round and turn* are two seeming contradictions of Taijiquan's essential body adjustments. *Round and turn,* as one side of the contradiction, is of primary importance, and is the unique essence of Taijiquan. All moves including *bend and stretch* are directed and limited by *round and turn*. Twisting, circling, advance and retreat, curve seeking straight, straight seeking curve, transform and release, attach and detach, all these moves cannot exist without *round and turn*.

Advanced Taijiquan practitioners often use *peng jing*[6] to confront the enemy first and change to other strategies as necessary. It is like building a fort to fend off the enemy first, and then deploying the army to attack. Using this analogy, as the first step, it is important to train one's body to be fit like a fort. *Peng jing* is inherent in each form of Taijiquan. That is why Taijiquan is also known as *Peng Quan*. When confronting the enemy, apply *peng jing* by adjusting the balance of the *yin* and *yang* force.

The path of *jing* is spiral. During any adjustment of *jing*, be it increase or decrease, the sum total is constant (100%, centred, round and full). It is important to note that just focusing on external techniques will not lead to the proper comprehension or interpretation of *jing*. *Peng* is the prevalent *jing* that all other jing forces rely on. *Peng jing* is applied in all situations.

Emptying the chest and the solidifying the abdomen will resolve the problem of "tense" hands. *Emptying the chest and the solidifying the abdomen* is a stage of internal adjustment. The extension and relaxation of the proper groups of chest muscles is a prerequisite for the diaphragm to be able to adjust up and down. The adjustment of muscle has two functions: the first one is a stationary (static) operation, which maintains the body's relative stationary posture and supports the skeletal kinetic operation during exercise. The second function is kinetic operation itself. Kinetic operation enables changing of the capacity of the chest cavity and the abdomen. In order to achieve an *empty* chest cavity and a *solid* abdomen as required by Taijiquan, regular training of this form of muscle kinetic operation is necessary.

The build up and release of *jing* is closely related to our body's respiratory system. The essential operation to achieve *empty chest and solid abdomen* is, in fact, the breathing mechanics of Taijiquan (known as Taijiquan Posture Respiration). This kind of breathing includes external

---

[6] *peng jing*: expansion force or fending-off, warding-off force.

breathing (exchange of external air), and body breathing (internal breathing). Taijiquan places special emphasis on internal breathing (circulation and functioning of *qi* inside the body), which enables the cultivation and nurturing of *qi*. It is important not to increase the rate of external breathing when practicing internal breathing exercise. Even when exercising vigorously, there is no lack of oxygen when there is plenty of internal *qi*. The goal of internal exercise is to cultivate, nurture and store *qi*, allowing for ease of use. Internal breathing marks the major distinction between the external martial arts and the internal forms.

Internal move/External release: without internal adjustment there is no external release. In other words, it is necessary to initiate internal movement before external release is possible. To exercise internal movement during daily practice, it is necessary to concentrate on moving *qi* down to the *dan tian*. Use *yi* (mind) to guide *qi* downward, without labouring and do not rely on external respiration. Nurture, build up and store *qi* below. Do not allow the *qi* to rise. Relax and quiet the abdomen. Feel the buoyancy of your *qi*.

My experience is that the concept of internal adjustment is not easy to comprehend. It is easier to pay attention to the active kinetic muscle exercises and to neglect the stationary operation of the muscles, which acts a balance and support. Without the stationary operation, the body looks slack, the sternum is unstable, and the *dai zhui* fails to pull up, resulting in the failure to achieve *relax the neck* to allow the energy to reach the *bai hui*. Taijiquan is an exercise that requires the continuous moving and weight shifting of the body in the act of offence and defence. It is necessary to maintain balance throughout. It is important to *use the hands to lead the body and use the body to lead the hands*, each responding to one another, extending, bending and stretching while maintaining body stability and equilibrium. It is only at this stage that one can exercise internal movement. Static and kinetic operations are two opposite exercises that control and facilitate each other. It is a typical Taijiquan exercise – the key to internal movement and external release.

The practice of internal movement of *jing* will result in *knowing others and knowing thyself*, especially *others don't know me but I alone know them*. This is the stage of *comprehending jing*. The internal exchange of *jing* begins with chest and waist, with the weight shifting from solid to empty legs. Chen Xin summarized this as *genius derived from knowing others; wisdom manifested in the application of hidden skills* which denotes the achievement of a high level of spontaneous movement. An empty chest and a solid abdomen are necessary requirements for the movements of chest and waist.

Try to achieve an empty chest, solid abdomen, solid leg, extended ankle (*jing* begins at the heel) while relaxing and resisting, folding and stacking, storing and ready to release. When extending the ankle, relax your sole and respond to the empty chest.

When employing the chest and waist movement, lead with the *dan tian*. This way the upper body is protected. When protecting the body, 'close' the rib cage on both sides of the chest; relax the inside. Without protection for the inside of the body, there is no energy in the spine and no direction. When releasing *jing*, both shoulders close and push forward. *Support jing* requires both shoulders to first close and then open.

In order for *qi* to sink to the *dan tian*, relaxing is a prerequisite. Without relaxation, you cannot sink the *qi*. Relax and sinking work together.

Holistic internal movement is to be guided by consciousness, including breathing exercises involving chest and abdomen, shoulder and back, muscles, joints, and internal organs. Turning and moving gently and skilfully. Focus on internal consciousness, leading by *yi*, using the body as a tool. Internal *jing* moving and changing is *jing change and move internally – internal qi sink and turn. Others don't know me but I alone know them*. This is the way to practise.

Force is released from the spine. Before release there must be internal movement. Internal movement is the process of cultivating the potential. According to body dynamics, *store energy as in drawing a bow*. Releasing *jing* is like releasing an arrow. *Releasing and shooting* is the process of turning loaded or stored energy into kinetic energy.

Recently, I became very interested in the essence of internal energy. According to the theories of dynamic mechanics, *jing* can be defined as a swift or agile force. But *jing* is neither equal to force, nor is it independent of force. Both are different and related at the same time. Force is a common element, whereas *jing* is a unique, special force. Force is a more generic term. Force has: (1) an action point, (2) magnitude and (3) direction. *Jing* has the same. Internal *jing*, according to the principle of *work and energy*, requires special practice methods in order for energy (as expressed in *elastic potential energy*) to perform action skilfully. Human beings have highly developed nervous systems. Excellent training of the brain will strengthen internal control (by raising the threshold of reacting to stimulus). *Potential qi circulating internally* means gathering potential energy but not showing it externally. *Jing exchange internally*, when poised to activate the potential energy there is a subtle change of *getting ready* that cannot be detected by others. This is the stage of *others don't know me but I alone know them* or *genius derived from knowing others; wisdom manifested in the application of hidden skills. Gather and release* is an organic linking and connecting process. Skilful gathering will result in skilful release. This is the highest level of Taijiquan. Upon reaching the peak zone of Taijiquan skills, one can manoeuvre, leading and forwarding at ease, seeking opportunities to attack wherever whenever by gathering and releasing skilfully. Human beings possess a secondary communication system, which acts as a conditioning device of our behaviour. It provides us with complex and detailed analysis of multiple stimuli, helps to maintain our self-awareness, and at the same time governs and conditions our behaviour. In push-hands practice, our feelings and senses, just as in any physical exercise, are the reflections of this secondary communication system (including language and thoughts). Chen Xin said, *use mind to reason, use reason to move qi*. In this context, the word 'reason' is understood as a function of our secondary communication system. *Internal jing*; the word 'internal' can be understood as a function, directed by the brain, working and balancing meticulously throughout our organs and during our various activities.

SECTION 4: *Co-relationship of "empty" "solid" and "double yang"* [雙重]

When the body reacts to external stimuli, there are two main reflections: the *Yang* and the *Yin*. The former is active, and the latter is passive. They are opposites of each other. When doing push-hands in Taijiquan, both reflections exist in various parts of the body, permeating, guiding and interacting with each other. For example, in *yang* forwarding and *yin* retreating, upper body is *yin* and lower body is *yang*. If both are *yang* or both are *yin*, this becomes double solid, the allocation of *yin* and *yang* is not in balance. This is known in Taijiquan classics as *there is empty and solid in every movement. Yang* reflection is *attach*, *yin* reflection is *detach*.

The objective of both is to reach the stage of *when others are hard and I am soft to reach the same goal*. According to Taijiquan classics, *attach is detach, detach is attach*. These are different means of reaching the same goal: self control and the control of others. Know the work and utility of *jing*. The limbs and different parts of the body are reacting; *yin* and *yang* complementing each other just perfectly. Upon reaching this seamless stage there are no errors to be found. Consequently, one will not lose the combat.

If you cannot circulate and change effectively you will be controlled by others. This problem is called *double yang (double-weightedness)*. Conversely, *if you can carry and transform effectively, you will be able to control others*. When others sink you follow. Follow free and expedient. Follow means smooth. Double *yang* signifies blockage and not free and nor expedient.

There is a saying; *a mind cannot be used in two places*. Using a mind in two places will denote double *yang*. Scattered attention cannot get things done. Releasing *jing* is like releasing an arrow; *focusing on one direction*. Focus is opposite of scattered. Where your body is, your mind follows, that is, paying attention to wherever you are. Focusing means *not missing nor going against[7];* which is a state of alertness that allows you to observe the cues elicited from your opponent. From this stage you can attach, glue, link and follow an opponent who is double-weighted and unfocussed.

Lost or giving up appears either before or after *going against*. When *going against*, one can immediately feel lost. Both are problems of the same cause. When you detect that your opponents is *lost*, or *going against*, according to Taijiquan principles, this is the moment you should release your *jing* on them.

In a daze momentarily is also a problem of *going against*. When one can *carry and transform* effectively, a momentary daze will not happen. *In a daze* is also a state of double *yang*. *Daze* is a moment when one's brain draws a blank, and the opponent can seize the chance. This is a fleeting moment and if you miss the opportunity, you have in fact   incurred a double *yang* yourself, and would be controlled by your opponent. Note that when *jing* is interrupted but the mind is not, this is not a case of *in a daze*. It is important to note the difference, and not fall into the trap. *Jing* may be hindered but the mind is still leading.

The problem of double-weightedness means that your centre is in the power of your opponent, and you cannot detect the centre of your opponent. You are not able to circulate and transform in any space, be it a foot, an inch, or less. The label double *yang* is used in a combat situation when you are under the influence of your opponent. It is used to describe how you handle your opponent.

Double *yang* can also be used to describe oneself when you are practicing and working on the forms. When you feel rigid and not loose and free, this is the problem of double-weightedness. When you are experiencing double *yang*, you will handle your opponent in the same state. Conversely, when you can handle your opponent without the problem of double *yang*, you yourself are not in the state of double *yang*. Cause and effect of double *yang* depends on how one handles the combat situation.

In theory, double *yang* depends on time and space. While one can be free from double-

[7] going against: meeting force with force.

weightedness at a certain time and space doesn't guarantee that double *yang* will not happen in a different situation at another time. The top martial artists are not exempt from this problem. The important thing is that when you are experiencing a momentary daze, it should not be detected by the opponent, and as such you will not face the problem of double-weightedness. In push-hands, the standard formula is as follows:

Know thyself   (Circulate and transform to avoid double *yang*, and not be
                  controlled by others)

Know thy opponent (Force him to experience double *yang*, block his circulation and
                  transformation, and put him under your control)

The concept of empty and solid is closely related to one's intent. *Intent is solid and without intent is empty*. However, empty and solid can be changing, transforming, and permeating and is each other's root. The magic application is, *solid with empty, and empty with solid*. This is why Taijiquan is so fascinating. In offence there is defence, and in defence there is also offence. Every move is circular; every move can also be linear.

Chairman Mao applied the empty and solid theory to the guerrilla warfare that he conducted, by summarizing his insights into 16 words: *Enemy advances, I retreat. Enemy stops, I disturb. Enemy tired, I attack. Enemy retreats, I chase. If the enemy advances* is solid, *I retreat* is empty. Through *enemy tired I attack...*, and a series of transformation from empty to solid, made it possible to attain success with fewer troops and a weaker force.

This is the magic of Taijiquan, employing less force to check the larger power, using soft to command the hard, and leisure awaiting the labour, quietness restraining the action. All these are results of changing and transforming solid and empty.

In practicing Taijiquan, the soles of your feet must experience empty and solid:

Soles differentiate empty and solid clearly
Pull back is empty; push out is solid
Toes loose when empty; grasping firmly when solid
Empty when appropriate; solid when timely
Yong Quan[8] [湧泉] is filled when empty;
Yong Quan is depleted when solid
Bow leg is ready with elasticity power;
Conserving and releasing is controlled by one's centre
When sitting the leg is solid and rooted,
Bow step allows moving forward gradually
Up and down forming a straight line, with the middle directing both ends

In practicing *push hands* recently, I had a further appreciation of the notions of *empty* and *quiet*. Empty will hold everything and quiet will permit one to respond to all. While these concepts are the fundamentals of Taijiquan, they can be followed as a way of life as well. The practice of Taijiquan is far beyond just a physical exercise. It has become a philosophy of life for me.

---

[8] *Yong Quan*: (literally Bubbling Spring) an acupuncture point located approximately in the centre of the sole of the foot.

Not understanding double yang. The problem lies in limiting your own movements at the wrong time and space, causing your own double-weightedness. There are external sources that cause double *yang* as well. There are in fact two kinds of double *yang*. The first one is self inflicted and the other is caused externally. The latter is produced externally first with the aim to generate internal impetus to cause double heavy. Point of action, direction and path are the unique features of Taijiquan's internal movements. The internal movement must not be detected by the opponent. It is like an inertia force that, with a slight touch, will turn instantly, first with intent, then as an instinctive internal movement. To be effective, your mind and intended movement must be ahead of your opponent. Otherwise you will lose control to your enemy. Movement is not just the change of form; it means the intent to change. Double *yang* is caused by the delay of intent, lagging behind your opponent, moving sluggishly, not grasping the right moment and situation, limiting one's own moves, not leaving and not blocking appropriately. Performance is based on the transformation of empty and solid, and not just based on the reception of the senses from the four auxiliary bows.

Wu (Hao) style requires a straight *central* posture. Spine and the center of the face are aligned. Both hip bones supporting (it is the same meaning as *waist and knee transitioning*). *Empty and solid* is strictly adhered to; at the same time each can permeate one another, without sudden break. Potential *qi* is buoyant, with a clear circular path. Master Hao Shao Ru said, *'Central concentration' does not mean 'Central stop'.* Upon further reflection, this means a straight body alignment, moving forward, backward and sideways. Transitional moves with and without direction require *hand leading, spirit following, body posture proper with steady steps.*

My most recent reflections: while elasticity and pliability denote two different substances, they are both soft and yielding in nature. Elasticity is primarily yielding, whereas pliability is mainly soft and supple. The application of softness is related to the transformation of empty and solid. Using softness to regulate hardness is a practical exercise of Taijiquan. Quoting Master Yao Fu Chun [姚馥春], *Taijiquan's every move has solid and empty, each point has solid and empty. In other words, Solid and empty is ubiquitous.* To grasp this empty and solid concept will depend on the alertness of one's senses.

SECTION 5: *Application of Techniques in Taijiquan*

The meaning of *Hua Yin* [化 引], *Na* [拿] and *Fa* [发][9]:

Hua Yin: dissolve (neutralize) and lure (lure your opponent into using his *jing* then neutralize his force to put him off balance).

Na: capture or seize (use one hand to seize, use both hands to capture. Techniques may differ but usage is the same. The point of capture is to lock the joints, terminate at the root, and break your opponent's posture).

Fa: release (add to your opponent's incoming *jing*, and when you feel that you are in control, release the combined *jing*.

---

[9] See also Chapter Three for another discussion on *na* and *fa*.

To summarize, dissolve (neutralize) and lure, capture, and release are the techniques of the Taijiquan principle *Lure incoming jing so that it misses the target, capture and release the combined jing.*

The purpose of *hua yin* is to enable yourself by disabling your opponent. Conversely if you are disabled by your opponent, you will not be able to *dissolve and lure*. Even if you try to *capture*, you will not be able to use the technique effectively as you are experiencing double *yang* and are under the control of your opponent. Subsequently there can be no *release*.

Three conditions must exist in order to *fa*: 1) potential opportunity (enabled or disabled); 2) timing, and 3) direction. These three conditions are created by using *hua yin* and *na*. In a situation when these three conditions are met, and you still cannot *fa*, it is because you are experiencing double *yang*. You are disabled as your force is *lured* by your opponent, and in effect facilitating his *releasing the combined force.*

Guarding the centre (my most recent reflections)

There are two situations:

1. Prior to *lure and let miss* (luring and causing your opponent to go off-balance)
   The *dan tian* should be shifted appropriately forward. This is the *guarding the centre* position prior to lure and let miss. The centre of gravity is directly in line with the centre of one's base centre of balance. This is essential to causing your opponent to be off balance.

   Conversely, a slight backward shift of the *dan tian* will affect your *guarding the centre* position. A backward shift will cause your centre of gravity to be off-line with your base centre of balance.

2. After *lure and let miss*

   After accomplishing *lure and let miss*, I am in the control of the situation. I can advance, retreat, move up or down, and I can do as I wish while *guarding the centre*.

   The meaning of *lure and let miss:*

   Lure your opponent to make his force miss the target, so that he loses his centre and, as a result, loses his rooting. At the same time *guard the centre*, enabling you to root to the ground. By disabling your opponent's force, he is under your control.

   Understanding the techniques of *hua yin, na* and *fa* will lead to a deeper appreciation of the principle of *lure and let miss*. *Combine to release*. *Hua yin* is essentially the same as *lure and let miss*. *Na* and *fa* use the combined force to advance.

   Na is the bridge between *hua yin* and *fa*. *Intent* occurs the split second prior to your opponent's missing. The action of *na* is conducted upon the moment of his missing (*five yang and five yin*[10]). When you grasp your opponent's exact moment of *missing*, your *fa* will be successful.

It is important to note that prior to *lure and let miss*, the *dan tian* must not retract backward. If the *dan tian* retreats backward, the centre of gravity is not perpendicular to the bottom, and is moved out of centre. You will fall before you can accomplish *lure and let miss*.

Yi (intent) summons *qi*, and *qi* summons *jing*. *Yi*, *qi* and *jing* become united. They can be hidden at will or appear on command. Your *yi* is always ahead of your opponent. Hide is soft; appear is firm. *Hide and appear are unpredictable, capture and let miss are under my control.*

My opponent has jing. So have I and my jing is ahead of his. My opponent appears without jing. So am I, but my yi is still leading. When I feel the power of my opponent, I immediately neutralize the power and get ahead of him, rendering his power useless. My dissolving of his power will put him under my control. In order to appreciate this principle it is important to pay attention to one's intention. Your *yi* must be ahead of your opponent in every move. Observe stillness and action. Where the point of contact seems quiet, be aware of action in other parts of the body, and know the transformation of open and close, empty and solid.

The folding and layering of *qi* must be done continuously and without stopping. The body posture is rounded, curved and seamless. This is especially significant in using *jing*, such as in transforming from soft to heavy and vice versa.

Follow the tempo of your opponent by controlling your own tempo. Slow him when he intends to be quick, and rush him when he intends to slow down. My opponent must not detect my tempo or rhythm. It is essential that only I know my own tempo.

The relationship of *slow and quick, light and heavy*: There is lightness in slow and lightness in quick; there is heavy in slow heavy in quick. These combinations appear unpredictable and are therefore difficult to control. *Use yi to direct Empty and Solid, and use hand movements to express Light and Heavy.*

The magic of *jing appears stopped but your intent is not* is used in conjunction with a flash attack. When you are advancing quickly your *jing* may appear to have stopped (a method of *quick empty*); as soon as your *jing* appears empty, you must attack with lightning speed to take your opponent by surprise. Focus on one direction. Don't hesitate. Quick open and swift close is essential.

Lure your opponent to attack and disable him: *I am enabled but my opponent is disabled* is one aspect of the folding and layering of *qi*.

Hit heavily but land lightly; hit lightly but land heavily. Become buoyant and transform continuously, totally mystifying (not delayed and not sluggish) to your opponent. *Observe stillness as movement; observe movement as stillness* is another important key to folding and layering.

Lock the joints and cut off communication. Use your *jing* to lock the shoulder joints of your opponent. The purpose is to prevent your opponent's *qi* from sinking to his *dan tian*.

---

[10] five *yang* and five *yin*: That exact moment; split second timing.

When *qi* is floating, the body falters, and your opponent is completely under your control. This particular move is called *qing*[11] [擎]. *Qing* allows you to borrow power from your opponent.

Lure your opponent to advance and to miss. Miss means not letting your opponent know the direction of your *jing* (action point and action path).

Power is to be borrowed— add to whatever is offered. The action of adding is for your own use and must not be used by your opponent. One way of adding to the offered power is to employ *Chan Si Jing* [纏絲勁]. *Using four ounces to deflect a thousand pounds* means that the capital is small but the interest is huge. Use the offered thousand pounds by your opponent, and add four ounces complementary force.

Sources of power offerings: Your opponent offers it, your opponent is tricked into offering it, and your opponent is forced to offer it. Accept all offers.

There are ten thousand applications, but there is only one *jing*. The intent may be different, and that is how *jing* can be used differently. *Jing* does not exist outside the *point of application*. When there is no application, *jing* cannot be expressed. Practical application is a medium through which *jing* can be performed. Therefore, practicing the basic form is one way to achieve the potential goal of expressing *jing*. Use practice and understanding to develop the ability to express *jing*.

Recently I did push hands with some people who demonstrated knowledge of Chang Quan[12] [長拳] and *san shou*[13] [散手]. Regardless of what they attempted, all I needed to do was focus my *yi* to attach and control their root, lure them to *show their hands*, and when they missed, use the moment to topple them to one side with both feet off the ground. It did not take too much effort to be successful. This confirmed my belief that Taijiquan is indeed an effective martial art. Of this, I have no doubts.

Push hands is like a spear and shield, both are effective but can only be used against the other. The application of push hands is continuous and changing. Attach is to restrain, detach is to dissolve; restrain then dissolve, dissolve then restrain. Cause is effect, effect is cause. Accordingly, internal reason uses external cause as a condition. An external cause on me results as internal reason on my opponent. External expression is directed by internal cause.

Like a spider in the centre of its web, one must always have control of the centre, so as to attend to any minute movement in the surrounding area with ease. A snake coiled with its head centred allows the greatest spread of control and is the quickest in offence. Snake hunters invariably have to wait for the snake to uncoil before they can capture the snake.

According to *The Psychology of Exercise* by a well known Russian professor, a *responding movement* can be divided into three stages: getting ready, performance, and taking effect. Applying this model to the principle of *internal cause external release*, it can be further divided into:

---

[11] *qing*: to lift or hold up.
[12] Chang Quan: Northern Fist. A style of wushu developed in northern China.
[13] *san shou*: free-style, full-contact combat.

I. Internal cause (Getting ready)
1. Prepare intent
2. Begin intent, no internal adjustment yet
3. Intent began, internal adjustment begins
4. Internal adjustment began, no external release yet (using *qi*)

II. External release (performing, and taking effect)
5. Prepare to release (receiving *jing* from opponent, and use *qi* to suppress it)
6. Ready to release
7. Begin to release
8. Released and mission accomplished (taking effect;transforming at the right moment)

Russian physiologist Pavlov's exercise theory should be helpful in the explanation of *knowing jing* in Taijiquan. *Genius is derived from knowing; wisdom is manifested in the application of hidden skills.* His theory helps to explain the concept of *without internal adjustment, there can be no external release.* This model applies even when the response is very swift (as if it is automatic). All stages would still need to happen, albeit at a much faster rate.

Chen Xin's theory, *Get a head start and strive for the upper stream 99% of the time* is based on the *Yi Jing*[14] [易經] principle of *Empty and Full.* When *qi* is at its fullest, it is at this precise moment the interchange of empty and full takes place. Sharp, alert, attentive and fully aware that *without internal adjustment, there can be no external release.* To be light is swift, swift is move, move is change, change is dissolve. Lightness is derived from empty and quiet. Chen Wei Ming [陳微明] said, *alight on emptiness, and appear to be light. Pay full attention to using one's waist and legs. As light as a feather...* In order to be in total control, you must be light and swift, and be able to react to your opponent's slightest movement in preparation for internal readiness.

SECTION 6: *Chan Si Jing [*纏 絲 勁*] (Silk Reeling Energy)*

[Editor's note: The contents of this section are excerpts from articles written by Luo Ji Hong during the great Spiral Force Debate of 1964 in the national magazine Sports Journal. See Chapter One.]

Chan Si Jing (Silk Reeling Energy) typifies the continuous metamorphoses from square to circle, and from circle to square. Points cumulate to form a line, lines cumulate to form an area, and areas cumulate to become a volume. The point is the basic element of all. A point will lead to the formation of a square or a circle. The condition of heavy or empty depends on this one point. A point is a minuscule circle, invisible to the eye; and while it may not convey the shape, it denotes the idea of a circle. Volume can be cubical or spherical in shape, its conversion caused by movement and dependant on one's will or intent.

Chan Si Jing utilizes spiral movement in its application[15]. The changes in rotation, path, distance and axis, conform to the theories of dynamic mechanics. In practice, Taijiquan forms use

---

[14] *Yi Jing*: (also written as I Ching) the *Yi Jing* or Book of Changes is an ancient Chinese divination manual and book of wisdom.

[15] *Chan Si Jing*: Silk Reeling Energy (Force) so named because it resembles the unraveling of a silkworm cocoon. The cocoon is constructed from a single continuous thread. When unraveling, the thread comes off in a spiral motion.

slow rhythm as a foundation and fast rhythm in its application.

Jing, based on kinetic theory, has a point of application or contact, direction and magnitude. Silk Reeling Energy is a spiral force manifested by a change in direction (according to the change in the radius of curve). The uniqueness of the rotational turn is that it has two simultaneous motions: a particle's translational motion and the particle's self-spinning movement. At a certain point in time, the self-spinning particle is in a different space than its displacement. Xu Zhi Yi[16], in his book *Wu's Taijiquan*, discussed a similar concept; that every move should be perceived as individual points joining. Thus, Taijiquan movements can be both linear and circular.

While Taijiquan has been well established as a circular activity, it must be understood that Taijiquan is not a two dimensional circular movement, nor should individual moves be viewed as a particle following an enclosed circular track. It is, rather, a complex spiral motion performed in a three dimensional space with up and down, left and right, back and forth, internal and external motions. Taijiquan precepts are *curve while seeking straight; curve in order to effect change; curve has no fixed orientation; straight in order to release; straight has direction; straight while seeking curve; the move is linear. However a slight touch will trigger a smooth rotational turn; turn softly and forcefully release; translational motion and rotational turn, combining and transforming; yin inseparable from yang; and yang inseparable from yin, each the root of the other*. All these principles are *sine qua non* (absolute prerequisites) of Taijiquan.

Chan Si Jing is an inherent characteristic present in all forms of Taijiquan, although it is more apparent in forms such as Chen style, and less so in other forms such as Wu (Hao) style. Without this common characteristic, no form can claim to be real Taijiquan. Taijiquan is a distinctive cultural wushu exercise.

What exactly is *Chan Si Jing*? Understanding *Chan Si Jing* will help us solve the perennial argument whether it is a common factor in all forms of Taijiquan.

Jing, according to dynamic mechanics, is essentially a spiral force, which consists of axial force, tangential force, and radial force. These components combine to form various types of resultant forces. *Jing* is not a two-dimensional but a three-dimensional or spiral force. As such, it has no fixed orientation but depends on the external force. *Jing* is swift and agile, *a force magical when confronting the enemy*. Spiral force is a combination of translational displacement and self-spinning motion. The two movements enact concurrently not separately. It should not be viewed simply as *joining contiguously* as indicated by Master Xu. Why is such an incorrect perception formed in the first place? In my view, it is because of the tendency to isolate each upper body movement from the rest, missing the important fact that *waist operates as an axis*. Each part is treated as an individual link of the *exercise chain*; each joint provides its own support, and each forms a *movement partner*. Thus, most students view the circular movement of Taijiquan as either translational or self-spinning, without the full understanding that both motions must act together.

Chan Si Jing should be viewed as the same as spiral force. Without spiral force, there is no Silk Reeling Force. Master Xu said he somewhat agreed with this principle but he maintained

---

[16] Xu Zhi Yi: see Chapter One. Master Xu introduced Luo Ji Hong to the great Zhang Da Quan.

that in compact fist forms such as Yang and Wu style, it is not necessary to worry about *Chan Si Jing*. This begs the question: How can one ignore such a basic principle of Taijiquan? My view is that there is no large without small. The compact forms of Taijiquan is using small to leverage large.

On October 21, 1962 Master Long Feng Wu [龍奉武] in his article *Another Discourse on Chan Si Jing* said; *a line is formed by points joining together; each point itself a circle*. This shows his in-depth knowledge of *Chan Si Jing*, far beyond the mere perceptual understanding level. Some schools use poetic terms to illustrate their philosophies, but readers have none. If a poem can negate the objective existence of matters, then researchers like us will be left to rely on straight translations of the Taiji classics in order to make a living.

This reminds me of a poem by Su Shi [蘇軾] of the Song [宋] dynasty…

> *Sideways behold a ridge, upwards a summit.*
> *Its height varies far and near.*
> *Not knowing the true beauty of Lu Shan*[17] *[盧山].*
> *Because I am in the midst.*

It is my belief that looking at things through a fixed perspective instead of being objective would prevent us from gaining a real understanding.

Mr. Yang Yu Ting [楊禹庭] in his book, *Comments on Movement in Taijquan*, said that the fundamental principles of Taijiquan are basically the same. Like calligraphy, styles may vary, word structures remain the same. Chen Xin stated that; *not knowing Chan Si Jing means not knowing Taijiquan*. I could not agree more.

Taijiquan is well recognized as having circular movements as a main characteristic. It is practiced in a three-dimensional space, and is not a two dimensional horizontal movement. As previously stated, the exercise consists of three components: axial force, tangential force and radial force. These components also form several combinations of resultant forces. One important factor of Taijiquan is *slight contact will trigger a smooth rotational turn*. During push hands, both sides are touching and turning. All muscles and joints work together as a *chain of motion*, each section linking and connecting. The body rotates as the axis, up and down, left and right, and back and forth. It is a combination of circular and spinning motions rotating in a three dimensional space. The upper limbs function like levers. Rotation of a limb can occur at one end while the arm is moving in a linear direction at the other. The range of movement is determined by the structure of the individual joints of the upper limb and the arrangement of the associated muscle and bone. The motion of extending the arm forward requires two groups of muscles producing movements in opposite directions, with the scapula acting as a force coupling point. The shoulder joint is a ball and socket joint type, providing the greatest range of movement, enabling the forearm to rotate out and forward with ease. It is thus important to maintain a *loose shoulder* when doing Taijiquan. The hinge joint of the elbow involves the articulation of the distal end of the humerus with the proximal end of the ulna, making it possible for the elbow to flex and extend. The pivot joint of the elbow permits a rotation. The gliding joint of the wrist allows a sliding movement. The condyloid (knuckle) joints of the hand permit movement in two planes. Understanding how the joints work together in the upper limb will lead us to truly appreciate how the arm and wrist

---

[17] Lu Shan: a famous mountain in China. The bottom half is nearly always shrouded in mist. Therefore, the mountain is best observed from a distance.

can rotate and turn accordingly. Without knowledge of anatomy, it is difficult to appreciate *touch and turn smoothly* and to fully launch the special efforts of: adhere and detach, detach and adhere; dissolve and attack, attack and dissolve; dissolve is attack, attack is dissolve. *Taiji is a sphere; Taiji is a cube; within the cube is a sphere, within the sphere is a cube. Within yin there is yang, within yang there is yin, yin and yang nurture each other*. It means a curve is straight, straight is a curve. A cube and a sphere are each other's root, each other's nourishment, and each helps the other. This is the magic of hard and soft. Master Xu, in his article *Soft Till the End* (published in the Sports Journal on August 20, 1962), emphasized the *yin* side of soft. He said it is empty and still, *motion seeking stillness* (i.e. solid seeking emptiness). He said to look for differentiation, a separation of 'two', yet the 'two' unite to form a whole. Master Xu's reasoning is different from the aforementioned Taiji concept. To consider Taiji as the *union of two to become one*, instead of *duality within one* is erroneous in my view.

Wu (Hao) style successor Li Yi Yu [李亦畬], in discussing the heritage of Wu (Hao) style, clearly discerned the significance of *a slight touch will trigger a smooth rotation*. He further explained the principle of using *jing*. By clarifying the fundamentals of *Chou Si Jing*[18] [抽絲勁], he deepened the definition of *pulling*, and yet, narrowed its context. Therefore it is important to practice spiral force to the extent that it becomes an involuntary or habitual reflex. The body will become like *each part is a moving round bead* (Chen Wei Ming [陳微明]); similarly *revolving into a round bead effortlessly* (Chen Xin). It is only at this level that one can launch the actions of adhere, detach, dissolve (neutralize) and release. *Adhere is detach, detach is adhere, dissolve is release, and release is dissolve*. Without spiral movement, *Chou Si Jing* is merely a translational move, a pull without rotation. This is not the true method of Taijiquan. Taijiquan is *motion and stillness not at the same time, yin and yang not in the same space, but an integral entity without separation. Exercise the body in the same space and simultaneously in a different space*. Taijiquan is an activity that unites the translational movement of a particle and its self-spinning motion; therefore *think of a particle with no fixed direction, but also with direction, and it becomes magical when encountering the enemy*. If there is only translational movement in Taijiquan, agility and flexibility will be greatly limited. Different interpretations of *Chou Si Jing* are the crux of the problem, and a bone of contention of many arguments.

Chan Si Jing is an inherent attribute of Taijiquan. The phrase *Chou Si Jing* is not as descriptive as *Chan Si Jing*. Although the two labels attempt to explain the same concept and both contain the notion of *extension and intersection*, it is not really up to us researchers to infer shared meaning from the classics. Our job is to understand the facts, observe the connection, to recognize the problem and to instruct and practice. Wu (Hao) style successor Hao Wei Zhen [郝為真] called *Chan Si Jing* "*Ma Hua*[19] *Jing*" [麻花勁]. These various metaphorical labels all attempt to describe the unique spiral characteristic of Taijiquan. Yang and Wu (Hao) styles originate from Chen style. The other Wu style originates from the compact forms of Yang. During his lifetime, Wu Jian Quan did not claim his Taijiquan as a unique style. It is said that Master Wu was very self-depreciative when asked about his form. He said; *my form is the Yang style compact form, this was what I learned and this is what I teach*. We can appreciate that, although there are various styles and characteristics of Taijiquan, *Chan Si Jing* remains a common attribute in all. It is simply more apparent in some forms than in others.

---

[18] *Chou Si Jing*: (Pulling Silk Force) similar to *Chan Si Jing* but here the emphasis is on a constant pressure and rate of jing.

[19] *Ma Hua*: a deep-fried pastry. The batter is slowly piped into the hot oil using a spiral motion resulting in a "knot" shaped delicacy.

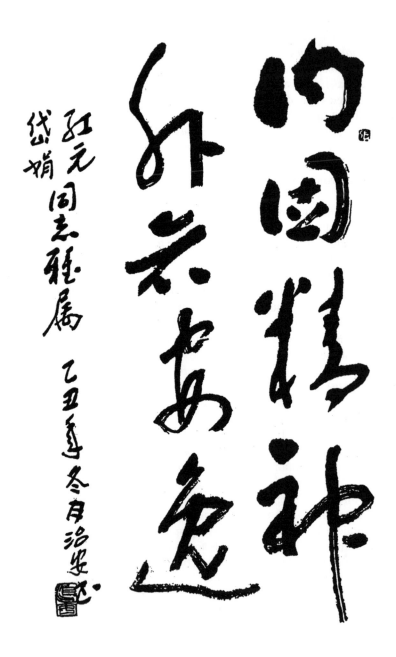

To: Hong Yuan and Dai Yuan
"Spirited Within, Relaxed and Tranquil Without"
From: Zhi An Zhang, Winter 1985
(Zhi An Zhang is a renowned Chinese Artist)

CHAPTER 3

My Journey on the Road of Taiji

My love for Taiji began under my father's influence, inspiration and instruction. Walking on the road of Taiji was difficult, but soothing at the same time. Every step on this journey is filled with my father's heart and hope, and every success I have is clearly marked with my father's fingerprints. (IIlustration.3-1-1)

Luo Ji Hong and Luo Hong Yuan (1983)
(Illustration. 3-1-1)

In my earliest memories, my father was already a legend and held the status of a celebrity. Suffering from a terminal disease his doctor had given up hope. But my father fought for his life by practicing Taiji and Qigong, with the result that he recovered his health and later became stronger and stronger. His *soft kung fu*, Taijiquan, was like magic. Even as a very young child, I was always very proud of such a father.

When I was very young, my father lived 40 kilometres from home in the Shantou Rehab Center to recover from his illness and to practice Taiji. Occasionally, he would come home and stay for a while. Every day, besides practicing his slow moving Taiji, he would immerse himself in writing, focusing on a Taiji principle written on the blackboard, or musing. He once brought home model human bones and spent a day trying to reconstruct a skeleton. Our family was large but our home was small, so he would put those bones under our beds during the night. We soon became used to them and were not scared any more. Sometimes my father asked us to help, like playing erectors, to put together a complete human skeleton frame up piece by piece. After dinner, in the evening, the procession of visitors coming to our home to learn Taiji never stopped. Normally a very shy man, my father would now become very eloquent, excited with words talking about Taijiquan. He also became as agile as a dragon and a tiger when pushing hands, throwing opponents at his will in any direction he wished. I was very impressed. I was five or six years of age then and imitated him from behind. I learned simplified Yang style and Taiji sword. I especially liked Taiji sword and put on a performance when I was in second grade at the elementary school.

I remember an event which left a lasting impression on me. I was playing spiral sea shells with other kids. We ground the spiral shell on all four sides to make a square tower, showing spiral lines on the shell like those round stairs. My Father saw our works, and became very interested. He asked for several of them. On the next day he mailed two of them to Master Gu Liu Xin. Several weeks later he asked for more. At that time I did not know why he was so interested in our toys, but we were happy and proud because our "works" were appreciated by adults. Recently, when I studied my father's correspondence with Master Gu, I discovered the reason behind his interest in our toys. Enclosed with the package of our spiral shell toys to Master Gu was his letter: *Along the seashore, kids like to play sea shells. They especially like to grind spiral shells to a tower. A circle has a square, a square has a circle, and a square and circle are mutual and coincide with Taiji's spiral force. What is spiral force? It is vortex power, to exist inside and outside, to have no beginning and no end. The spiral line can extend infinitely, tangentially, centrifugally, radially, centripetally, circumvolutory, up and down, correlated with each other, forming a multi-dimensional force system. The radius can be considered a spiral line in space; points make a line, but points themselves are circles. A non-closed curve line is also a spiral circle.* Master Gu replied: *The package with the two spiral seashells is very interesting. Chen Xin, I remember, also mentioned spiral force; he might also have been inspired by the same thing. Whenever it is convenient for you please send me two more, one original without grinding, and the other ground.*

My father not only studied Taiji theory from books. He also tried to observe the most elementary, most simple, and most common instances in daily life, and use them to explain the profound theory of Taiji. His approach had a far-reaching influence on me. When I studied Taiji theory later, I would also absorb principles from daily life into practical examples.

My father spoke of Master Gu a lot. After he returned from Shanghai for his Taiji studies, he often mentioned Master Hao Shao Ru, Master Shao Pin Gen and many others. I liked to listen to Taiji stories from my father. The more I heard, the more I was attracted to the Taiji circle.

My father was swept up in the Great Cultural Revolution in China and was arrested and jailed in *Buffalo Hut*[1]. At the time of his arrest, he did not think about his own safety but sought to preserve the collection of books and materials on Taiji which he had gathered with much effort over the years. He kept admonishing his students to keep the collection safe, over and over. At that time I was only 12 years of age, and though I did not quite understand my father's intent, I was deeply moved by his love for Taiji. It was then when I started to love what my father loved. For a time, my mother was also held in a concentration camp. As the children of *enemies of the People*, my brothers and I were often persecuted. It was commonly believed that *the sins of the father visited upon the progeny*. We would be punished for the slightest infractions, real or otherwise. I remember several times being made to *ride the airplane*[2] as punishment. I became determined to learn to protect myself and my family. I organized several other teens and we practiced in secret. Late at night we punched and kicked banana trees until we were exhausted. I became single-minded and extremely focused on my training. I learned to channel my energy

---

[1] *Buffalo Hut*: a notorious concentration camp set up for the "re-education" of those deemed as enemies.
[2] *"ride the airplane"*: a particularly painful punishment. A victim was made to stand on a chair with his arms tied behind his back with one end of rope. The other end of the rope was thrown over a rafter and secured. The chair was then kicked out from under the victim, leaving him swinging in the air.

into the study of Taiji.

In 1970, our family moved back to our countryside home town of Xingning where I continued my high school education. Soon after our return, my father's books were recovered and sent to us. An artist friend of ours helped us wrap all the books, sort them into categories, and catalogue them. Whenever I had time I would read those books.

Though I did not understand the profound and mysterious classic Taiji theory, I enjoyed the stories of famous Taiji masters. When my father had a chance to come home he was overjoyed to see the care we had taken with his "beloved books." It was then, that I formally requested to study Taiji from my father. Surprised with joy he said: *I thought my Taiji would have no one to inherit, and I would have to give all these books to the library. Now it is good I can bequeath them to you.*

That same night, my father brought me to a piece of flat land where we started our formal master-student relationship. At the first enlightenment class, father said: *Young man, now I will let you try to see what Taijiquan really is.* He widened his stance, and lowered himself a little. He then asked me to push him. At the time I was sixteen and I loved sports. I trained in track and field and basketball at the Amateur Athletic Education School and my physical condition and athletic quality was at its prime. By contrast, my father's health was not that good and after those years of hardship, he looked thin and weak. When I pushed against him, I did not go all out and my father moved me easily sideways. However, he saw through me, and said: *Young man, do not worry about me. Do all you can. I want to know how powerful you are.* I then wound up and pushed with as much force as I could. The next thing I remember was I was on the ground on all fours. When I stood up, my father lifted up his right leg, and, standing only on his left leg, asked me to try once more. This time I put everything into it and charged. As soon as I made contact, both of my legs left the ground, and I landed on my head. My father stretched his hand to get hold of my shoulder to hold me up. Later I realized that my father used *cai jing* [采劲] (pull down power), which was his favourite. It took me a while to recover from this sudden disorientation. Those three pushes by my father showed me the wonderful charm of Taiji. I was greatly attracted: *This is Taiji!* I told myself then and there: *I must master Taiji!*

Thereafter, my father used his two weeks leave to explain Taiji theory to me, showing me the basic entrance level training of *Five Bows*, and a series of basic moves and basic postures. Finally he taught me the single move training of Yang style. He said: *Yang style Taijiquan is decently stretched out in comfort, like the standard style in calligraphy. Once you have a good foundation in Yang style, the other styles will be easier to learn. Single move training is to repeat and train each single move. This practice is simple and repetitive, easy for people to master the principles and internal feeling of the move.*

After my father left, I spent at least two hours a day on the basketball court or the track field practicing what my father assigned to me as homework (in addition to my school studies and my athletic training). Sometimes I would practice along the 400 meter track such Yang style moves as *Part the Wild Horse's Mane, Brush Knee and Twist Step, Step Back* and *Repulse Monkey* and so on. Six months earlier I had dislocated my hip joint during a baseball game, which had never fully healed. After a period of Taiji training, not only was the injury gone, but my body was stronger and more flexible. My athletic sports performance greatly improved. This was even more of an incentive to practice Taiji. In 1973, I successfully competed in the Guangdong Provincial

Junior Track and Field Tournament. After the competition, I decided to take a temporary absence from school for a year so I could concentrate on my Taiji studies with my father. After seeing my determination, my father agreed.

At that time, my father was being *reformed through labour* at the mine site he had once managed, and was not permitted to teach Taiji. He asked me to go to Shantou to study the Yang style form from his senior students. I spent three days in intensive study and practice, completed the whole set, and then rushed back to my father. My father's residence was approximately a dozen square meters. We used it as a home and a Taiji classroom. In the political climate of the day, we were not supposed to practice Taiji. We had to cover the windows with newspapers for the spies not to see inside. The next day my father set out a detailed study plan. Early in the morning, I would use the gasoline stove to make breakfast, and my father would practice in the small room and let me observe him. I would practice after him and let him correct and coach me. Then we would push hands together. In this way we utilized both the short time and the small space.

According to the traditional way of teaching Taiji, one must study the form for at least four years before starting push-hands practice. My father, in contrast, taught me both at the same time. Push hands training is a means to test the form's postures. When form and application are practiced simultaneously both benefit mutually and progress is made in both areas. This training procedure was an important reform to shorten the learning cycle, and enhance study efficiency. When my father went to work, I was left home to practice and study Taiji's classical theories. When my father returned, he would ask probing questions, test me, or provide further explanations. This gave me a systematic knowledge of Taiji theory.

We lived half way up a hill. After dinner, my father would take me for a walk along the small path through the hill, discussing Taiji principles, talking about his training experience, and even more interestingly, telling me stories of famous masters. When it became dark we would go to practice in a nearby cemetery. For us, this was a big undisturbed space free of spies. Even the Red Guard was reluctant to come near the place. Today, when I close my eyes, I can still see the profile of my father practicing Taiji in the moonlight. Sometimes after practice, we would watch the tranquil spacious sky, the stars and the moon, breathing the fresh and sweet air. One time my father said emotionally: *If I had the chance, I would pick a deep jungle mountain to practice Taiji for a period of time.* (Illustration.3-1-2)

Luo Ji Hong pushing hands with Luo Hong Yuan (1976)
(Illustration 3-1-2)

Before the Great Cultural Revolution, my father had spent almost ten years seriously studying Taiji's theory and technique. He studied with famous masters in Shanghai and had learned many new techniques and principles. He had enhanced his Taiji abilities to a very high level. Even though he was still on full time sick leave, he attracted many students. They were, however, temporary and part-time students. Father had to improvise and adjust his teaching methods to each class. It was therefore very difficult to devise a training system with measurable results. Later, during the Great Cultural Revolution, he was not free to openly practice or teach Taiji. I was the only student on whom he could test and refine his teaching methods. I, who stayed day and night with him, was the first student who trained under what became known as the Ji Hong Taiji system.

My father designed a very complete training system. First, he divided Taijiquan into the two parts of *control of the self* and *control of others*. Since I was in very good athletic condition, he concentrated my training on developing internal power and on posture and single move practice. Every day I was training *Buffalo Strength*, which was a very demanding energetic training in both quality and quantity. This type of training laid down a very solid foundation towards the quality of my internal power.

My father believed that speed and internal power were key elements in competitive sports. After my body adjusted to the correct postures and I had developed a certain quality of *yi* (intent), *qi* (internal energy), and *jing* (internal power), my father trained me to improve my speed. According to the principle of "store energy like stretching a bow, and *fa jing* like shooting an arrow", he required me to always be in a state of a *fully stretched bow and fully pulled string ready to touch and shoot*. He tested the quality of my state of stored energy and my state of readiness by observing my *fa jing*. First I trained to store energy and explode in a single move or posture. Then I applied the same state to the entire form. I was required to *fa jing* on every movement in the form. Finally I was required to *fa jing* at any moment on receiving a signal. When I was practicing, my father sat behind me and gave signals by knocking on the tea table, demanding I respond immediately. In addition, he required me to use different parts of my body to do *fa jing* training in different situations.

This training was often misinterpreted by outsiders. One time, I was challenged by a senior student of a famous master who was renowned for his Taiji staff. As I had no staff handy, I used a broomstick. We squared off, and on the first move, I sent his staff flying. My father had trained me to anticipate and react faster with *fa jing* training. My opponent wrote to his master describing the match. His master wrote back accusing me of not using real Taiji as *authentic Taiji does not use fast moves.*

One day, after spending a period of time on internal power and speed training, my father told me: *You have developed 'control of self'. Now I will start teaching you how to 'control others'.* He then taught me *locking force.* My father said: *How can a little boy control and drive a huge buffalo? The key is to connect to and pull on its nose, which, in turn, controls the buffalo. Man's 'buffalo nose' is located on the lower back, called the 'ming men' point. Once you connect to and lock up your opponent's ming men, your opponent would be unable to utilize and transmit his own power, and thus would be under your control. This is the secret of Taiji's 'four ounces move a thousand pounds'.* To explain the principle of *locking force*, my father first used anatomical pictures and medical skeletons to explain the structure of the collar bones and the vertebrae. Then he taught me how to practice and apply the different forms of *locking force* and how to master the readiness state. He also helped me improve the quality of internal power under different conditions.

He instructed me in push hands not to care too much about winning or losing, but to concentrate on applying *locking force*. After much practice, I could usually apply *locking force* on an opponent in push hands. I became very confident, thinking that I had mastered *locking force*. However, in one push hands contest, the opponent was very quick and refused to connect to my force. I was upset. I tried very hard but was not able to lock his force. When my father heard about it, he told me a story about a young cat and an old cat: *One day there was a young cat who spotted a lizard. After carefully stalking his prey, the cat leapt on the lizard's writhing tail and sunk his claws. The lizard instinctively dropped its tail and ran away. Some time later an old cat came upon another lizard. The old cat focused on the lizard's body and disregarded the wiggling tail. Finally, he pounced and caught both the lizard and its tail.* He used this story to explain to me that I must get rid of the distraction from the contact point and concentrate on the *Main Bow*[3]. At the same time, he taught me techniques like *use cold force[4] (vibratory force) to penetrate a solid opponent*, and *sense an opening, attack immediately*. This greatly enriched my control technique. He also encouraged me to practice more, to analyze problems in practice, and solve them by developing an organic relationship between theory and practice.

Besides teaching me push hands, my father paid special attention to *sanshou* (free fighting) training. He helped me develop an even stronger state of readiness in *sanshou* training, how to use *yi* (intent) to control an opponent at a distance, how to anticipate an opponent's intent, and how to judge the range of reach and distance. He said: *Before contact we must wrap up the opponent with our intent to control him.* This was the meaning of *fu* [敷] (control). Ten years later,

---

[3] For an explanation of the Five Bow Module see Chapter Five
[4] See footnote 7 in Chapter One

at a symposium, Master Lei Mu Ni asked me what the meaning of *fu* was. I gave him my father's explanation of control. Impressed, Master Lei said: *This is a very advanced level explanation.* My father was very strict with me during *sanshou* training. He required that at all times I must be like a cat ready to jump on a mouse, store full energy, and use intent to control my opponent. This way, as soon as he entered my range, I could speedily explode to lock him up. One time, as my father sparred with me, I slowly approached him, inside his reaching range. A fly came by in front of his face. He drove the fly away with his hand and I did not respond. He immediately scolded me: *I moved my hand. Why did you not respond? If I had not moved to drive the fly away, but to attack you instead, what would have been the result?* I never forgot that lesson.

My father was good at explaining the Taiji principles using modern scientific observations. He especially liked to use every day examples to vividly complement his teaching. For instance, he used bows, springs, and rubber bands as training tools. He used a water bag half full of water to explain *empty chest and solid belly* and *energy sinks to dan tian*. On one occasion, to illustrate the requirements *originates from the waist, from inside to out, all sections connected*, he lit up incense on his *ming men* and on his joints. He turned off all the lights so that I could see the *ming men* and all other joints moving from one point to the other which was really explicit and impressive. He would relate any natural phenomena to Taiji. He told me that animals displayed the best stored energy and pressured state when they were approaching their prey. At night, he brought me to see how lizards caught their prey. Lizards would first move very lightly to get close to their prey, a mosquito or worm. My father said this was the state of *moving while being still*. When the lizard was in range, its body curved to an "S" shape which represented *store energy like a pulled bow*. Finally, it jumped, extending its tongue to catch the prey; this was *fa jing like shooting the arrow*. Examples like this created in me a vivid understanding and feeling for several principle elements prevalent in the martial arts.

As the political atmosphere relaxed, more and more students came to learn. There were also masters of different disciplines and styles who came for a challenge. Often I saw my father separate his legs and lower his torso a little, both hands stretched out in front of his chest, his expression peaceful but full of confidence, showing an aggressive aura. As soon as the opponent moved, father would seal him off with his *fa jing*. This showed me the principle of *slow training and fast application* in Taiji.

When I first started to do push hands, I practiced mostly with fellow students. Among them was a senior student of a large build, who had trained in "hard" martial arts, and who was once an army commando. At first, I often lost to him because of his power. Over time, my training and practice caused my push hands level to surpass his. One day, he asked me whether I did free fighting. I never had done that before and asked him to explain. He said we would not contact each other's hands first but would attack as we got close to each other. Feeling brave I agreed to the fight. He assumed a posture and I adjusted myself according to the way my father taught me. As my opponent entered within my range, I used *fa jing* to lock his force and neutralize his attacks. He was shaking his head, saying *I cannot use it.* I asked him what he meant. He showed me several movements he had planned to use to attack me but was not able to penetrate my defence. It scared me. If he had been successful in pressing his attack, I could have been seriously injured. This trial greatly increased my confidence in applying Taiji in free fighting.

My father taught me *non sequence move hits sequence move*[5]. It worked. He also

---

[5] *non sequence move hits sequence move*: do not follow/practice a preset series of moves to counter an attack. Be ready to change and adapt on a moment's notice.

allowed me to study from masters of other martial arts, to understand the principles and features of other disciplines. After this, he showed me how to combine the hard martial arts with Taiji, thus creating a unique training methodology.

For one year, I stayed with my father day and night and had an intense and in-depth period of study. I learnt from his experience and he shared with me the results of his many years of research. He systematically trained me in all aspects and laid down a very solid foundation for me.

When I returned to school, I continued my Taiji study. I was especially interested in *sanshou* training. At that time, China did not have *sanshou* tournaments. There was no formal training program to study free fighting, so I could only study by challenging the good fighters wherever they were. I went around the area challenging all the masters I could find. After a well publicized battle I had with a traditional kung-fu sifu (instructor), my father sent word forbidding me from continuing the challenges. He wrote, *Why take away his livelihood? If you lose, you lose nothing. If he loses, he loses the respect of his students.* I realized my father was right. Still, I had gained much valuable experience.

In 1975, after I graduated from high school and while waiting for employment, I accepted a teaching position in an Amateur Junior Martial Art Class. I also attended the Guangdong Martial Art Coaches Training Course and had a chance to learn from the Head Coach Chen Chang Mian [陳昌棉] and other coaches. This gave me a new point of view and helped to raise my understanding of the martial arts. During the classes, I had an opportunity to meet Hong Quan [洪拳], Cai Li Fo [蔡李佛], and several good Yang Chun [詠春] fighters. Again I learned a lot.

That same year, my father was allowed to go back to work for the same company as my mother. He came back to live with us. He could again train me day and night. He started to teach me the basic postures of the Wu and Wu/Hao styles. Besides the forms practice, my father paid close attention to my theoretical studies. In addition to Taiji theory, my father encouraged me to study human physiology. He required me to keep a Taiji diary, and he would review it periodically. When I sorted through my father's papers after he passed away, I found a letter I had written to him. The letter mentioned that I had a "stiff contact" with an opponent during push-hand. I analyzed the causes and summed up my experience which helped me to make progress. My father's response to the letter was: *This letter reflects the progress Hong Yuan made in his Taiji studies. He has gained an important understanding of the principle of 'rotating and leading to shift gravity' and the organic relationship between radius force, tangent force and axis force in Taiji.* In a letter to a new student, father commented, *My younger son Hong Yuan loves martial arts, especially Taiji. He follows the rules, is well rooted, quietly pursues and progresses daily. He has the quality of purity, but not vanity. His learning is fine and I feel satisfied.*

From 1976 to 1977, I worked in a shop. In 1977, The Department of Higher Education reinstated the practice of entrance examinations and colleges stopped taking freshmen on political recommendations only. I was looking forward to this opportunity and studied for the entry exams. I passed the exams to the Guangzhou Physical Education Institute, with a major in martial arts. I belonged to the first group of college students who were admitted by entrance exams after the Great Cultural Revolution. A dream had come true for two generations, my father's and mine. Before the Cultural Revolution, my father had written to Master Gu: *How I wish I could have a year in the Physical Education Institute to study basic subjects such as anatomy, physiology, and athletic body dynamics. I could develop a new phase on our research and at the same time to intensify my philosophical studies. Training while studying. I have an urgent need to study. Unlike most students, I would expend extraordinary efforts and would expect good results. However, it is but a dream.* He often told me, *It would be nice if you could study in the Physical Education Institute, to study and command the knowledge of contemporary physiology and athletic science, which have far reaching influence on research of Taijiquan theory and training.* My father could not realize this dream for himself, but he passed his dream on to me. It was his profound insight and persistent pursuit that made my accomplishments possible. When I graduated from Junior High School our whole family lived still in the countryside. A factory hired me to play basketball and that would have allowed us to change our residence back to the city. It would have been a move of great fortune. While we were celebrating this new opportunity, we reported the news to my father, who was still on the "Fifth Seventh" Commune for Labour Reform. The next day, to our surprise, we received my father's reply, saying *Continue with your school education.* Had my father not intervened, my life today would have been very different and, I suspect, not as rewarding.

When my father learned that I was admitted to the Physical Education Institute, he was overjoyed. He advised me on several occasions to appreciate the opportunity. He wanted me to diligently study basic theory and gain special knowledge to advance my education to a new level. It was my father's expectation that I would go to the Institute with questions and a need to study. During the four years in college I can say I was thirsty to absorb knowledge. I achieved excellent academic scores, and thus laid a solid theoretical foundation for my later research. In my martial arts training, I also broadened my horizons by studying different martial art disciplines. One of the teachers was Professor Zhang Deng Kui [張登魁]. Professor Zhang taught us his favourite forms such as Ba Ji Quan [八極拳], Xing Yi Quan [形意拳], Ba Gua Zhang [八卦掌][6] boxing and wrestling. In addition, I studied Southern Fists and Northern Legs, various weapons forms, martial art theories, and so forth. Among all these martial arts, I especially liked the widely open, very aggressive Xia Quan [俠拳] (White Crane Fist) and also Single Head Stick. I felt that Xia Quan enhanced my long range skills. Single Head Stick was similar to Taiji staff. By adding Taiji's *fa jing* to my practice of the stick I discovered a fine way to increase my Taiji power. Once our College had a test competition and invited the senior generation of Guangzhou's martial artists as judges. When they saw my adaptation of Single Head Stick, they were confused. The form was a traditional southern staff form, but I applied *fa jing* to several of the movements. However, they gave me a very high score in recognition of my innovation.

In 1979, the National Sports Committee picked Guangzhou and Wuhan as experimental areas for *sanshou*. My fellow students and I were very excited despite our college's apparent reluctance. A student got hold of a pair of boxing gloves and we took turns using them. Soon, people throughout our area started training for *sanshou*. My father was happy to receive such news. He advised me to completely and solidly train myself according to *sanshou* requirements. When I mastered the free fighting techniques, I could combine them with Taiji's power and principles to improve on them.

Prior to the relaxation on the restrictions on *san shou* training[7], my free-style fighting techniques consisted mainly of sealing and controlling of the opponent. My father advised me to use the opportunity to train hard, and to develop the capability of high kicks, punches and ground wrestling. Over a period of time, I formed my own style in *sanshou*. In competition, I could vary from seal-up and control, to kicks, strikes, and wrestling with excellent results. Soon, many

---

[6] *Ba Ji Quan, Xing Yi Quan* and *Ba Gua Zhang* are three famous *internal* martial arts.
[7] *San shou* or "free-style fighting" was banned in the People's Republic of China until 1979.

martial art practitioners came to challenge our college and we gained some valuable experience.

I spent the last vacation before my college graduation at home. I was challenged by a very aggressive street fighter who considered himself a master of the martial arts. At first, I used sealing and controlling techniques to neutralize him. This only angered him and I soon found myself in a very dangerous situation. It became apparent that this was now no-holds barred; a fight to the finish. I began to use the punching and kicking techniques from my *sanshou* training to defeat my opponent. A senior student of my father's watched the fight and, disappointedly, reported to my father: *It looks like Hong Yuan has lost confidence in Taiji, and changed to sanshou already.* My father replied humorously, *You only saw the wine bottle of Hong Yuan's hitting and kicking, but you did not taste the Taiji wine inside the bottle. Taijiquan is not limited to push hands. Do not assume that Taiji is only about touching hands and making circles. Taiji's martial art is more complex than that. The nature of Taiji is to control your opponent and to control him by any means.*

While my father enjoyed my progress, he admonished me not to be conceited. Every time when I came home from college on vacation and as soon as I put down my luggage my father would say: *Come on, let us see if the college student has made any progress.* Then he would resume my *buffalo strength* training. After my father was retired, he had more time to practice and study Taiji, and his martial art level became even higher. With his guidance I developed new ways of looking at Taiji and its various components. My graduation dissertation was *About the Organic System of Internal Power of Taiji.* In the article, I stated that internal power is the essence of Taijiquan sport. Taiji focuses its theory and training around the forming and applying of internal power. My father supported my topic greatly, and gave me several valuable suggestions. As soon as I completed the dissertation, I mailed a copy to Master Gu for his review. Master Gu promptly replied and gave me very high praise on my efforts to reveal the organic system of Taiji's internal power using contemporary science and knowledge. My dissertation was rated as excellent and so closed my college study life on a satisfactory note. (Illustration.3-1-3)

(L-R) Luo Hong Yuan, Master Gu's wife, Gu Liu Xin (1986)
(Illustration 3-1-3)

In early 1982, after my graduation from the Guangzhou Physical Education Institute, I was hired by the South China Normal University, as a professional martial arts teacher. A new journey in my life began and the position as a martial arts teacher placed higher demands on my teaching abilities as well as my specialty level and it was a great opportunity for further self development. During that period, I participated in competitions at city and provincial levels and won championships in Taijiquan.

In May of 1982, not long after I accepted the teaching position, I went to Xian [西安] for the National Martial Arts Performance Tournament. Elite masters from all over the country came together. To my great delight, Master Gu Liu Xin was invited to be the chief judge of the conference. My dream of studying with Master Gu finally came true. At the time, Master Gu stayed at the accommodation center right by the stadium. I could not wait to visit the Grand Master. This was the first time we met and he was very pleased to see me. He again praised my dissertation and encouraged me to continue to work hard using contemporary science and knowledge to study Taijiquan. He told me it was especially important to work hard when young in order to lay a solid foundation for future advancement. Then I pleaded with Master Gu to teach me his Taiji form. Master Gu said, *Time is short, chances are hard to go by. Let us push hands first!* Thus he led me through the four-corner push hands exercise.

Master Gu's push hands posture was rather high and upright, and his movements were not large. Yet his internal power was very strong. He locked my main bow and caused my legs to stiffen. I was not able to sink down. During the circles, my centre of gravity was shifted again and again. He liked to use small circle submitting force, forcing me to kneel down by blocking my force and twisting some joints. We pushed for a while and then rested. He then asked me to try free-form push hands—no circling, no formal hand contact. He ordered me to try to attack him. However, every time, before I could begin, he was all over me. He said initiating contact should be like the blowing of the northeast wind, penetrating through any crack. His hands were like a pair of big pliers, piercing my defences straight to my chest. As soon as I made contact, it felt like I was trying to move a small mountain. I then felt a tremendous force straight pushing to my back bone. Then he would do a short *fa jing* by bending the wrist, like bouncing a ball, pushing the force to my feet. I would rebound up severing my roots, and then he would *fa jing* upwards, sending me to either the couch or the bed. Quick and decisive, once, twice, three times, the same thing happened. Each time I would try to adjust differently, but the result was always the same. In the final contest, when he was ready to attack, I withdrew first, but he reacted even faster. He changed the angle of attack, sending me crashing heavily into the door.

Master Gu used his tremendous internal power, caused by the pressure from his *dan tian*, to quickly link force with the opponent on first contact, and to immediately control him. Then he used a small circle to *link force* (chuan [串]), *twist* (na [拿]) and *expel* (fa [發]), all combined into one. The move was simple without any exaggeration, and overcame the opponent within seconds.

During the conference, I had several opportunities to learn push hands from Master Gu. I sought his secret to enhance the quality of my internal power, and to do the small frame *chuan-na-fa* technique. This revered Master generously shared his teaching and I have benefited from his wisdom my whole life. Between 1982 and 1987, I was fortunate to be able to study with Master Gu on several occasions.

In April 1984, Wuhan organized an unprecedented large scale tournament. The Wuhan International Taijiquan and Sword Performance and Tournament Conference inspired several major cities in China to organize teams to participate. They also invited countries all over the world to send in their teams. The Conference invited the 13 most famous masters to participate. It was a huge event. Ms. Gu Dai Juan (Jennifer), who was still a student in the Guangzhou Physical Education Institute, and I were selected to represent the Guangzhou Team in the traditional Taiji men's and women's competition.

Ms. Gu started training martial arts at very early age. She was selected for the Guangdong Provincial Wushu Team and studied Taiji from my father. My father was very happy to hear the news and he decided to go with us to Wuhan. He told us to cancel the winter martial art workshops we had originally planned to teach and that he would be our coach to prepare for the competition.

At the end of March, my father wrote to us: *You and Dai Juan should intensify your training, think constantly about the competition, and earnestly face the event. Fajing frequency should be as large as possible and easy to reach out. Dai Juan must pay attention to the aura when performing. An aura full of power leads to good performance. You should be cool and relaxed. Store energy while keeping agile, storing and exploding energy should show a great contrast. Make internal power connected throughout. Turning should be agile, and exploding would be complete. You should have enough confidence and don't feel intimidated among those famous martial artists.*

After a period of preparation, we finally went to Wuhan. My father also arrived with our team and as soon as we settled down in our lodging, my father brought us to visit Master Gu Liu Xin. Master Gu was kind enough to polish our form performance before the competition. He recommended we lower our posture to show the characteristics of Chen Style. He also corrected our hand movements according to Chen Style requirements. (Illustration.3-1-4)

(L-R) Luo Hong Yuan, Luo Ji Hong, Gu Liu Xin, Master Gu's niece, Gu Dai Juan (1984)
(Illustration 3-1-4)

Finally it was our turn at the tournament. Facing all the famous masters and the whole audience, Ms. Gu and I had an extraordinary performance from posture, internal power, to *fa jing*. We were applauded and cheered by the whole audience. We each won the gold medal in men's and women's traditional Taijiquan Performance. (Illustration.3-1-5) When we went up to the podium to receive the medals, my father, who sat at the VIP area, shed tears, as he seldom did in his life. He was happy and proud of our performance. Our success proved that his research on Taiji theory and practice through all these years was not in vain.

Team Guangzhou in Wuhan (1984)
Gu Dai Juan (2nd from left bottom row) Luo Hong Yuan (4th from left upper row)
(Illustration 3-1-5)

During the conference, my father brought us to meet Masters like Ma Yueh Liang, Wu Ying Hua, Wu Tu Nan [吳圖南], Fu Zhong Wen, Sun Jian Yun, and Yao Ji Zu [姚繼祖]. (Illustration. 3-1-6)

(L-R) Sun Jian Yun, Gu Dai Juan, Gu Liu Xin (1984)
(Illustration 3-1-6)

After the conference, Ms. Gu and I returned to Guangzhou to work and study. My father, on the other hand, went back to Shanghai to visit his teachers and friends he met 20 years ago. While he was in Shanghai, he wrote me a letter, describing his experience in Shanghai. He greatly regretted not being able to see Masters Hao Shao Ru and Zhang Da Quan[8]. However, he was very excited to see a lot of friends and masters after 20 years. They came together, exchanged experiences, talked about their successes through all those years. In his letter to me, he said: *This gold medal is good, it is in time. However, the gold medal can only tell the past. From now on, you should start a new quest. Humbly study, solidly train, and you will have great success!* In the letter, he also mentioned Master Gu had great expectations from me. *He has great hopes for you. One must have both theory and practice to be able to become a master. He is concerned about the successors of Taijiquan.* The expectations of the senior generation of masters became my incentive to strive for greater understanding and ability.

My father wrote me several letters from Shanghai, describing his Shanghai tour and his plans to write a book. Then, on June 15, 1984, while I was training the University's martial arts team, I received the sad news that my father had passed away. It was like a bolt of lightning hitting me. I took a bus home that night, and learned that my father had passed away the previous midday. The doctor said that he had died from exhaustion after so many days of continuous teaching. He had devoted his last breath and spark of life to the cause of Taijiquan. I could not accept this fact for a long time. His voice and his smile; his shadow in the moonlight when teaching me Taiji; feeling the pressure of his *buffalo strength*; his vivid and lively teaching methods; his kind generosity in teaching without discrimination; unconcerned with his own exhaustion; his love and devotion to Taiji...... all these memories remain with me to this day.

At the funeral ceremony, I put my gold medal on his chest, for he was the real winner of the medal. I then performed a set of a Taiji in front of my father for the last time. Later, while sorting through his effects, I came across the writing tools he had purchased. I made up my mind to carry on his legacy, and to contribute to the development of Taijiquan.

Master Gu Liu Xin passed away in 1990 at the age of 83. Another martial artist left us, who had lived and breathed Taiji with his whole heart. However, his contribution to Taijiquan will be everlasting. After Master Gu had passed away, I received a letter from his son, Mr. Gu Yuan Zhuang [顧元莊]. In his letter, he informed me that he had found a lot of correspondence between Master Gu and my father. When he was sorting through the Grand Master's belongings he also found drafts for publications. This was like a surprise sent from heaven and I was full of joy. Soon afterwards, I received a parcel from Mr. Gu comprising of eighty letters which my father wrote to Master Gu, forty letters which Master Gu wrote to my father together with a lot of other valuable materials. It turned out that their correspondence was all about Taiji. At that time they did not have copy machines and therefore had to write their letters twice to keep a copy for themselves. One was mailed out and the copy was kept on file. All of my father's correspondence was burned during the Great Cultural Revolution. However, Master Gu's correspondence was fortunately preserved by the Red Guards as "Criminal Evidence" and returned to Master Gu after the Cultural Revolution. The discovery of these valuable documents not only shows the deep friendship between two generations of our families, but also our respect towards the contribution of our senior generations.

Being a professional teacher at South China Normal University provided me with many

---

[8] Both revered masters had recently passed away.

opportunities for study and exchange. Using my father's old connections, I had the opportunity to seek instruction from many famous masters

In 1983, in Guangzhou, I learned Wu style Taiji sword from Master Ma Yueh Liang and Wu style Taijiquan from Master Wu Ying Hua. While visiting Shanghai in 1963, my father learned also from both masters and a friendship had developed between teachers and student. With my father's introduction, I was fortunate to learn Wu style push hands from Master Ma. Master Ma and Master Wu wrote to my father: *Your son's martial art foundation is very good, his future is unlimited.* This gave me much encouragement. In addition, Ms. Gu and I also had the opportunity to learn Sun [孫] Style Taiji from Master Sun Jian Yun. Studying with all these Masters enabled us to understand the principles of the various styles of Taiji.

In 1985, I was invited to give a seminar at the Hong Kong Chinese University. That same year, I went to Shanghai to invite some famous masters for a Taiji workshop in Guangzhou. I visited Master Fu Zhong Wen, Master Gu and other famous masters. Later, I visited my father's good friend, the miraculous person I had been looking forward to meeting — Master Shao Pin Gen. Master Shao was a simple, honest man. He started to talk about his friendship with my father. They had both persisted in the pursuit of Taijiquan and also both had hoped that I would study Taiji well, so Taiji would have a successor. He happily agreed to push hands with me the next morning in Sea Shore Park. Next morning it was cold to the bones, yet there was a group of people pushing hands. Master Shao appeared weak and small, but he became quite different in push hands. His abundant energy and his agile movements surprised me greatly. Master Shao did not have formal students, but would welcome anyone to practice with him. Master Gu told me an interesting story. One time Master Gu led a Japanese delegation to show them our martial arts activities among non professionals. They watched how a disabled old man[9] pushed a big man around like a magician. The delegation thought it was a prearranged performance, and one member of the delegation of the Judo discipline wanted to have a try. Master Shao gladly agreed. The Japanese stepped up and started to attack but he looked like catching the wind and grabbing the shadow. Several times he was put on the ground. He came to worship Master Shao for his advanced martial arts skills. I had heard about Master Shao's perfect "understanding force" (*dong jing*) in push hands and on this cold morning I had the opportunity to experience it for myself. I thought I had some internal power and the ability to control it but I could not catch him, I knew I must not *rush down the cliff like a wild buffalo.* I wanted to learn how he would control my force. At the first contact, I felt empty and drifting. I could not get any sense of his force. I calmed myself down and approached him solidly and safely. Master Shao's posture was very high and casual. He saw that I was not rushing and he did not yield or withdraw but drew my power towards his chest. All of a sudden, he made a very short movement with his wrist. His power was both focused and sharp like the blade of a knife. Immediately, I felt an electric shock running from my wrist all the way down to my feet. I felt my right knee bend and knelt down, like bowing to the new master. Very impressive! We continued for several rounds, and I still could not feel anything. I felt like I was falling into five miles of fog. He was everywhere, attacking and controlling from any direction. Several times, he pulled, turned swiftly, disappeared and then he appeared again behind me. He then used his fingers hooking on my collar bones, pulled a little bit and suddenly I was on the ground. Later, I discovered this was *Big Body Change.* Master Shao's push hands was agile with a perfect understanding of power. After he gained the advantage, I also felt the character of his *fa jing.* First, it was cold and short, like a flashlight, flash and gone, with no

---

[9] Shao Pin Gen had contracted polio as a child and had a withered right leg.

warning. Second, the direction was very focused, highly pressurized, and extremely penetrating. I was on the receiving end of this power and it felt like cutting or piercing as if a steel wire was irresistibly cutting through my body. I really admired this magical technique. (Illustration.3-1-7)

Shao Pin Gen
(Illustration.3-1-7)

Master Shao promised that, while I was in Shanghai, he would try his best to teach me his techniques. Over the course of several days, he systematically taught me his push hands techniques: four squares, head part, middle part, small body change, large body change, *random stepping on flowers*[10] and so forth.

By learning from Master Gu and Master Shao, I quickly absorbed the two contrary push hands styles. Again, I wondered about the profound study of Taiji, and how these two Masters' completely different ways reached the same purpose. During this visit to Shanghai, I also met my father's fellow Hao Style students. They received me with a warm welcome and entertained me. This trip was my most beneficial trip ever.

After Shanghai I was introduced to Master Lei Mu Ni by a student of his from the railroad department. Upon my return from Shanghai, we invited Master Lei to come to Guangzhou. Master Lei had studied Chen style Taiji with Chen Fa Ke [陳發科] for over thirty years. When debating *Spiral Force*, Master Lei and my father became close friends. He told me that my father was his soul mate in addition to being an old friend. Master Lei was a kind and honest senior martial artist who had followed the most famous masters for decades. His Taijiquan was at a very high level and his standards were very strict. (Illustration.3-1-8)

His movements were precise and exact, detailed and circularly agile. He taught us day and night for nearly three months and under his careful guidance, Ms. Gu and I systematically enhanced the quality of our Chen style. It is worth mentioning that Master Lei was very fond of the art of swordsmanship. We were greatly attracted to his Chen style sword performance and he taught us the complete Chen style sword form. Later this sword form became one of our favourite Taiji weapon forms.

---

[10] *"random stepping on flowers"*: Moving Step Push hands

54

Lei Mu Ni (1986)
(Illustration. 3-1-8)

Master Lei showed his love for me by going all out to teach me all he knew. He told one of my students that I was his most accomplished student during his entire teaching career. It was a great loss when the 76 year old master suddenly fell sick and passed away. My students and I, along with students from the Guangzhou Wushu Association organized a huge memorial service. Master Lei's daughter came all the way from Beijing to join the funeral and requested: *My father studied martial arts for fifty years. Through the ups and downs of his life he devoted all his heart and soul to Taijiquan. You are his favourite student and I beg you to perform his most loved Taiji form in front of his spirits, to see him off.* I agreed and reverently performed the Chen style form in front of the spirit of this respected Grand Master. (Illustration.3-1-9)

Lei Mu Ni teaching a Chen Style class (1986)
(Illustration. 3-1-9)

In 1986, I went to Chengdu [成都] to attend the First National Taiji Research Dissertation Conference. Elite Taiji practitioners and masters from all over the nation were at the conference and I had the opportunity to learn from many of them. I learned the Wu (Hao) style push hands from Master Liu Ji Shun [劉積順], a fellow student of my father. After the conference, I was able to commission him to teach in Guangzhou for a period of time. The chairman of the Shanghai Wu (Hao) Style Research Association, Master Pu Gong Da [浦公達], was also a fellow student and good friend of my father. He was skinny and slight of build, but his martial art level was very high. He had a very strong finger force and once filled with *qi*, his fingers would be like steel claws. Besides teaching me Wu (Hao) style techniques, he also taught me how to train finger power. During the conference, I got to know Master Jiang Jia Jun [蔣家俊], who had studied Chen style Taiji with Master Chen Zhao Pi [陳照丕] and Master Hong Jun Sheng [洪均生]. Master Jiang had a very profound and comprehensive understanding of Chen style Taijiquan, push hands, and *sanshou*. After the conference, I invited Master Jiang to teach at my home for several months. I learned from him Chen style push hands, forms, and basic training. He especially introduced us to the favourite techniques of Master Hong Jun Sheng.

Master Hong Jun Sheng was a very open and creative Taiji martial artist. He had submitted an article on Spiral Force during the great debate of 1964. Through that article, he and my father corresponded regularly. Master Hong would use examples from every day life to explain Taiji theory and techniques. He generated a whole group of excellent students. In 1985, I planned to invite him to come to Guangzhou to teach, which did not work out for some reason. Though we never met, we corresponded with each other quite often. In November 1985 he wrote: *Though I never met either you or your father we came to know each other through Taiji, and became friends through our correspondence. Taijiquan, especially Chen style Taijiquan is extremely profound in theory and principles. People with a limited education can not learn it, or cannot learn it well. College students are trained in philosophy and science. If you understand the theory, and combine that with great effort, you will achieve a high level. Because you have proven yourself to be a willing pupil, I want to assist you with your development so you will not only just inherit Taiji, but will work to advance it.* Through the words of this Taiji Grand Master, I could perceive his generosity, his encouragement and his expectation from our new generation. In 1988, Ms. Gu and I compiled our book titled "Taijiquan - Theory and Training". When we were ready to publish it, we asked Master Hong Jun Sheng to write a foreword. He wrote: *Accurate in theory and profound in principle* thus expressing his consideration and love for us. (Illustration.3-1-10)

Hong Jun Sheng (1986)
(Illustration. 3-1-10)

During the Dissertation Conference the attendees held very valuable discussions. Information was exchanged and different opinions about the Taiji theory were expressed. It soon became apparent that many practitioners still clung to the principle *use intent but not force*. These same people disputed the nature of Taiji's *jing* (internal power) and the application of Taiji's technique and speed. My father's concern was being proved correct. Many schools had persisted in their approach to try and make Taiji mysterious, even magical, and proclaimed Taiji to have a "supernatural force". I had the opportunity to push hands against many of these proponents of *no force*, some of whom were very senior and experienced masters. I easily controlled them, thus disproving their theories.

During my tenure at the South China Normal University, I continued to study Taiji theory, especially the organic structure of its internal power. In order to analyze the biological effects of *spiral force* on the bones during body adjustments, I subjected myself to many x-rays. Too much exposure to x-rays over a short period of time affected my health temporarily. I also partnered with a teacher in the Faculty of Medicine at Ji Nan [暨南] University to monitor the muscle function during Taiji practice by using a muscle electronic pulse machine. We gathered some worthy results and published our research in the Shanghai Wu (Hao) Style Research Journal, the South China Normal University Journal and the Science and Technology Journal. The article was later selected to be included in the First National Taijiquan Theory and Dissertation Conference in 1986, and the First National Martial Arts Theory and Dissertation Conference in 1987. Upon the request of the Guangdong Higher Education Publishing Department, Ms. Gu and I compiled in 1988 the book *Taijiquan - Theory and Training* using contemporary language and knowledge to introduce Taijiquan Theory.

I continue to practice and gain more experience. Increasing numbers of foreign students began to seek me out in order to challenge and to learn from me. I was exposed to many foreign martial arts from Japan, Korea and many other countries throughout Asia. I started to review and summarize my father's teaching theory and methods to combine them with my own teaching practice. I also adapted contemporary sports training models to teach and train young students. In 1985, my students participated for the first time in the Guangzhou Tuishou Competition. Most of them had started training only two years previously, but they received excellent scores and took most of the medals. We continued to be successful in competition for several years, even after I left China in 1988. In 1992, at the Guangdong and Hong Kong Taiji Push Hands Tournament, my students and their students won four gold medals by using my training methods. These results proved the benefits of applying contemporary training methods to traditional sports; at the same time I was encouraged to continue my hard work to develop new methods.

Contrary to standard policy, I was promoted in 1985 as a Lecturer based on my professional level, my results in research and teaching. At the same time, Gu Dai Juan graduated from the Guangzhou Physical Education Institute with the highest academic scores in her class. She was hired as my associate teacher at the South China Normal University. We married the following year and became not only a family but partners in the development of Taijiquan.

In June, 1988, we published *Taijiquan - Theory and Training* and I was invited to hold a Taiji Seminar in Newberry College, South Carolina, USA. In August, Ms. Gu Dai Quan was invited to teach in Calgary, Alberta, Canada. By the end of October, I was also invited to teach in Calgary and Edmonton, Canada.

In the beginning of 1989, we founded the Ji Hong Taiji College. Our intent was to fulfill my father's dream to have a Taiji college and to create a comprehensive Taiji theory and training system by using the research results gathered by two generations. We tested and refined the mode of teaching in this college and finally, after a year's hard work, we attracted many interested students. With the generous help from friends we established our headquarters in Edmonton and set up subsidiary colleges in Calgary and Toronto. Ji Hong Taiji College soon became one of the largest advanced level Taiji schools in North America.

The first problem that we encountered in North America was how to teach so our students would understand our Taijiquan teaching system. Although the level of education in Canada is quite high, there were few people who understood traditional Chinese culture. To bridge the cultural gap, we applied contemporary theory, teaching methods and organizational models of modern sports schools to teach a classical and traditional sport like Taijiquan. Our approach enabled our students to achieve satisfactory results in the understanding of the basic principles of Taiji. We began to attract many students from various walks of life to our classes. In addition, we associated Taijiquan's free fighting aspect with competitive sports which attracted another group of students that liked competition. In the beginning, many Westerners did not appreciate the martial art functionality of Taiji. They regarded Taiji as a "soft exercise". They believed it to be very mysterious and exotic and or it was *too high a mountain to climb*. So at the beginning of our teaching, we often had some doubters and martial artists of other styles come to challenge us. This gave me the opportunity to become familiar with different types of Western free fighting techniques. Two very significant incidents occurred at this time.

The first incident involved a police self-defence instructor who believed that Taiji was only for seniors to maintain their health. He doubted the fighting aspects of Taiji. He brought several large young officers to visit our school. I asked them to use whatever submission techniques they wanted to try to subdue me. As these four husky young men approached, I "readied" myself. I allowed one to put me in a headlock, two pinned my arms behind me and the fourth grabbed hold of my legs. Using *vibratory* force, three of them ended up on the floor and the fourth was thrown several feet away. They were shaking their heads saying *Incredible!* That day their opinion of Taiji changed.

The other incident involved a big and strong student who trained in different martial arts, but especially in Jiu Jitsu. One day at class, he raised a sharp question: *Taiji wins by upsetting an opponent's balance to bring him on the ground, but on the ground is the beginning of Jiu Jitsu.* I bravely agreed to give it a try following Jiu Jitsu rules. First, I focused on keeping myself on the *Taiji State of Readiness*, filling up my whole body with power to avoid being controlled and be ready to control. Because the rule was to fight until one opponent submitted, all moves were potentially lethal and there were several dangerous moments. After ten minutes the contest came to an end, becoming one of the fiercest fights in my career. Even though I won, I realized the importance of maintaining the *State of Readiness* in Taiji more deeply and I found a brand new research topic. Besides training in kicking, punching, wrestling, *chin na* (joint locks), and *tuishou* in Taiji, we need to apply the Taiji principles to ground fighting.

Canada's pace of life was very conducive to my research. First, I intensified my analysis to systematically sort and summarize all I had learned from my father and many other famous masters. I hoped to absorb and digest the details quickly, to add them to my own knowledge, and to apply them in my own practice and teaching. I realized that self control "internal power" and control of the opponent "understanding power" are the two keys to enhance the training level. In regard to this, my father wrote during his second visit to Shanghai: *Master Gu Liu Xin's internal power + Master Shao Pin Gen's understanding power = Superior Level. This is the path for us to pursue.*

Increasing the quality of Taiji's internal power has always been a concept we were most concerned with. Techniques like *lead the body by intent, five bows into one,* and *pull from both sides to stretch and generate flexibility* are the elementary phase of developing Taiji's internal power. While teaching in China, I instructed students in this phase, made them understand the principles in a short period of time, and trained them successfully to win competitions. However, when the intent and the energy can be combined with body adjustments (*to lead qi by the body*), in such a way that the body is transformed into an Air Bag-Like Elasticity[11], one can generate a great deal more pressure. The pressure formed by the internal power is more flexible, has a better capability to dissolve outer force and thus brings internal power to another level. Based on this finding, I reformed some of my teaching methods. For those students whose goal was to learn martial art techniques, I shortened the training gap between *lead the body by intent* and *lead the qi by the body.* As soon as the students had some basic foundation on body adjustment, they would be required to practice *intent and energy* training methods. Some even trained simultaneously in both body adjustment and *intent and energy* training and thus further shortened the training cycle. The development of these methods for the *control the opponent* was based on my experience in push hands with my father, Master Gu and Master Shao. I developed the *Theory of Rootlessness* and the method of *using the opponent's spine as a turning axis to control the force.* These new techniques were then added to my new teaching model for *self-control* and *control of the opponent.*

I put this new and reformed teaching system into practice for a whole year. Then I brought the students to participate in the Toronto Tournament held by the Canadian-Chinese Kuo Shu (Martial Arts) Federation and we won almost all the medals. Since that year, we have maintained our winning streak. During the 1998 Pan American Wushu Championships (with competitors from North, Central and South America), we took away 11 gold medals out of 13 Push hands categories. Also in 1998, a student from our Toronto branch competed at the Taiji Legacy Tournament held in Dallas, and won four gold medals in lightweight and middleweight fixed and moving step push hands. In 1999, I personally led our team to the Taste of China Taiji Tournament held in Virginia. United States. We competed in four out of five push hands competitions and won all four gold medals. In the final double elimination competition for the Grand Champion title, our heavyweight student and middleweight student defeated their opponents. Especially exciting was the fight where our middleweight student overcame his opponent who was a super heavyweight. That match brought the whole audience to their feet. Our two students ended up facing each other in the final round.

The above accomplishments were all competitions against outsiders. However, it would be more convincing to compare my teaching results between the pre-reformed method and post-reformed method of training.

There was an unpleasant episode that accidentally created the opportunity for such a comparison. In 1991, one of my students from China came to us because he could not obtain a visa to immigrate to Canada. He was a graduate from South China Normal University but did not major in martial arts. In China, I had interviewed him when I was recruiting a team in 1983.

---

[11] The *ABLE* concept is discussed more fully in Chapter Five.

Later, upon his request, I taught him Taiji in my spare time. After several years of studying with me, with no prior martial arts training, he won the 70 kilo Taiji push hands gold medal in the Guangzhou Taiji Push Hands Competitions every year from 1985 to 1987.

Seeing his immigration difficulties after he came to Canada, I hired an expensive attorney to file an appeal for him, using my Calgary College as his sponsor and hiring him as teaching assistant for this college. I also gave him 75% of the college's income. His appeal was successful and he got his residency permit. I was happy I was able to help him once again. This student came from a poor rural family and in China I often housed and fed him and generally supported him during the tough times. I never charged him for teaching. Unexpectedly, however, after he had settled in, he requested outright ownership of the Calgary College. This was the first school we established after our own immigration to Canada. We could not accede to his demands so we dissolved our business association and went our separate ways. He set up his own school, called himself "Grand Master" and included in his advertising a slogan that read *Learning does not count later or first, but the stronger deserves the first[12]*. The implication was very obvious and, in addition to my hurt feelings, I had to face a new challenge. He was not a professional Taiji teacher, and since I left China, he had not had the opportunity to learn the new training methods. He only remained at the old level, improving only by quantity, but not quality. His students also learned only the old techniques. Finally, we met in a tournament. Both teams came from the same roots, but ours had developed new methods of training. Now they would have to face each other in competition. The result? Our team took all the gold medals. After the tournament, my former student removed his "Grand Master" title from his advertising and took down his sign *Learning does not count later and first, but the stronger deserves the first.* We had proven the effectiveness of our new and reformed teaching methods. It also made me appreciate the truth of the old saying: *Learning has no limits.* There has been a positive result from this unfortunate incident. First, it gave me the incentive to re-double my efforts in refining the Ji Hong system.

Secondly, I also realized I had a good nucleus of dedicated students who were worthy of our new training system. I opened myself to these students and concentrated on their training. They have made remarkable progress and have earned our college much respect from the Taiji community.

During the course of my teaching, my students would ask me how I could continue to progress now that I do not have senior masters beside me. I would answer: *Once you reach a certain level, teaching does happen by having someone beside you.*

The senior generation masters wrote down their theories and their practical experience. I also gained experience by learning from all these masters. All masters left deep impressions in my mind and those memories are my never-ending resources.

Students are also my best teachers. To teach a student well, I must ponder and solve all problems and questions that arise from various aspects and different levels. Tournaments require focused training, observing players' performances with a post-competition review of progress. These are all my resources and incentives that make me persist in my learning and help me to progress. Finally, my love of Taijiquan directs my brain and my body, thus inspiring me to continue to research and progress.

---

[12] *"learning does not count later or first, but the stronger deserves the first"* The inference here was that the student (who had trained for a shorter time) had surpassed the master.

As my students' Taiji level improved, they sought even greater challenges. We turned our focus on China. Taiji originated in China and there are excellent trainers and athletes. It remains the best place to learn and advance.

In the year 2000, I brought eight students to participate in the 1st International Taijiquan Biannual Conference in Jiaozuo [焦作], China. Facing new rules and strong opponents with rich experience and fine training, we only had one student advance into the top three. This tournament opened our eyes and showed us our shortcomings. We learned a lot, and we returned home full of ideas and enthusiasm.

Back home, I spent some time in reviewing and analyzing, and we set up new training plans. Since all of our students were part time Taiji students, spending a couple of hours per week training at class, it really was like *Smart wife could not cook without rice*[13]. We could only *eat rice according to the dishes* or to work with the time and resources available to us, to improve our efficiency in training.

First, I intensified the basic training on *sinking and heaviness*. Then I applied *Qi Shi* (expression of *qi*/internal energy) to push hands training, which I acquired from Wu (Hao) style Taiji practice. This training produces a bigger *airbag* thus increasing the quality of the internal power. It extends the controlling range, and magnifies the quality of the *Taiji State of Readiness*.

In 2002, I brought 12 students to participate in the 2nd International Taijiquan Biannual Conference in Jiaozuo. Before the tournament, we went to Taiji's place of origin, Chenjiagou [陳家溝] (Chen Village), to pay our respects to Taiji's ancestors. There we benefited greatly by receiving instruction from Master Wang Xian [王西安]. We also made great progress in this competition. We had 12 students participate, and 8 of them fought into the top four of their respective categories. The final result was two gold medals, two silver, and three bronze. One of our Canadian students ended the competition winning 71 points and losing only 6. He won the championship with these excellent scores. Observers remarked: *This young Westerner really expresses the flavour of Taiji*. He received a warm appreciation from the audience.

In 2005, I returned to Jiaozuo with 3 students. Two students took gold and silver medals in Chen Style Taiji Forms. A third student won a silver medal in forms competition and, once again, took a gold medal in the Push Hands category.

While I was busy with forms and push hands training, I also applied the techniques of Taiji's conditioning and *control of the opponent* training to the development of free fighting. Within a short time, five of our students fought in the Selection Competition for the Canadian National Sanshou Team. This experience enriched all of us.

I have trained many Taiji practitioners during the last 17 years of teaching in Canada. Due to the limitation of student resources and training time, I have had to treat my colleges as a laboratory or experimental plant. In the future, I hope to have better training environments, to apply and test the Taiji theory and training methodology that I acquired over the years.

Looking back at the Taiji road that I traveled during the last 30 years, I realize that I

---

[13] *"Smart wife could not cook without rice"*: A Chinese expression meaning you must have the basics before you can create anything.

have been very fortunate. When I was young, I was influenced by my father to fall in love with Taiji, this Chinese national treasure. Then my father taught me what he had learned, showing me the way. He also taught me the new approach, which benefited me greatly and set up my direction of scientific research. Later on, I had the opportunity to study at the Physical Education Institute, and then teach at the South China Normal University, laying down a foundation of contemporary scientific knowledge, which created fine research conditions. In addition, I was very lucky to receive instruction and encouragement from numerous senior masters. These provided me with valuable experience and incentives for later inheriting, studying, and researching Taiji.

Since my immigration to Canada 17 years ago, my life and work have been stable. A group of warm-hearted, high quality students with a thirst for knowledge have joined in, providing an ideal environment for me to research and review Taiji's theory and principles. *Heaven times, ground fits, and people endorse*[14]. My progress advances daily, strengthening my confidence in walking through this road of modernizing Taiji. I often regarded myself a *soldier crossing the river*[15]. I will advance forward; confidently pursue, to contribute my own light and wisdom to the development of Taijiquan.

Luo Hong Yuan
Edmonton, Alberta
October, 2005

---

[14] "*Heaven times, ground fits, and people endorse*": Anyone can learn if they have enough time to invest and the proper environment.
[15] "*soldier crossing the river*": A Chinese chess expression meaning you can advance but never retreat.

The Ji Hong Taiji System

EVOLUTIONARY THEORY   APPLICATION   METHODOLOGY

PRINCIPLES
AND
THEORIES

Master Luo in Yang Style "Single Whip" Posture (1998)

CHAPTER 4

Taijiquan and the Theory of Yin and Yang

The theory of *Yin-Yang* is an ancient Chinese philosophy which permeates all aspects of the Chinese culture. There is no doubt that martial art, as a form of traditional Chinese culture, finds its roots in the theory of *Yin-Yang*. *Yin-Yang* can be regarded as the soul of Taiji. The name *Taiji* itself is suggestive of the co-existence of *Yin-Yang*. The symbol of Taiji is illustrative of the cyclical nature of *Yin-Yang*, and the ever-changing characteristics of Taiji. The practice of Taiji observes the co-existence of *Yin-Yang*, the *Yin* exists in the *Yang* and the *Yang* exists in the *Yin*. Therefore, the understanding of the meaning of *Yin-Yang* is of foremost importance in Taiji practice.

Yin-Yang is an abstract, philosophical and broad concept. The opposites in Taiji, like solid and empty (substantial & insubstantial), open and closed, hard and soft, strong and weak, move and hold (motion and stillness), external and internal, expand and compress, inhale and exhale, are, in fact, part of the general concept of *Yin-Yang*. In this chapter, we will discuss some of these opposites within the parameters of *Yin-Yang*.

SECTION 1: *The Relationship of Solid and Empty*

The concept of solid and empty (substantial and insubstantial) is a general concept in Taiji. It takes on different meanings from different points of view. In terms of body weight, when the body shifts to the left, the left side of the body becomes solid, and the right side empty and vice versa. In terms of direction, when the body moves forward, the front of the body becomes solid, and the rear empty and so on. In terms of *jing*, when force is released, the point of application of force becomes solid and the rest of the body becomes empty. In terms of mental concentration, the focus of concentration becomes solid, the rest empty. In terms of fighting strategy, the act of luring the enemy is empty and the act of attack is solid. To divert (neutralize) one's force is empty, and to release one's force is solid. Proper understanding of the concept of solid and empty is an important, yet difficult aspect of Taiji practice.

According to Taiji literature, *Yin* and *Yang* co-exist. Solid and empty is only a pair of opposites within the parameters of *Yin-Yang*. Similarly, they exist in time and space simultaneously. In solid, one finds the existence of empty and in empty, one finds the existence of solid. The two cannot be isolated. For example, prior to any movement, there is no *Yin* or *Yang*, and there is no external expression of solid or empty. *However, solid and empty remain in all the movements and are in a ready state to be expressed when called upon.* Whether one should take a solid or empty stance all depends on and is in response to the movement of the opponent. In the mind one should avoid having any predisposition about where *Yin* is and where *Yang* is. In movement, *Yin* and *Yang* as well as solid and empty become apparent. However, one should bear in mind the advantages of solid and empty and make the best out of their interchangeability in any part of the body.

When applying the concept of solid and empty, the mind plays a very important role. Ensure that the mind is in a neutral state, not predisposed to solid or empty, so that it can change from solid to empty or vice versa more promptly. Besides, the mind is the control of the expression of solid or empty. The mind gives direction and the body follows. According to Master Luo Ji Hong: *The relationship between the mind, and solid and empty, is interwoven and closely connected. When the mind is called upon, it is solid, otherwise it is empty. In view of their interchangeability, there is solid in the empty and empty in the solid.* According to Master Luo, the neutral state is similar to the "zero" point on a number line, positive or negative values can be attained efficiently if you are there. On the other hand, if you are already in a positive or negative state, you must go back to "zero" in order to go into a different state.

Having discussed solid and empty from a theoretical point of view, we will now talk about its application in Taiji practice. There is a saying, *when the left feels heavy, the left becomes empty and the right will launch,* which illustrates the fundamental principle of solid and empty in *push hands. When the left feels heavy* means that when the left side comes in contact with an opponent's attack it feels heavy. *The left side becomes empty* means that the left side becomes empty to divert an opponent's attack. However, this strategy is not a way to avoid the opponent's attack by simply diverting his energy because at the same time *the right will launch* meaning the right side will become solid and fight back. At this moment, *the empty left* and the *solid right* will have to co-exist at the same time. If not, the opponent will be aware of it and easily discontinue his attack, then the *empty left* and *solid right* will become ineffective. We are actually using leverage (mechanical advantage); using the opponent's incoming force to act upon the opponent. If the opponent's force and your own force do not co-exist at the same time, we can not create leverage by using the opponent's force plus my force or jing to return opponent's attack.

Perhaps a further elaboration of the meaning of *solid* is helpful. When we talk about the weight of an object, we often refer to a set of standards in order to judge how heavy the object is. For instance, if a weight of 5 grams is placed on one side of a scale, another weight has to be placed on the other side in order to balance the two sides. If the two sides balance, then the object on the other side of the scale has also a weight of 5 grams. In Taiji, when we talk about solid and empty, it refers to the set of standard of energy or *jing* we put out in order to judge the *heaviness* of the *jing* of the opponent. The standard of energy or *jing* that is extended is just like the weight put on one side of the scale, and the energy or *jing* of the opponent is the unknown weight placed on the other side of the scale. In push hands, once your hand is in contact with the opponent's hand, you will feel the comparative *heavy* or *not heavy* of the *jing* of your opponent. The saying *when the left is heavy, the left becomes empty and the right will launch* means, when you are in contact with your opponent, if your opponent's *jing* is greater than the standard put out by yourself then you will feel heavy at the contact point. If your opponent's *jing* is less than your standard of *jing*, then you will not feel it to be heavy and you do not have to use *the left becomes empty and the right will launch* in order to deal with your opponent. Great Taiji masters inevitably possess great intrinsic energy or *jing* as if they have placed a very heavy weight on their scales. Untrained people cannot counterbalance such a weight. Thus, once in contact, beginners would be easily thrown off balance by the masters. However, some masters deliberately set their standard at a lower rate, just like placing a very light weight on their scales, so when in contact, the opponent can only feel the *lightness* of a master and cannot detect their actual *jing*. Conversely, such masters are able to detect any slight change in the opponent's energy. Both methods are effective and determined by one's personal preference.

Another saying that we come across in the traditional Taiji literature is *to stick (adhere) is to follow and to follow is to stick.* This saying refers to the existence of both solid and empty at the same time and in the same place. *To follow* is to divert the opponent's *jing* and is therefore empty. *To stick* is to control the redirection of an opponent's *jing* and causes it to move in accordance with one's own will and it is therefore solid. *To follow* and *to stick* need to co-exist. *To follow* appears to be the expression of *empty*, but, in fact, it contains the element of *stick* or in other words, there is solid in the empty. In this process of an interchange of empty and solid, it is important to note that this interchange can take place at will. This has a similar meaning as the saying *Yin and Yang should not be isolated from each other. When you understand and are able to comprehend the complementary nature of Yin and Yang, then it can be said that you understand the nature of jing.* In Taiji *push hands*, we easily commit the error of *double-weightedness*[1] because of a failure to apply the interchange of solid and empty appropriately.

Taiji talks about *the point of contact moves in circles*. It is another illustration of the interchange of solid and empty or *Yin* and *Yang*. In push hands, the point of contact can be solid or empty; however, in order to facilitate the interchange from empty to solid or vice versa, the movement has to go in a circular direction. If the point of contact does not move spirally, your opponent may be able to restrict your attempt to achieve this interchange. You will find yourself unable to adopt the strategy of *to stick is to follow and to follow is to stick*. When this happens, you will be confronting force with force, and all your movements will be determined by the stronger opponent.

SECTION 2: *The Relationship of Strong and Weak*

In most physical contests, the general rule is that the strong will overcome the weak. Taiji, as a martial art, is no exception to this rule. However, Taiji literature often talks about the principle of *moving a thousand pounds with four ounces*, that is, one can use a smaller force to prevail over a greater one. As most Taiji practitioners are not usually distinguished by a strong physical build, the misconception has evolved that Taiji enables the weak to overcome a stronger opponent.

We will first talk about the meaning of strong and weak. Strong and weak is a general concept. In the martial arts, it takes on different meanings from different perspectives. From the physiological point of view, it can refer to a type of body physique or the difference in one's physique from youth to old age. From the psychological point of view, it is courage or fear. In terms of techniques and skills, it is the ability of varying degrees to use jing within applications. From the athletic point of view, it is swift or sluggish, quick or slow, greater or lesser power of jing. All the above can be grouped under the static perspective. From the dynamic perspective, strong and weak can interchange under certain circumstances. In the example of *four ounces versus a thousand pounds*, it is obvious that the former is weak and the latter is strong. However, when the *four ounces* is able to move the *thousand pounds*, the *four ounces,* once in motion, has shifted from the weak to the strong and the *thousand pounds* from the strong to the weak. The two have reversed their positions. This dynamic view of strong and weak is critical to the understanding of strong and weak in Taiji.

Like all other martial arts, Taiji pursues the goal of becoming strong. However, Taiji

---

[1] *Double-weightedness*: equal distribution of weight/*qi*/intent between left and right sides of the body, front and back, upper and lower sections of your frame.

offers a unique method of training to achieve this goal. In comparison with "hard" martial arts, Taiji does not demand as high a level of physical strength and power. Instead, Taiji focuses on training *the soft to become the hard*, emphasizing the development of a person's internal strength and potential. It is a very effective method of becoming strong from the weak which can be achieved with insight, practice and persistence. When internal strength or *jing* is cultivated and a high level of skill is acquired, then one can become strong. It is only at this stage that one can achieve *moving a thousand pounds with four ounces*. Although one can apply the principle of force to achieve the same goal with a lever, this is effective only if the opponent is stationary and not constantly changing and in motion. If one does not have great internal strength, it will not be possible to adopt the strategy of *to stick is to follow and to follow is to stick* in order to divert and control the direction of the opponent's *jing*. According to Master Luo Ji Hong, *if we wish to move a thousand pounds with four ounces, we must develop a thousand pound of internal strength in ourselves. In doing so, we have to equip ourselves in all the aspects of physical, psychological, technical as well as athletic. Among these, the development of great internal strength is the most important.* In his later years, Master Luo was able to demonstrate his immense internal strength and high level of skills by defeating many younger and physically stronger opponents.

The best way to facilitate the interchange of strong and weak is to recognize the optimal time to create the conditions to force the opponent to shift from strong to weak. An example is using the *to stick is to follow and to follow is to stick* strategy to divert the opponent's *jing*, push him off balance and then strike back. Another example is using *lock-up jing* to lock up the attacking force and control the opponent's balance. The effect is like holding up the opponent's body and borrowing his momentum to strike back. As a result, the opponent is shifted to a weak position. It is similar to controlling a buffalo by leading his nose.

In conclusion, the goal of Taiji is to train practitioners to become strong and at the same time force the opponent to become weak. Taiji training should be focussed on these interchanges.

SECTION 3: *The Relationship of Hard and Soft*

The relationship of hard and soft is an important topic in Taiji. According to Taiji Master Chen Xin: *People tend to regard Taiji as a soft form of exercise. In fact, hard and soft co-exist and are interrelated. It is only by appearance that it looks like soft. The techniques of Taiji include both hard and soft although they may not be visible at all times. It requires a lot of practice and mastery of the skills is not easy.*

Master Chen clearly pointed out that Taiji is neither hard nor soft. The two co-exist. Hard and soft is a pair of opposites within the parameters of *Yin-Yang* in Taiji. In practice, hard and soft are complementary in nature and should not be isolated from each other. Therefore, it is not right to say that Taiji is a soft form of exercise and the goal of Taiji is to achieve soft and gentle.

The concept of hard and soft can have different meanings from the perspective of 1) when we mastered the Taiji skill and attained the *Taiji condition*, 2) the application of Taiji techniques and 3) the learning process.

The co-existence of hard and soft can be seen at the level of mind and body. When the skills are mastered, the mind should be in a neutral state and not predispose itself to hard or soft which helps to facilitate the interchange of the two. The Taiji Classics state that: *At this stage, there is qi inside the body which can be hard or soft. It flows in such a natural way that it is neither hard nor soft. It is only when the mind is in a neutral state and hard and soft co-exist that one can achieve the interchange of the two at will.* According to Master Luo Ji Hong: *The mind directs the qi and the qi generates the jing. When the mind and qi are in harmony, they control the disposition of the jing, overtly or covertly. When the jing is demonstrated overtly, it is hard. When the jing is manifested covertly, it is soft. When one can manipulate the interchange at will, the opponent will be at your mercy.*

Apart from the mind, the five bows of the body are linked together to form one elastic entity. The entity is soft on the outside but hard inside. When force acts on this entity, it can absorb and store any outside force. The greater the force, the greater the elasticity and kinetic pressure. It is similar to the potential force of a compressed spring. The opponent will feel the reaction or hardness from the spring. This is the state of *wrapping a piece of iron in cotton* or *hiding a needle in wool*. This exhibits the co-existence of hard and soft. When there is no movement, no hard or soft can be seen. When in motion, it can be hard as stone or soft as a willow. The hard appears to be soft and the soft appears to be hard. This is the goal in the pursuit of excellence in Taiji.

The co-existence of hard and soft is a unique technique in the practice of Taiji. According to literature: *When proficiency in Taiji is achieved with diligent practice, all the movement and the interchange of heavy or light, solid or empty, hard or soft can be called upon at will. Hard and soft must co-exist. Without soft, we cannot go in circles swiftly. Without hard, we lose speed. With both, we can apply all the Taiji movements and skills freely and naturally.* In confrontations, we have to apply the interchange of hard and soft wisely. Facing a hard attack, we use soft to divert it and never try to respond with hard. When the opponent is off balance, we can attack with a hard blow. Whichever strategy we use, we have to bear in mind the hard and the soft co-exist and they can interchange freely at will.

The co-existence of hard and soft can also be understood as three stages in the learning process: 1) from stiff and rigid to soft; 2) accumulation of softness to form hardness; 3) from hardness back to softness and eventually hardness and softness compliment each other.

i)   Stage of Stiff and Rigid to Soft
When people exert force, the tendency is to contract and tighten their muscles resulting in stiffness, rigid movement and poor co-ordination. Practising this way will lead to localization of stress to a few joints or muscle groups. We call this kind of strength *stiffness jing*. In Taiji, the objective is for the body to form an elastic entity under the direction of the mind and the *qi* for the release of *jing*. Therefore the first step is to disregard the former tendency and learn a new way to relax and control the body as an entity in all movements.

ii)   Stage of Accumulation of Softness to Form Hardness
Based on the foundation of the previous stage, while maintaining softness and gentleness, we need to use our mind to focus on exerting *jing* consciously in the daily practice. This will add a feeling of heaviness in the softness and gentleness, making the *jing* both elastic and hard. With proper posture (extending all joints and preparing all the muscles), this *jing* originates from the waist and releases evenly through every section of the body. This *jing* can be so powerful that it can penetrate any hardness.

iii) Stage of Hardness Back to Softness and Both Compliment Each Other

The question often asked is why we have to go back to softness. In fact, at this stage our softness is a higher level of softness. At this level, our mind can control this softness freely whenever we need it. According to an old Taiji doctrine: *It appears to be soft, in fact, it is extremely rigid; it may appear to be rigid, in fact, it is extremely soft; hardness and softness compliment each other; there is no way to determine which is which.* At this stage, hardness and softness compliment each other. Hardness and softness can be manipulated at will and there can be unlimited variations. It is this stage every Taiji practitioner must strive to attain.

Finally, we will talk about defeating the hard with the soft which is widely spoken and pursued in Taiji. The *hard* here means the hard force and not the *jing* in Taiji. This kind of hardness is blunt, inflexible and not able to change directions. The *soft* here is flexible and extendable. It can neutralize and adhere. In brief, it means using controllable softness in Taiji to defeat any blunt and inflexible hard force.

SECTION 4: *The Relationship of Fast and Slow*

One of the characteristics of Taiji is its fast and slow movements. The slow movements can be as slow as extracting silk threads and fast movements can be as quick as a flash of lightning.

However, people tend to focus on the soft and slow side of Taiji and miss the complimentary side of hard and quick. They generally accept that they have to practice Taiji at a slow pace but they are not aware of the rationale behind this guideline. Additionally, most of the Taiji literature is not comprehensive or seldom explores this aspect of training. As a result, misunderstanding occurs which adversely affects the attainment of higher levels of Taiji.

There is no doubt that quick movements exist in Taiji. We can trace these back to the traditional Chen Style Taiji which is the oldest form of Taiji. However, the subsequent modifications derived from Chen style Taiji tend to emphasize the soft and slow movements. Nevertheless, all schools of Taiji have developed their own methods for training speed and quick movements in order to raise their level of practice. In the Taiji Classics, the description of quick movements is always related to slow movements, which further demonstrates the co-existence of *Yin-Yang* in Taiji.

At the beginning of basic training, the emphasis is on the slow movements, the slower the better. However, as a form of martial art, Taiji requires speed and quick movements to defeat an opponent. In other words, Taijiquan martial art training is to achieve quickness (as opposed to practicing Taiji as a form of exercise). Contrary to the end result of training and its effectiveness in confrontation, Taiji adopts a unique method of training – slow motion. This is due to the sophisticated and complicated nature of Taiji. Only by slow motion we can appreciate and integrate all the intricate aspects of its theory and practice, to attain the state of *directing the body with mind, guiding the qi with the body and the body with qi.* With slow motion, we can note the imperfections in our movements, adjust the body posture, and correct our mistakes resulting in successful integration of the mind, *qi* and *jing.* On the other hand, with slow motion as a foundation, we also need high speed trigger force training (*fa jing*). Failure to release *jing* properly indicates an inability to accumulate sufficient energy. Slow motion training is, in fact, the most effective method of training high speed and power movements. This kind of slow motion workout let us properly co-ordinate our mind, *qi*, posture and internal energy. It is similar to repeatedly opening a bow with proper posture. Once we can open it fully, all we need is to place an arrow in the notch. The results are extremely powerful and the high speed release of the arrow is similar to the desired release of *jing*. According to an old saying in Taiji: *No matter where my opponent contacts me, my mind and qi are there. My opponent will feel being shocked by high power electricity.* When we are at this stage, we have completed our training from slow to fast; we will enter into a higher level: *Slow to extreme slow; fast to extreme fast.*

The paradox of Taiji training is that while practicing in slow motion we can achieve speed and quick movements. This can be explained by the unique method of body alignment in Taiji and the theory of force and momentum in Physics. Taiji requires "section linkages" in the body and the *jing* must originate from the *dan tian* when it is released. According to the theory of force, the force can be passed on in a whipping and rippling action. When force is applied on one end, it is passed on; reaching its maximum magnitude in speed and power at the other end. In the body, the force originates from the waist and passes on to the shoulder, the elbow and finally to the hand. Therefore the release of *jing* can be very powerful.

Understanding the reasons behind between slow motion and speed training will improve our understanding towards the direction we are taking in our Taiji training.

SECTION 5: *The Concepts of Move and Hold in Taijiquan*

Almost all literature on Taijiquan covers the topics of *Move-Hold* and their interrelationship. For example we find concepts such as: *The principle of Yin-Yang applies to the entire body and it is natural to have Move and Hold, Move and Hold are of a cyclical nature, The beauty of Taijiquan is embedded in the move and hold and open and close, Move is the moving of the whole body, Hold is the holding of all the parts of the body, Taiji involves fighting the Move with Hold, but the Hold is in the Move as well, We hold when the opponent holds but we move sooner than him when the opponent starts to move.* From these examples, we can see that in addition to void and real, hard and soft, and quick and slow, the equilibrium of Move and Hold and the concept of fighting the move with hold are also characteristics of Taijiquan. Appreciation of these characteristics, understanding of the meaning of Move and Hold and acquisition of the techniques of fighting the Move with Hold are very important in the practice of Taijiquan.

In some literature, the elaboration of the concept of the Move and Hold and the explanation of their interrelationship is either too simple or too abstract for readers to understand. Quite often it will cause misunderstanding. For example, the sayings: *There is Move in the Hold, and Hold in the Move,*[2] and *Move is the moving of the whole body, Hold is the holding of all parts of the body* are not easy to understand, not to mention to practice. Other examples: *Fighting the move with hold* and *We hold when the opponent holds but we move ahead of him when he starts to move* can bring about the misunderstanding that Taijiquan only reacts to being attacked and does not initiate a move. All these have a negative impact on the daily practice and application of Taijiquan. For this reason, I feel it is essential that I can share with our readers my experience and understanding of *Motion and Stillness*.

---

[2] *"There is Move in the Hold, and Hold in the Move"*: An example of *Yin-Yang* as represented by the Taiji symbol. These states are interrelated and one cannot exist without the other.

First, let's discuss the meaning of Move and Hold. The Move and Hold in Taijiquan is not simply the moving and holding from the physical point of view. The Move in Taijiquan comprises the move of the mind, the *qi* and the *jing* together (*Yang* state). *Move is the moving of the whole body* cannot be interpreted simply as the moving of all the external body parts (that kind of move is loose and not powerful). In fact, it should be seen as being directed by the mind and the *qi*, the jing exhibits itself physically in the full coordination of the body. In the same way, the Hold in Taijiquan is not simply the holding of the physical body. The Hold is a condition of great concentration, a high state of alert and the ability to react to input from the environment at any time (*Yin* state). *Hold is the holding of all the parts of the body* can be explained as the preparation and disposition of the whole body to a state of readiness to act or react. This condition of Hold can have an intimidating effect on an opponent.

Regarding the interrelationship of the Move and the Hold, there are the sayings of *There is Move in the Hold and Hold in the Move* and *Move exists in the Hold*. Using the meaning of the Move and the Hold previously explained; consider the example of an arrow notched in the string of a bow. When the arrow is pulled back ready to be shot, the arrow is in a state of Hold, although motion is imminent. We can say there is Move in the state of Hold. Similarly, we can use examples to explain the phenomenon of incorporating the Hold in the Move. There is the saying that *Disposition as the eagle after the rabbit* and *Concentration as the cat after the rat* which best illustrates the two ideas of having the Hold in the Move. When the eagle is after the rabbit, its motion and speed changes according to the speed and direction the rabbit runs. The eagle demonstrates calmness from a proactive approach. When the cat is after the rat, its eyes watch the rat closely and it approaches its prey silently. The cat demonstrates calmness with high concentration. These two examples help to illustrate the idea of having the Hold in the Move.

After clarifying the meaning of *Move* and *Hold* in Taijiquan and their interrelationship from a theoretical point of view, it is easier to comprehend the principle of *Fighting the Move with Hold* in Taiji practice. In practice, there are the circumstances of having an opponent or not having any opponent at all. I will talk about the circumstances of having an opponent first. When the opponent makes an advance to attack, I can adopt the principle of *Fighting the Move with the Hold* to achieve *Acting promptly when the attack is quick, acting leisurely when the attack is slow*. When the opponent confronts me and does not advance, I can initiate an advance forcing the opponent to react. It is a*cting in an appropriate manner to collect information*. In other words, it is to induce a response from the opponent, to adopt a proactive approach like the eagle after the rabbit, to move in a state of calmness, or *Staying calm in Move* or *having the Hold in the Move*. In addition, I make subsequent modifications with the information collected, switch quickly from Hold to Move and act ahead of the opponent to defeat him. It is a*cting ahead when the opponent starts to move* and *Reacting can become ahead*. Therefore, this kind of move is a good application of the principle of *Fighting the Move with Hold* in Taijiquan.

In the circumstances of having no opponent or self-practice, we should still apply the principle of the Move and the Hold to appreciate the intertwining relationship in *There is Move in the Hold and Hold in the Move*. Although there is no real opponent, we can pretend one exists, that is, *Assuming there is an opponent when there is none in reality*. Always bear in mind the principles of *Fighting the Move with the Hold* and *Having Numerous Assumptions* when we move in order to capture the qualities of the eagle which is skilled at catching rabbits. Once the relationship between Move and Hold are understood and one can control the degree of Move and Hold with the mind, the practitioner will be able to advance to the highest levels of Taijiquan.

CHAPTER 5

The Technique of Self-Control in Taijiquan
(internal adjustment, co-ordination and self maintenance)

Taijiquan is an internal martial art form. The understanding and feeling during the attainment of the higher stages in Taiji depends on one's physical fitness and educational background. For this reason, although there have been many great masters or instructors throughout the development of Taiji, each master or instructor has a different description of the highest stage in Taiji.

The Chen school of Taijiquan defines its ultimate form in terms of the ratio of *Yin* to *Yang*. A ratio of one *Yin* to nine *Yang* is considered poor, and a ratio of five *Yin* to five *Yang* superb. Other schools of Taijiquan apply the skills of one practitioner at his different stages and levels of training as a yardstick to measure the competence of another practitioner. And there are still others who describe the ultimate form in terms of a blow-up air balloon, capable of expanding and contracting. Finally, traditional writings describe the process of Taiji training in terms of the *diligently practising stage to the understanding of the use of jing, and from the understanding of the use of jing to reaching the ultimate stage of complete understanding (the Goddess stage).*

All of the above expressions are applied to describe the different levels of competence of a Taijiquan practitioner at a particular moment in their training, and as such, fail to give a comprehensive view for the overall training of Taijiquan, which, in its final form, exudes the interaction of *yi*, *body*, *qi*, and *jing*, as well as the internal development in the substance and essence of *yi*, *body*, *qi*, and *jing*. It is not surprising that many practitioners give up training in Taijiquan as a martial art form, and satisfy themselves in the practice of the forms only.

In view of the present trend in the training of Taijiquan, the author wishes to offer the following training module, which is based on the lessons that he has learned from his former instructors, and on the experience he personally has acquired in his own training. Like the lighthouse lending light to guide the ships, it is the author's sincerest wish that his training module may hopefully lend some light to the comprehensive training of Taijiquan.

What follows is a discussion of the *Basic Principles of Taijiquan*, the *Principle of Self-Control*, and the *Characteristics of the Final Form of Taijiquan*. To facilitate a thorough comprehension of these concepts, the author will discuss in detail the three topics:

- The Principle of *Air Bag-Like Elasticity* (*ABLE*) and its relevance to the *Principle of Qi Shi* (or Presence of *Qi*);

- The Principle of *Taiji Readiness*; and

- The Characteristics of the *Quality and Substance (QS)* of Taijiquan.

TOPIC 1: <u>The Principle of Air Bag-Like Elasticity and its Relevance to the Principle of *Qi-Shi* (Presence of *Qi*)</u>

SECTION 1: *Principle of Air Bag-Like Elasticity (ABLE)*

An *Air Bag-Like Elasticity* in Taijiquan is defined as an elastic, solid body, created in an orderly, purposeful and closely-knit manner as a result of the inter-workings of the three Taiji elements *yi*, *qi*, and *body*. The process in the formation of **ABLE** involves three separate stages.

In the first stage, the body structure is adjusted under the direction of the mind *(yi)* as outlined in the theory of the *Five-Bow Module*[1], as a result of which the body is capable of pulling and stretching, thus becoming one unit filled with elastic power.

The second stage involves the movement of *qi* under the direction of *yi*, whereby *qi* will fill up the inner space of the body, and when combined with the movement of the body, will create a pressure system or energy field from within.

The third stage is the manipulation of the energy field within the body and the projection of such energy outside the physical confine of the body such that the air space enclosed by the four limbs of the body will form another field of energy. When the body is well adjusted in a curved manner, as in a bent bow, the air space created by the enclosing limbs (the air space under the hip area is enclosed by the legs and the air space above the waist area is enclosed by the arms) will form an energy field wherein *qi* can move and function. The limbs will form the outside wall of the energy field, with *qi* functioning within the physical confines of the limbs, just like an air-filled car tire or an air-filled air-bag, thereby creating a self-operative pressure system.

This unique structure, created as a result of the close workings of the *body*, *yi*, and *qi* in the combined movement of the body and movement of *qi* acting within and outside the body's physical confine, is henceforth called the Module of **<u>Air Bag-Like Elasticity</u> (ABLE)**[2].

Formation of Air Bag-Like Elasticity (ABLE).

The formation of ABLE depends on the adjustment of the *body*, the mind (*yi*) and the internal energy (*qi*). To achieve this unification of the internal and external movements, Master Luo Ji Hong explains: *Common understanding of the unification of the three elements is that the yi directs qi, and qi directs jing. Such however, is only a self-awareness of the workings of the three elements, but not the understanding of the actual working relationship of them. The fact is that the mind directs the body, the body directs qi, and qi re-directs the body, resulting in release of jing. Upon such unification, the process is then abbreviated to read: mind directing qi, and qi directing yi.* This explanation illustrates the connection between *yi*, *qi* and *jing*.

---

[1] The *Five-Bow Module* refers to the body structure comprising of the spine as the main bow, the hands as front bows, and the legs as low bows.
[2] An *Air Bag-Like Elasticity* is simply an ideal of Taiji operation consisting of (a) a well-adjusted body capable of elastic power, and (b) an energy column outside the physical confine of the body but enclosed by the physical limbs. Combined, the system operates like an elastic body filled with *qi* or energy both within and without.

For better comprehension, one needs to understand the training process of this tri-party connection. Traditionally, the training process is directed as *from the outside to the inside*, that is to say, the body is adjusted in such a way as to result in the flow of *qi*. After the proper adjustment of the body, the emphasis of training then changes *from the inside to the outside*; that is, *qi* directing the body movement and ultimately culminating in the *unification or co-existence of the external and the internal*.

The sequence in the formation of the *Air Bag-Like Elasticity* (*ABLE*) is as follows:

(a) *mind* directing *body*,
(b) *body* directing *qi*, and
(c) *qi* re-directing *body*.

The first and the second stages are designed to establish the platform for the construction of Module *ABLE*; the third stage activates the operation of *ABLE*, or the *internal energy of Taijiquan*.

(a)   <u>*Mind* directing *body*</u>

Training in *mind directing body* is the very basic stage in Taijiquan training. It represents the first stage in the creation of *ABLE*, and its objective is to adjust the body structure by applying certain pre-determined guidelines and requirements. Traditionally, adjustments are applied to different body parts, such as the spine (as in *lifting the head and hanging the hips, gently leading the head and lifting up the energy, maintaining tail-bone at the centre, sucking in of the chest and up-lifting of the back, relaxing the waist and rounding the hips*, etc), the upper limbs, (as in *sinking the shoulders and lowering the elbows,* and *resting the wrist and stretching the fingers*, etc.) and the lower limbs (as in *opening the hips and bending the knees,* and *turning the ankles and twisting the knees*, etc.).

Unfortunately, all of the above requirements basically tend to describe the external appearance of the movements without any logical or rational explanation for doing so; and as a result, many practitioners find such concepts disconnected and confusing.

It is therefore imperative to draw a clearly defined outline for the overall training such that practitioners can follow a proper methodology. In other words, it is critical to provide a rational criteria that lead to the formation of the module *ABLE*.

Five-Bow Module

The requirements for alignment of the body structure for Taijiquan training can be found in the traditional *Five-Bow Module*, which not only illustrates the adjustments of all the various body parts, but also explains the underlying rationale.

To establish the Module of *ABLE*, the body needs to be adjusted in such a way that the body trunk and the four limbs will operate like a five-bow structure containing elastic power.

In the training in *mind directing body*, the *ming men* acts as the central point from which all the internal energy emanates, reaching out to the farthest points of the four limbs, culminating into one single unified five-bow structure. This describes the ideal unit of *ABLE*. With the *ming men* acting as the central point, the main bow (spine) extends and stretches longitudinally and latitudinally, reaching out to the upper and lower limbs, and setting the stage for the operation of the second process, *body directing qi* , when *qi* sinks and settles in the *dan tian*. When the main bow extends and stretches, the upper and the lower limbs will open up and form an elastic net or energy column (Illustration.5-1-2) filled with elastic power (Illustration.5-1-1). This is the basic objective of *mind directing body* in the formulation of *ABLE*.

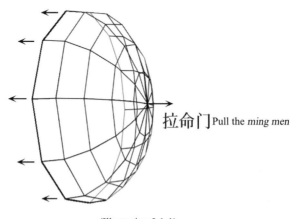

拉命门Pull the *ming men*

(Illustration.5-1-1)

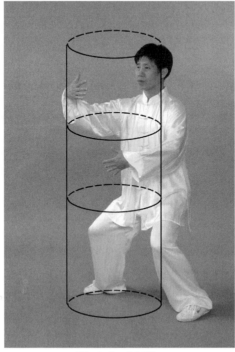

(Illustration.5-1-2)

The second objective of the body structure adjustment in the formation of *ABLE* is that, when the five bows (i.e., the spine and the four limbs) extend and stretch, elastic power will result. Taiji master Shen Jia Jiang once said: *In Taijiquan practice, the limbs must necessarily be stretched such that they will contain elastic power. With such elastic power is in place peng jing [掤勁][3] will result. In other words, peng jing originates from elastic power, and elastic power originates from stretching of the body.*

In the training of *mind directing body*, the body structure adjustments will result in elastic power, and this lays down the foundation for the formation of *Taiji Qi Shi* or *Presence of Qi* which will be discussed later.

(b)　　*Body* directing *qi*

Body directing qi is the second stage in the formation of *ABLE*. After the body parts are well adjusted and aligned in the procedure as explained under *mind directing body* following the Five-bow Module, the *mind* can now direct the flow and distribution of *qi* in an orderly fashion inside the body, which, in conjunction with the movements of the body parts, will result in the ideal form of *Taiji Readiness*.

Taijiquan is a unique martial art in that it is a combination of fighting techniques, induction of *qi*, and breathing techniques. It emphasises the importance of the movement of the body parts, as well as the internal movements of *qi*. When studying traditional Taiji treatises, one comes across sayings such as *the heart directing qi, qi flowing around the body*. The concept of *qi* in the Taiji treatise is the same concept of *qi* as it is used in the study of the meridians in the traditional Chinese medicine. Martial art practitioners call it *internal qi*. The existence of *qi* has already been proven in the study of Acupuncture, Qigong, and Taijiquan.

Qi is a form of energy. It not only maintains the vitality of human beings, but also expresses itself in the form of power as a result of its close working with the body. We call it the internal power of Taijiquan. In the study of Taijiquan, one can for a moment set aside the inquiry of the real substance of *qi*. Let us use the example that *qi* is a substance contained in a black box. Using the analogy of input/output, the mind is the input to the black box and the output of the black box is *jing* or power.

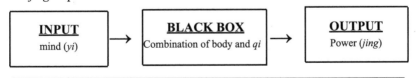

Body and *Qi*'s connection and adjustment

The above illustration shows the connection between *body* and *qi* in the training of Taijiquan. The output or result is expressed as the internal energy of Taijiquan and its quality is an elastic power and pressure. In the training process of *mind directing body*, the body framework will be adjusted into an elastic body, defining an enclosed air volume outside the body frame, just like an air-bag, which, when charged with *qi*, will produce power under adjusted pressure.

---

[3] *peng jing:* internal power

77

Qi sinking into *dan tian*

When training *body directing qi*, the technique of directing *qi* into the *dan tian* cavity is critical. The process of adjusting the body frame as well as the movement of *qi* will create a pressure centre inside the abdominal cavity. This pressure centre will be the source of all the internal energy, directing the movement of *qi* and *jing*. To direct *qi* into the *dan tian* cavity, the body's frame or *main bow* (spine) must be well adjusted. To achieve this, the *ming men* needs to be pulled back; the hip bones open up, such that a well-rounded concave structure is created. Forming this concave structure will not only enlarge the size of the pelvic cavity when the outside wall of the pelvic cavity is stretched, but will also create an energy field when the inside wall of the pelvic cavity exerts pressure towards its centre.

To create a well-rounded concave structure in the body's upper part, a similar procedure is applied by *tucking in the chest and stretching the spine*. The back of the body will now be stretched, inducing the feeling of *qi on the back*, and the inside walls of the chest will exert pressure on the chest cavity, thus creating another energy field. At the same time, the muscle groups around the shoulders, the chest and the back will be totally relaxed, directing the flow of *qi* from the chest cavity into the pelvic cavity. This process is analogous to placing two water bags one on top of the other. The water pressure from the upper bag will be directed to the lower water bag and the combined pressure of both the upper and the lower bags will be stored at the bottom of the lower water bag, thereby creating a high pressure centre. In other words, as a result of the relaxing of the muscle groups from top to bottom, a high pressure centre will be formed at the bottom of the pelvic cavity. This is the explanation of the theory of *emptying the chest and solidifying the abdomen*.

The technique of *emptying the chest and solidifying the abdomen* directs the flow of energy from top to bottom and thereby creates a downward movement of energy. When combined with the *pulling of the ming men, opening of hips and the pelvis* , the elastic power of the muscle groups under the hips and the pelvis will create an energy field inside the pelvic cavity, totally confined and compressed. Within such an energy field enclosed by the pelvic cavity, energy from all parts of the body will converge at its centre, thereby creating a centre of pressure and compression. This centre is the location of *the dan tian*. (Illustration. 5-1-3)

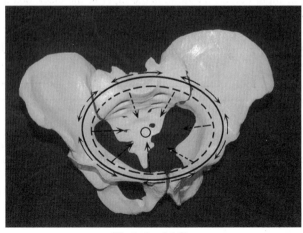

(Illustration.5-1-3)

The objective of *qi sinking into dan tian* in the process of body directing *qi*, is to create an energy field within the *dan tian* by:

    i.   adjusting the body parts following the Five-Bow Module,
    ii.   directing the flow of internal energy or *qi* inside the body from top to bottom, and
    iii.   collecting and converging all the internal energy in the *dan tian* cavity.

Taiji Master Chen Xin once described the importance of the *dan tian* as the *headquarters of an army*, or *the repository of qi from the whole body*.

During the process of *mind directing body* in the formation of ABLE, the *ming men* and other parts of the body such as the spine and the four limbs are stretched and extended, just like laying down a fire hose. When the hose is properly laid out, water will flow along the hose after the hydrant is turned on. Likewise, when the body parts are properly stretched and adjusted, *qi* emanating from the *dan tian* will flow inside the body, resulting in an outward expression of energy filled with pressure. The result of *mind directing body* is to enable our body to operate like an elastic entity. And in the process of *body directing qi*, *qi* is now directed to sink into the *dan tian* cavity, creating an energy field where all energy and pressure is found. Combined, the body will operate like an elastic body charged with internal energy.

(c)   *Qi* directing *body*

The third stage in the formulation of Module *ABLE*, or *Air Bag-Like Elasticity*, is the creation of an energy field outside the physical confine of the body when the mind directs the internal energy or *qi* to act or react on the air space enclosed by the body parts.

The result of *mind directing qi* not only creates a body with elastic power; but it also, through the interaction of the body and *qi* movement, enables the combined potential power of the elastic body and the *qi* energy to affect the air space outside the body's physical confine, resulting in a highly pressurized field of energy. This external field of energy is sometimes described as the *qi column* or *Qi Shi* (Presence of *Qi*).

The concept of *Qi Shi* was once described by Taiji Grand Master Hao Shao Ru as follows: *In order to express the fullest effect of qi, (or Qi Shi), there must be a certain confinement to such expression, and at no time should the qi be left in disarray. To establish such a confinement, there must be a centre and a certain imaginary edge or a border to the scope of qi within which qi can operate. In our practice, the waist becomes the centre of the qi expression. We should try to respect this limitation of qi and all our movements should be directed to reach this edge or outer limit of qi, but not beyond. This way, the expression of qi will become full and without defects. When the imaginary edge of the qi expression is farthest away from the centre, the expression of qi will become the fullest. However, within the scope of the qi expression, qi needs to be supported by a Vital Spirit (energy). Without the support of this energy, the qi expression will collapse. On the other hand, the qi expression should enclose the Vital Spirit (energy) from within, such that the energy will not leak outside the confinement of qi. If you can do this, then qi can find its fullest expression, filled with and surrounded by a lively energy.*

Master Hao's view on *Qi Shi* clearly outlines the theoretical basis of Module *ABLE*. In the sense described by Master Hao, the edge of the scope of *Qi Shi* now becomes the inside wall of *ABLE*. Through the workings of *qi directing body*; the air space enclosed by our limbs outside the body becomes an enclosed energy field; and the centre of *Qi Shi* now becomes the centre of the *qi* column to which all our energy is directed.

In result, we have created an operative system filled with elastic power and charged with energy, able to expand and contract, and to remain calm in the midst of action. Hence, we call this system the Taiji Module of *Air Bag-Like Elasticity*, or *ABLE*.

SECTION 2: *Taiji Concept of Qi Shi or Presence of Qi*

In the preceding section we already discussed the formulation of Module *ABLE*, a system made up of *body, qi* and *yi*, the interaction of these three elements, and the three major stages in the formulation process. A careful reader will probably appreciate that in the final stage of the formulation process, one has already created an energy system outside the confine of the physical body. This energy system, which serves as the ultimate goal of Taijiquan, has already been described by Master Hao in his dissertation on *Qi Shi*. In all the years of training and teaching, the author has come to fully understand and appreciate the correctness of Master Hao's view. Below the author presents his findings.

A.   **The Concept of *Qi Shi* or *Presence of Qi*, and the Formulation of *Qi Shi***

Master Hao Shao Ru was one of the leading masters in the Wu (Hao) school of Taijiquan. In his book "Wu's Taijiquan", he said: *The presence of qi in its fullest expression is determined by one's training in Taijiquan. It is an indicator of one's prowess in the pursuit of Taiji. The greater the scope of Qi Shi, the greater is one's skills. The emphasis of training in Taijiquan is on the substance and not on the form. In your daily training, you should endeavour to achieve the maximum expression of qi.*

a.   **Scope of *Qi* or *Qi Shi***

The formulation of *Qi Shi* is therefore a matter of internal adjustment. To begin with, one must adjust the body and open it up like a bow, such that it contains springy or elastic power. This is the first stage in the formation of the module *Air Bag-Like Elasticity*.

The adjustment of the body includes all of the elements of the *five-bow module*. The arms, legs and the main bow (back bone) become stretched, with the *ming men* on the lower spine operating as the initiating factor. Once the limbs become properly stretched, springy or elastic power will result. The limbs will curve slightly outwards in a web-like projectile manner. The upper part of the body trunk remains upright; the two arms will open up as if holding an imaginary air-bag in front of the chest area. The hips in the lower part of the body, assisted by the adjustment of the *ming men*, will likewise open up and enclose another imaginary air-bag below the *dan tian* cavity.

The properly adjusted body, which is now under a stretched condition, as a result of the workings of the *ming men* on the lower spine, is now enclosing an imaginary air-bag in front of and below the trunk. Such air-bags however are not an open but an enclosed space confined by the arms and legs. The *mind* will now direct the flow of energy into these two imaginary air-bags, just like filling up a car tire or a balloon with air, which, when under compression, becomes a *field of energy*. Within this environment, *qi* or internal energy can find its fullest expression. This *field of energy* within the confine of the air space formulated by the combined adjustment of the body parts and the influx of internal energy is hence called **Qi Shi.**

b.   **The Effective Scope of *qi* or *Qi Shi* or *Presence of qi***

Within the confine of the air space, internal energy will find its fullest expression. But the internal energy is not working in a random, directionless and listless manner. The *mind (or yi)* will, at this time, direct all the energy to converge into a central focal point within the enclosed air space.

To achieve this, all the muscle groups in the body will become totally relaxed. This includes the muscle groups in the shoulder area, the arms, the chest, the waist and the hips. Under relaxed condition, all the energy will be directed downwards, like the falling of snow from a mountain top (avalanche) or lava flowing from a burning crater. The *mind* will then direct all the energy to converge into one central point within the confine of the air space above and below. The limbs, which are now in a web-like concave form, will help direct the flow of energy into this imaginary focal point. When all the energy particles are collected and contained inside this air space, a *field of energy* containing highly pressurized energy is hence created.

The central point within the air space to which all the energy particles converge is called the **Centre of Qi Shi.** Master Luo Ji Hong pointed out that in any movement in any Taiji form, the center is not our body but rather it is the center of the posture (i.e. in Lazily Tying Coat, the mind is not set at the ends of the limbs, it is in the center between the two extended hands). He had named this as the Centre of *Qi Shi*. This center expands with movement and contracts when resting.

Such an energy-charged air space however is not stagnant. It can be charged and re-charged, compressed or expanded, just like the air space inside a balloon. When external pressure is applied to an air balloon, the shape of the balloon is changed, and the air pressure inside the balloon is increased. At the same time, the external pressure dissipates evenly around the periphery of the balloon. If, under a compressed condition, the external pressure recedes, the reaction from the compressed air inside the balloon will become greater. In other words, the greater the compression from the outside, the greater is the pressure from within, and the more effective would be the reaction.

Likewise, when the body is well adjusted, the limbs will form an elastic web-like structure, enclosing an air space outside the body, charged with energy collected at the centre. When external pressure applies to the body, the body will change its shape, thereby increasing the elastic or springy power contained within, and directly increasing the pressure within the confine of the air space. When external pressure recedes, the compressed energy will react more effectively than in the pre-compressed condition, and will consequently affect any object in a wider and broader space.

The space in which *Qi Shi* can find its fullest expression is called the ***Effective Scope of Qi Shi.***

c.   The Effective Scope of Mind Control

The effectiveness of the presence of *qi* within the scope of *Qi Shi* is not limited to the air space created by the adjustment of the body parts. It can very well work outside such a confinement. The *mind* takes on the leading role in this regard.

When the *mind* projects its attention outside the *Effective Scope of Qi Shi* it operates like a radar trap, sending its signals to catch any incoming objects. When an opponent enters into this radar field, one can react immediately. This space in which the mind operates outside the confine of the *Effective Scope of Qi* is called the ***Effective Scope of Mind Control***.

d.   The Co-relationship of *Qi Shi* and *ABLE*

Having discussed the concepts of *Qi Shi* as explained by Master Hao, the formulation of *Qi Shi* and its structure, one can come to appreciate that the Module *ABLE* is the theoretical module for *Qi Shi*.

The air-bag in this module is the air space within which *qi* functions. The edge of *Qi Shi*, as defined by Master Hao, is the inside wall of the modular air bag. The energy that is needed to support *qi,* as explained by Master Hao, is the compressed energy as a result of the application of external force or self-adjustment of the body parts.

To make a reaction more effective, the scope of *Qi Shi* needs be expanded by increasing the energy pressure from within. To increase the internal pressure is to increase the elastic power emanating from the arms and legs as a result of the construction of the *five-bow module* and to direct all energy particles towards the centre of the air space in a compressed condition which has now become a *field of energy*. To mobilize *Qi Shi* is to expand the scope of *mind* control beyond the effective scope of *Qi Shi*. In short, the Module *Air Bag-Like Elasticity* is the modular structure for the expression of *qi*.

**B.   The *Quality and Substance (QS)* of *Taiji Qi Shi* and its Mode of
         Distribution** - *Qi directing Body*

The process of *qi directing body* in the formulation of module ABLE is designed to collect and distribute *qi*, under the guidance of the *yi* in an orderly manner. Such a process can be found in the final presentation of *Qi Shi*.

In Taijiquan training, all the requirements such as *emptying the chest and filling abdomen, qi sinking into dan tian, sinking shoulder and lowering elbow, relaxing waist and sinking hips*, have their distinctive purposes.

The collective objective is to relax our body parts in such a way that all energy particles can move downwards, resulting in a structure in which the top part is empty and the lower part is solid. This represents the main objective of the technique of *relaxing*: to relax is the means, and to enable the energy to sink is the end. Through proper training, the internal energy may then be collected and directed in an orderly manner, just like collecting water or mercury, both of which exhibit the quality of heaviness. The body, operating like an *Air Bag-Like Elasticity*, contains internal energy (*qi*) occupying the lower part of the body structure. Master Luo Ji Hong likens this phenomenon to a plastic bag half-filled with water. The upper part of the plastic bag is empty with air, while the lower part is heavy with water. This graphic image vividly explains the manner of distribution of *qi* within the body. In fact, the distribution of *qi* within the body takes on a sectional, progressive and sequential manner, with each section of the body exerting pressure on the next section below it, thereby cumulating in a total pressure system at the lowest section of the body.

To explain this process in more detail, we may divide the body into three areas, the chest area, the abdomen area, and the hip area. Each area is holding a water bag. When *qi* in the upper-most chest area exerts pressure on the next lower area, like water in the upper-most water bag exerting pressure on the next lower water bag, the lowest water-bag, which is the hip area, will contain the greatest pressure and form a highly pressurized field of compressed energy.

The end result is that the upper part of the body becomes empty, and the lower part becomes compressed and solid, like Humpty-Dumpty- light on the top and heavy on the bottom. This form of bottom heavy and light on the top is ultimately best suited in the offensive and defensive mode of Taijiquan.

As a result of *qi directing body*, a pressure differential is being created from top to bottom with *qi* being contained at the bottom of the module. As well, energy is being evenly distributed from the inside to the outside. Under the direction of the mind, the *dan tian* becomes the focal point where all energy converges and hence the centre of pressure and compressed energy. Within this system, energy will be distributed from the inside to the outside with the energy closest to the *dan tian* being the most compressed and the energy farthest away being the least compressed. Such orderly distribution of the *substance of energy* is critical in the movement of Taijiquan.

While the overall distribution of the substance of energy takes place in the aforementioned manner, each individual part of the body also distributes substance of energy by adopting the rule of *qi collected inside the bones*.

Under the direction of the *mind*, all muscle groups are and must remain totally relaxed; *qi* however, under the direction of *yi*, is being collected from the muscle groups to the bone marrow and then guided to flow along the bone structure, like electricity flowing along a wire insulated by a plastic covering. The end result of this uneven *qi* distribution process is often described as *steel inside a cotton ball*, or *needle inside cotton*. In this context, Master Gu Liu Xin once said: *If you follow this practice, you would acquire the feeling of internal energy, for qi will flow along the veins and the muscles, and later, inside the bone marrow. When this happens, the bone lines inside your limbs and the spine would feel like a guitar string being picked. This internal feeling of movement of qi is what the 'Treatise of Taiji' describes as 'qi collected inside the bones'. As a result of this training in 'the yi moving qi, and qi moving body', 'where the mind directs, that is where the qi flows', 'the movement of qi is as refined as in the movements of nine pearls', and you will improve the explosive power in offensive action.*

C.   Taiji *Qi Shi* - its Pattern of Movement and Operation

Upon the formation of *Taiji Qi Shi*, the *dan tian* becomes the centre of activity within the body, which now operates like an air-bag with elastic power. To start with, the pelvis cavity is the place where *dan tian* resides which now becomes a highly pressurized area in which *qi* operates. When *dan tian* moves, a pressure differential is created, affecting the substance and quality of *qi*. Such an effect is distributed from the inside to the outside, in a sectional, progressive and orderly manner, and at the end, affecting the entire movement of *Qi Shi*. Such is the operational mode of *qi directing body*.

As a result of *qi* sinking into *dan tian*, all the internal energy will now be collected and focussed in the *dan tian* cavity, which now becomes the *headquarters of the army*, or *the residence of qi*. To disperse the army or *qi*, the *mind* will turn on the *dan tian system* (or, *internal rotation of dan tian*), just like opening an air compressor. The *dan tian* is therefore an area or a field of high pressure, where all the internal energy converges. When the *dan tian* moves, it takes on the mode of flowing in and out, up and down, and from side to side, it operates similar to the movements of valves in an air compressor, thereby creating changes in pressure through these movements. When the *dan tian* expands, it creates a positive pressure on its surroundings (compression), enlarging the shape and form of the inside wall of the cavity containing it. And when the *dan tian* contracts or closes up, it creates a negative pressure (suction) on its surroundings, contracting the shape and form of the inside wall of the cavity containing it. Or, when the *dan tian* moves to the right, it creates a positive pressure on the right side; but at the same time, it creates a negative pressure on the left side of the cavity which accordingly changes its shape and form. In other words, when the *dan tian* moves in any direction, it will create a positive pressure on the side of the direction to where it moves, and correspondingly, it will create a negative pressure on the opposite direction, thereby creating a positive and negative pressure differential within the confine of the pelvis cavity. When the *dan tian* moves back and forth in an over-lapping manner, it will create a rippling effect in the movement of *qi*. When the *dan tian* revolves and turns inside the pelvis cavity, it will set forth a spiral current of internal *qi*, just like the turning movement of the agitator inside a washing machine (spinning on the center axis) sets up a spiral (vortex) current of water inside the drum.

As a result of the aforementioned movement of the *dan tian*, a rippling *jing* and a spiral *jing* will be generated. Such generation of *jing* however will proceed from the inside to the outside, section by section, and increasing its pressure in the process. When our body is adjusted into an *Air Bag-Like Elasticity*, and using the diaphragm as the dividing line of the upper and the lower sections, we now connect our four limbs to the central torso. The resulting structure would become one unified pressure system, with the *dan tian* operating as the central motivating force, spreading the energy from within to reach the far ends of the four limbs. When the *dan tian* expands, thus creating a positive pressure (compression), like opening an air compressor, energy or *qi* will be distributed to the four limbs. This is what is known as *dan tian reaching out to the four limbs*. Conversely, when the *dan tian* contracts, thus creating a negative pressure (suction) grid, energy or *qi* will be collected from the four limbs. This is what is known as *dan tian returning from the four limbs*. Or, when *dan tian* moves to a certain direction, the direction to which the *dan tian* moves will set up a positive pressure; and correspondingly, the direction away from which the *dan tian* moves will set up a negative pressure. Or, when the *dan tian* revolves and turns, it will set up a positive and negative pressure; and when spread to other parts of the body, it will create a spiral current effect.

Through the described manner of *dan tian* operation, the internal energy (*qi*) may now be distributed to other parts of the body. Such distribution of energy, however, may be directed to the outer part of the body, thus expanding the scope of *Qi Shi*, and affecting the air space in its vicinity. The process can be shown as follows:

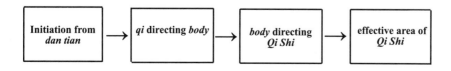

Such chain of action or reaction leads to the *State of Taiji Readiness*. In Taiji practice, it is the last section in the action chain of the scope of *Qi Shi* that affects its effective area. (Effective area is where our target or opponent is within the reach of our *Qi Shi*).

To summarize:

a. When the *mind* sets up a pressure system within the scope of *Qi Shi*, a pressure differential will be created in the area outside the scope of *Qi Shi but within the effective area of Qi Shi*. Such pressure differential can ultimately be utilized to release explosive power (*fa jing*) so as to control your opponent.

b. When *Qi Shi* expands, it will set up a positive pressure. If a target comes near the effective area of *Qi Shi*, it will be affected by the positive pressure created inside the scope of *Qi Shi*.

c. When *Qi Shi* contracts, it will set up a negative pressure. If a target comes near the effective area of *Qi Shi*, it will be affected by the negative pressure created inside the scope of *Qi Shi*.

d. When *Qi Shi* moves from side to side, inside the scope of *Qi Shi*, it will set up a positive pressure in the direction it moves to. When a target enters into this effective area, it will be affected by the positive pressure created inside, just like being run over by a moving locomotive. Correspondingly, a negative pressure system will be set up in the direction that it moves away from. When a target enters into this effective area, it will likewise be affected by the negative pressure created, just like being drawn in to the current of a fast moving train.

e. When *Qi Shi* moves back and forth, it will set up a rippling effect affecting an object at the perimeter of the effective scope of *Shi* with an overlapping *jing*. And when *Qi Shi* turns and revolves, it will set up a spiral current effect, affecting all the objects within the effective scope with a spiral current.

TOPIC 2: <u>The Principle of *Taiji Readiness*</u>

In the first Sections, we spent some time in exploring the concept of *Air Bag-Like Elasticity*, its relationship to *Taiji Qi Shi*, the formulation thereof, and the resultant module of operation. If one follows this procedural training closely with a clear understanding of the conceptual basis, one can eventually create a system of energy comprised of the movements of *body, qi and jing*; in other words, an *Air Bag-Like Elasticity*. And when combined with the operation of *qi* within the confine of this system, one will eventually be able to achieve *Self-Control* in the training of Taijiquan. The next logical level of training is how to apply this system of *Self-Control* in a confrontational situation. For this second level of training, we call it the **Training of** *the* **Taiji Readiness State.**

Taiji Readiness actually is another term for the ideal fighting form. It is characterized as a condition resulting from the creation of the *Air Bag-Like Elasticity* in conjunction with the workings of the *mind* and *qi* in an orderly, controlled and repeated manner. To attain this state of readiness when practicing alone, one must keep focussed on an imaginary opponent. When one is in a *State of Taiji Readiness*, a number of phenomena will become manifest.

(1)   The *mind* will be maintaining a central position at all times. Master Luo Ji Hong once said: *The mind, when focussed, operates like holding a zero point on a mathematical scale……it can easily move to the positive side or the negative side. It can direct the movement of the limbs and the body in any direction; it can strengthen the body parts like solid iron; or it can operate the body parts like feathers; and in the end, your opponent can hardly tell if you are in a solid or empty state.*

(2)   One has become so sensitive that one can sense *the falling of a feather, or landing of a fly or insect.*

(3)   One can react swiftly; as described in a Taiji treatise, *before the opponent comes into contact with my body, my mind has already detected his intention and my internal energy will act immediately, quick as lightning.* In other words, *explosion upon contact, like setting skin on fire, or water gushing out of a fountain.*

(4)   One's internal energy has acquired such a solid strength and power that *when confronted with an opponent, one's internal power will explode, like wind and fire destroying anything in their way.*

The above are just some illustrations of phenomenon occurring in the *State of Taiji Readiness*. Upon closely following this training procedure, one will eventually acquire this *State of Taiji Readiness*, or the ideal Taiji fighting readiness form.

TOPIC 3: <u>The relationship between the Taiji Readiness</u>
<u>State and the Characteristics of the Quality and</u>
<u>Substance (QS) of Taijiquan</u>

The *Quality and Substance* of athletic movements (*QS*) is defined as the state of one's potential energy resulting from the movements of the physical parts of the body under the direction of the mind. Generally speaking, the *Quality and Substance* of athletic movements is based on the primary substance of which the body parts are made of. For instance, the *QS* of physical force depends on the development and training of the muscle groups; the *QS* of the elasticity of the body joints depends on the elastic strength of the ligaments, muscle groups and all related parts; and the *QS* of Taiji movements depends on the state and condition of *Taiji Readiness*. And the *State of Taiji Readiness* is the resultant product of the working of the *mind* (*yi*), *qi* (energy) and the *body* in a cohesive manner. It is analogous to the building of a motor vehicle when all the individual components and parts are assembled together in a well-defined procedure. The *QS* of Taiji movements is the resultant product of such a procedure.

a.   *Quality and Substance* **of Taiji Energy**

The general concept of the *Quality and Substance* of physical force refers to the quality and substance of the physical power contained in the human body or body parts that may be utilized to overcome external force. In the context of Taijiquan, the concept of the *Quality and Substance of Taiji Energy* refers to the quality and substance of the resultant elastic power derived from the formation of the *Air Bag-Like Elasticity* and *Qi Shi* discussed earlier. To distinguish Taiji Energy from other muscular forms of energy, Taiji Energy is traditionally described as *internal energy*, or *peng* energy. The training in the quality and substance of Taiji Energy has therefore become a specialized training in Taijiquan.

In this regard Master Luo said: *Peng energy is a common form of energy. All other forms of energy are derived from it. One cannot operate without peng energy.... therefore all experienced Taiji masters use peng energy, or a modified form thereof, to deal with their opponents. It is like hiding soldiers behind a strong fortress in a battle. You use the fortress as the first line of defence; then you send the soldiers in the attack. It is therefore important that we acquire both the strong and the soft aspects in our training. All Taiji moves contain peng energy. This is why Taijiquan is sometimes known as Peng Quan [掤拳]. Insofar as the practical application is concerned, it is just a matter of combining the strong and the soft aspects of peng energy.*

The module of *Air Bag-Like Elasticity* (*ABLE*) is the basic format for the creation of *Taiji energy*. When the outside wall of the air-bag like structure is being stretched, an elastic power will ensue; when the inside cavity of the air-bag structure is filled with *qi*, pressure will appear; and combined, a strong springy or elastic power will result. This is the fundamental concept of the creation of *Taiji energy*. When *ABLE* is properly adjusted, just like when the tire of a car is properly inflated at proper pressure, all external force will be evenly and uniformly dealt with by the elastic body operating as one single unit.

The operational aspects of this process can be described as follows:

When external pressure is applied to the external surface of a well adjusted *ABLE*, the external surface of the *ABLE* will react like a stretched trampoline; that is to say, the elastic body will change its shape and form to accommodate the external pressure, which will be evenly dissipated away from the point of contact in a projectile manner. At the same time, as a result of the application of the external pressure, the modified form of the elastic body will increase the pressure contained in the field of force within the elastic body and the enhanced pressure will simultaneously be evenly distributed to all other parts inside the elastic body. In result, while external pressure is being dissipated along the outside wall of the elastic body, the inside wall of the elastic body will be simultaneously pressurized, thereby enhancing its internal power. The resultant pressure can then be utilized to act on the external object. At this point, external pressure has been converted to enhance the internal pressure of the elastic body to react on the external object. In other words, *Taiji energy* is not simply intended to overcome external power; but, based on its elastic power, it serves to effectively dissipate and convert external power for one's use to overcome an external object. This explains the traditional sayings that *to run is to stick; to stick is to run,* or *power within dissipation, and dissipation within power*, and the theory of borrowing the opponent's power for one's use in offensive moves.

Apart from the characteristics of elasticity in the *quality and substance* of *Taiji energy*, one also finds that within the confine of *Taiji Qi Shi*, energy is being distributed from the top to the bottom, resulting in the top level being empty and the bottom level solid. Hence, one other characteristic of the *QS* of *Taiji energy* is that energy tends to sink to the bottom of one's base area. The distribution of energy from top to bottom not only enhances the balance of one's stance, but also directs and transfers external pressure from the top to the bottom of one's base area, like water coming down from a waterfall or snow in an avalanche , thereby solidifying the balance of one's base. And when the collected energy is re-directed from one's base to the base of the opponent, one completes the *circuit of energy transfer*, resulting in the up-rooting of the opponent.

One other characteristic of the *QS* of *Taji energy* is that the outside is soft and the inside is solid, like a *cotton ball wrapped around a piece of iron*. With the *dan tian,* operating as the central force, transfers energy from the inside to the outside in a wave-like manner, from section to section, layer to layer, sequentially and continuously, a time differential between each section or layer will be created during this process. By the time the energy reaches the surface layer of the point of contact with the opponent, one's energy would have reached its maximum output and can be used to upset the opponent without him becoming aware of this chain of reaction. This perhaps explains the traditional requirement to *shield one's internal energy from the knowledge of the opponent.* The reverse of the process is also true. That is to say, when the opponent applies pressure on our *dan tian*, the external pressure will be absorbed sequentially, from the outside to the inside, layer after layer; and by the time when the external pressure reaches our *dan tian*, the pressure would have been reduced or dissolved to the minimum, posing no threat to our *dan tian*.

To summarize:

When the *dan tian* expands, energy is being transferred from the inside to the outside, increasing its strength in the process; and when the *dan tian* contracts, external energy is being collected and absorbed from the outside to the inside, decreasing its pressure layer after layer. *Taiji energy* therefore finds its expression not only in terms of the *quality and substance* of its force, but also in terms of its flexibility in defence and fighting techniques. Such is the basis for achieving the ultimate condition *My opponent does not know me; but I know my opponent; hence the Invincible One.*

b.   Quality and Substance of Speed in Taijiquan

The *Quality and Substance of speed* in terms of human actions refers to the ability of a human being to complete a move at the fastest speed. Generally speaking, it refers to the speed in reaction, the speed in completing a certain action, and the speed in moving from one point to another point. The *Quality and Substance* of speed in Taiji movements refers to the speed in action and in reaction.

The speed in reaction of a human being to certain external signals and sensations, such as light, sound and touch, refers to the speed in reacting and responding to such signals and sensations. The speed in movements refers to the speed in completing a certain move.

In terms of the strategic requirements of Taijiquan, the *QS of speed* can be further broken down into three different stages: the commencing stage, the proceeding stage, and the effective final stage. And with this in mind, the formation of *Taiji Readiness* is the best platform to accomplish the requirements of speed and to demonstrate the *QS of speed* in Taijiquan.

i.   Speed of reaction:

The *speed of reaction* in Taijiquan refers to the speed in reacting to the moves or the intention of the opponent in his moves. This speed of reaction includes the ability to receive the signals of the intention of the opponent in his action, to make a judgement of the intention of the opponent from the signals, and to make a decision as to how to react to such signals. In the confrontational process, the sight and touch are the basic means to receive the signals of the opponent. In Taijiquan, the training in reaction from touch and the application of it therefore form an important part of the training program. Such training in touch reaction includes not only close contact, but also remote contact. The process goes as follows:

Before coming into contact, one firstly holds the opponent under close surveillance within the confine of the *Scope of Mind Control*. Upon contact, one then reacts immediately from the body touch. In order to be in a position to do so, one must be in the state of *Taiji Readiness* when the *mind, body* and *qi* operate under optimum condition. At this point, one's body will function like an air-bag filled with elastic power, ready to strike at any time. According to a research study, when energy within a body is under compression, the speed of reaction and the release of power will be 60% faster than that in a body which is placed under relaxed condition.

In confrontation, before contact, we firstly apply our *Qi Shi* to press against the opponent. We will endeavour to place the opponent within the confine of the *Scope of Mind Control* and the *Scope of Qi Shi*, such that the opponent will become part of our *qi* system. Within this combined enclosed system, our *mind* will operate like radar waves to detect and uncover the moves of the opponent. This would enhance our ability to receive the signals of the opponent and to react against them in result.

ii.   Speed of commencement of action

In the complete process of offensive movement, the time required for the commencement of action and the speed of delivery of the action are critical in order to achieve the optimum results. Taijiquan emphasises the importance of internal adjustments as exemplified in sayings such as *internal adjustment without external expression*, or *containment of energy within (internally) and expression of power externally*. Under the condition of *Taiji Readiness*, energy is being contained under immense pressure, capable of discharge at any instance. The formation of *Taiji Qi Shi* results in the top being empty and the bottom being firm, the external soft and the internal strong. As a result, a pressure differential is being created between the top and the bottom, the internal and the external, like a fully charged air gun, capable of discharging power at any time. The end result is that an opponent can hardly detect the commencing stage or the process of the transfer of energy when power is released in an instant moment. The sudden release of power is called *cold power* which can often create a surprise effect.

iii.   Speed of action in progress

In the delivery of *Taiji's power*, one must not only be able to release *cold power*, but also be able to deliver *speed* and *substance* in the process. With the *dan tian* acting as the central power house, based on the requirements of *sectional movement* and *from within (internal) to external*, internal energy or *qi* will be delivered in a wave-like manner from the inside to the outside, like the operation of a sport chain. The *dan tian* then acts like the last section of a sport chain. When the *dan tian* activates, energy will be transferred from the inside to the outside, sectionally and progressively, like the movement of a sectional rocket, until energy is fully discharged at the very last section of the chain, or the extremity of the limbs. The result is a lightning effect on the opponent.

iv.   Speed in the final and effective stage of action

Generally speaking, when power is applied on a subject in the final effective stage of action, the resulting effect on your opponent will often be reduced by the opposing quality, substance or resistance of the opponent. However, as a result of the formation of *Taiji Qi Shi*, an *Air-Bag-Like Elasticity* is created, containing different layers of differentiating elastic power, just like different layers of bags containing different kinds of liquids. When the outside layer comes into contact with an external force, the outside layer will react by changing its elastic shape, thereby increasing the elastic power of the underlying layers, resulting in the enhancement of power and momentum of moving forward. As well, the reaction of the outside layer will prolong the time of its action on the subject, increasing the rate of acceleration and propulsion. The attack or counter attack on the incoming force becomes more effective. This explains the theory of *borrowing the opponent's power in offensive moves*.

c.   **The Quality and Substance of Taiji Energy Preservation or Endurance**

The Quality and Substance of energy preservation refers to one's ability to withstand exhaustion during long hours of work. Such quality and substance of energy preservation depends on the basic built of one's body and the manner of operation of its parts. Taijiquan training in this regard has an obvious advantage in the improvement of one's health. Unlike all other forms of physical exercises, which result in the ultimate exhaustion of one's energy, Taijiquan emphasises on preservation of energy or *qi*. This is more particularly so in the movement of *qi*, which takes on a wave-like process when *qi* is being preserved and not spent, energy being contained and not released. In result, energy exhaustion is being held at the minimum. In *Taiji Readiness*, therefore, *the inside is energized, while the outside is relaxed; the solid is clearly defined from the empty; the strong and the soft are being combined.* The emphasis on relaxing is to avoid the over-exhaustion of energy resulting in the *double-weightedness* condition, or some other undesirable effects. In this sense, the key concept of Taiji movements is to *preserve* and to *contain*, but not to exhaust and to spend, and in the end would greatly enhance the quality and substance of Taiji energy preservation.

d.   The Quality and Substance of Taiji's Elastic Power

The general concept of the quality and substance of elasticity refers to the magnitude of the movement of the joints. Generally speaking, the magnitude of the movement of the joints depends on the ability of the joints, the ligaments and other soft tissues to stretch and to retract. In the training of Taijiquan, the requirements of the elastic quality of the parts are strict. In addition to the basic movements of the joints, in the process of formation of *mind directing body*, all body parts, under the direction of the *mind*, become extended and stretched, resulting in the enhancement of elastic power and the ability to anticipate incoming signals. And more importantly, all movements in Taiji are based on the concept *when one part moves, all part move together,* or *the totality of movements.* Within the confines of *ABLE*, the movements are not restricted to any one single joint. Rather, the movements involve the totality of the workings of the body parts. In the constant changing of the shape and position of the elastic body, no one single point of the body would become a fixed position and be controlled. Instead, all parts of the body move at the same time, thus expanding the scope of movement and enlarging the ability to accommodate external power. At the end, the opponent will experience *the more one advances, the further one goes; the quicker one retreats, the faster one withdraws; the lower one bends, the deeper one dips; and the higher one projects, the further one extends.* Such is another characteristic of the quality and substance of *Taiji's elastic power*.

Master Jennifer Gu in Yang Style Sword Posture (1998)

CHAPTER 6

Techniques of Control

Techniques of control in Taijiquan are based on a number of factors: the condition of one's Taiji Readiness State, the quality and substance of one's physical prowess, the ability to employ specific techniques and strategies to control others. Consequently, training to control others in Taijiquan consists of, firstly, technique of control, secondly, strategies of control, and thirdly, psychological control.

SECTION 1: *The Characteristics of Taiji Techniques of Control*

The technique of control of the opponent is based on one's state of Taiji Readiness, and the ultimate development of one's skills in Taijiquan training.

In order to acquire the skills and techniques to control one's opponent, one needs to be in a well-founded State of Taiji Readiness. Skills and techniques to control others, on the other hand, are the basis for the development of strategies in confrontation. It is only through hard training in skills and techniques that one can employ different strategies in confrontation. Without the basic training in skills and techniques, strategies per se would become meaningless and useless.

Traditionally, skills and techniques to effectively control others are often referred to as *practical applications (zhao fa)* ［着法］[1]. To control is the purpose behind *zhao fa*. To control is to block the opponent's *jing lu*[2]. As in an automobile, to control the energy of the vehicle is to block the flow of energy emanating from the engine, the transmission and other parts of the vehicle. In confrontation, to control is to employ different skills and techniques in order to block and ultimately destroy the energy flow of the opponent.

In traditional Taiji training, there are a multitude of *practical applications* employed in the control of the opponent. However, the basic principles underlying all these moves are the same. Our duty is to simplify the process and to find some common rational grounds. It is like a locksmith employing one single master key to open a number of doors.

In traditional Taijiquan training, there are four basic moves summarizing all the skills and techniques in control of the opponent:

1.   lift and hold up, (*qing jing*)［擎勁］
2.   lead and stretch, (*yin jing*) ［引 勁］
3.   grip and grab, (*na jing*) ［拿勁］
4.   explode and release power (*fa jing*) ［發勁］

---

[1] *practical applications:* See Chapter Two –Section Five
[2] *jing lu:* literally "path of energy". In this context, the principle means to control your opponent's total energy (in all its forms) while hiding the source of your own energy.

To uplift and to lead are part of *chuan jing* [串勁], or a form of penetrating energy that links, connects and locks the joints of the opponent. It forms the first station of the Move in the process of control of the opponent.

To grip and grab is the second station in the process of control. The objective is to block the energy flow of the opponent by applying a spiral or rotational twist at the point of contact, thereby forcing the opponent to yield and surrender.

To explode is the last station in the process, the final expression of release of power, sending the opponent off the ground, just like kicking the football or shooting the basketball into the net.

1. *"Chuan jing" –Theory and Characteristics*

What then is *chuan jing*?

Chuan is an action word, meaning to contact, to pierce through, to connect, and to tighten up all the parts in between. In Taijiquan, to *chuan* is to contact, pierce through, connect and tighten up two or more parts or joints of the opponent's body, such that energy cannot flow through the joints or parts in the normal fashion. To *chuan* is an important skill in the control of the opponent. As Master Luo Ji Hong once said: *To chuan is to block the flow of qi into the dan tian. When qi stays on the upper chamber of the chest, the body would then be separated into two different parts. When this happens, your opponent would become totally submissive. This is the essence of 'qang'. Without 'qang jing', one cannot borrow energy from the opponent.*

In real practice, *chuan jing* takes on two separate formats.

The first format is to employ the power of *uplifting* or *sticking* to compress against the pressure point of the *ming men*, or centre of energy of the opponent, by linking, connecting and locking all the parts and joints of the opponent from the point of contact to the *ming men*. The process of compression is one that is directed to the centre. In practice, using the opponent's collar bone as the reference point, one will apply sufficient energy to stiffen up all the joints and parts from the point of contact to the collar bone. Hence, from the collar bone, one will continue with the application of pressure to the lower *ming men*, thereby stiffening up the entire bone structure and blocking the flow of energy through it. The application of *uplifting* or *sticking* energy in the process of *chuan* is most effective when the opponent has not yet released his energy. However, when the opponent has already released his energy in opposition, then one can apply another technique, *to lead*, in order to stiffen up his joints by stretching all the parts and joints of the opponent to the maximum limit such that the entire structure would become one solid rigid piece.

The second form of *chuan jing* is to *lead*, *stretch* and *extend* the joint structure of the opponent such that the entire structure becomes one solid piece as a result of which *qi* cannot flow through. *To lead* is to apply energy away from the centre of the opponent; *to uplift* or *to stick* is to apply energy towards the centre of the opponent. The objective of both applications is the same. That is to say, to connect and lock the joints and parts in between such that *qi* cannot flow through. The question then becomes what is the most opportune time to apply which technique.

The answer is all depends on the movement and reaction of the opponent. The fact is, there is no clear definition as to when to apply the *uplifting power* or the *leading power*. For in every uplifting moment, one should be ready to employ the leading energy if the opponent suddenly charges towards you; or in the moment of leading, if the opponent suddenly withdraws, you should then apply the *uplifting* towards his centre of energy. The combination of the employment of both *uplifting* and *leading* is a matter of continuous practice and training. Traditionally, we characterize such employments as *first leading then compressing; half leading, half entering; immediate leading, immediate entering; when the left side is heavy, the left side becomes heavy and the right side enters; when the right side is light, the right side becomes light, and the left side enters*. For in every uplifting movement, there contains a leading energy; and for every leading energy, there contains an uplifting energy. *Yin* can never be totally separated from *Yang*; and *Yang* can never be totally separated from *Yin*. *Yin* and *Yang* always co-exist.

2.   *The Theory and Characteristics of "na jing" or the power to grip and grab*

What is *na jing*? Master Luo Ji Hong once explained: '*Na' is the common term for grip and grab or 'Qin na'* [擒拿]. *Single hand grip is called 'Qin'; using two hands to manipulate the joints is called 'na'. Although the techniques are different, the usage is common. To grip, or 'na', is to control the joints and root of the opponent, to compel the opponent to submit. 'Na jing' is based on and part of chuan jing. Having made connection with the joints of the opponent by application of chuan jing, 'na jing' is applied to make a rotational twist on the joint of the opponent to block the passage of energy, thereby controlling the flow of energy of the opponent at the end. If 'na jing' is applied to the opponent's joints, the opponent's joints will be controlled and broken (control of joints); if applied to the whole system of the opponent, the opponent's stability will be uprooted (control of roots).*

The basic quality and substance of *na jing* however is internal energy; and to apply *na jing* effectively, one needs to operate *na jing* in a spiral or silk-reeling manner. Master Hong Jun Sheng once said: *Taiji is 'peng jing'; the moves are spiral.* In other words, movement of Taiji internal energy takes on a spiral or silk-reeling manner, or what is commonly known as *spiral energy*. The application is as follows: first, apply *chuan jing* to connect with and block the joints of the opponent; then apply *na jing* in a rotational, spiral manner to control the joint. In this process, it is important to connect and make contact with the *ming men* of the opponent, and then use the opponent's *ming men* as the focal point for the operation of the *na jing*. One example is as follows: first make connection with the opponent's *ming men*; then following a vertical axis leading to the *ming men*, apply the spiral energy to the *ming men* as the focal point to break the *ming men*. If the spiral energy is applied to the right or left axis of the opponent at the point of *ming men*, the opponent will be carried left and right. In actual practice, the operation of spiral energy is volumetric, working at different axis of the opponent, vertical or horizontal, and focusing at different joints or parts of the body of the opponent at the same time, resulting in complete control of the energy flow of the opponent, thereby upsetting the balance and stability of the opponent.

In the application of spiral energy, one must take reference to the amount of energy output of the opponent, and then apply spiral energy in varying circles containing different radii. If the opponent's force is heavy, then one may apply energy in the form of a circle with a longer radius (*big circle* application) such that the opponent's energy may be stretched to the maximum extent and becomes blocked; or if the opponent's force is small, then one may apply energy in the form of a circle with a shorter radius (*small circle* application) to compress and press against the opponent. In confrontation, it is critical that you sense your opponent's energy and react accordingly by application of the appropriate circles of energy, big-circle, small-circle, or otherwise.

In the process of control of the opponent, *na jing* operates as the mid station after the initial station of *yang* or *yin,* and prepares for the operation of the last station of control, the release of explosive power or *fa jing*. This is why in this process, *chuan jing* and *na jing* become inseparable. *Chuan contains na, and na contains chuan.* This is one characteristic of Taiji energy in the matter of control.

3. *The Theory and Characteristics of "fa jing" or Explosive Power Release*

Fa jing, or explosive power release, is the final stage in the process of control and is based on the operation of *chuan* and *na* energy. Depending on the circumstances, conditions and purposes, *fa jing* is utilized to finally control the opponent and make him yield. Just like playing soccer, *fa jing* is the final kick of the football into the goal. In this sense, *fa jing* is the anticipated and calculated movement on your part to finally achieve the pre-meditated result in confrontation, and hence, the ultimate expression of one's power and control.

In classic martial art theory, *to store one's energy is like opening a bow; and to release one's power is like shooting an arrow.* The quality and substance of *fa jing* is based on a number of factors:

    a.   the degree of one's ability to store and maintain power and energy; and
    b.   the condition of one's *Taiji Readiness State.*

The condition of stored energy is the ultimate expression of the combined workings of the mind (*yi*) and body within our body operating as an Air Bag-Like Elasticity (ABLE), resulting in the movement of *qi* or internal energy within the confine of Taiji *Qi Shi* and the Effective Scope of *Qi Shi*, thereby creating a pressure differential and a powerful elastic energy which may be utilized to do work at any time. To be more exact, *fa jing* is the final expression of the release of the stored energy at its maximum after the opponent's flow of energy has been blocked, stopped or disconnected by the application of one's *chuan jing* or *na jing*.

Fa jing takes on a number of formats, typically, the linear and the rippling formats. In the linear format, *fa jing* follows the forward or backward direction of the application of *chuan jing* or *na jing* on the opponent. For instance, after the opponent's joints are connected by one's application of *chuan jing*, and thereafter *na jing*, one can release the final power along the same linear direction when the opponent recedes backward. Or, if the opponent moves forward after your application of leading energy thereby connecting the *ming men* of the opponent, then you can release the power along the same linear direction when the opponent moves and tumbles forward.

The second format, the rippling format, in the release of power is applied when the opponent reacts aggressively. When this happens, one could lead the opponent's energy along the same linear direction as the opponent's energy is exerting, relent the pressure a little, and then, applying *yin jing*, re-direct one's energy against the opponent in a rippling manner.

Chuan and *na jing* are utilized to connect and block the joints of the opponent. Once the joints are connected, and using the opponent's *ming men* as the focal or pivotal point, one can apply *sticky jing* along the same path as the opponent's energy either in the linear or rippling format to control the opponent.

In short, the application of *jing* on the opponent, whether in the linear or rippling formats, depends on the initiatives of the opponent, and cannot be pre-planned.

In the application of *jing* on the opponent, however, one needs to make sure the application of *jing* takes on a spiral turn. If the application is exercised at one particular joint of the opponent, and when worked along an imaginary axis along which the joint functions in a sudden spiral turn, one can break the joint or the sinew of the opponent. Or, if the application of *jing* is applied on the whole body of the opponent, and when worked along an imaginary axis along which the opponent's body functions in a sudden spiral turn, one can upset the balance of the opponent and throw him off his base.

In a real confrontation, *chuan*, *na*, and *fa jing* are often applied in a split second. The initial control and the final destruction of the opponent require a combination of the application of *chuan*, *na* and *fa jing*, such that in every execution, *chuan jing* contains *na jing*, and finally *fa jing*.

The order of control, as explained previously, is as follows:

a.   to connect or *chuan*,
b.   to twist or *na*, and finally
c.   to release power or *fa jing*.

However, at times, one may reverse the order such that one can apply *fa jing* as the initial order of the control event. If the opponent is fairly powerful and well conditioned, sometimes, the application of *chuan* and *na* may not be successful. Then one can apply *fa jing* at the first instance in order to shatter the defensive mechanism of the opponent, just like shattering the armour of the opponent by use of explosives. When the armour is opened up, one can then apply *chuan* and *na* to connect and control the flow of energy of the opponent via the joints and *ming men*. This initial application of *fa jing* is sometimes called *shaking power*, often applied when the opponent puts on a strong static defensive posture. A secondary purpose of the application of shaking power is to retard and momentarily produce a numbing effect on the mind of the opponent. Master Luo Ji Hong characterizes this reaction as a form of double-*yang* or double confrontation, which is to be avoided in confrontation. The use of this shaking power or *shocking power* is a very useful tool in confrontation; but one needs to have acquired a powerful *qi* base before one can apply this shaking or shocking power effectively.

To conclude, to control one's opponent is to control the flow of energy of the opponent. This is basically the essence of Taijiquan.

SECTION 2: *Characteristics of Strategies of Taiji Control*

Strategy is defined as *a plan of action in confrontation, based on the condition of the competitors, to distribute and motivate one's energy such that the weaknesses of the opponent may be exposed and ultimately overcome, and one's strength may be concealed and hidden.* Training in strategy is a major study in Taijiquan. In confrontation, the competitor has to be in his best form in terms of condition, strategies and psychological readiness. Both competitors will attempt to expose and control the weaknesses of the other; and at the same time, to conceal and hide their own intention.

The main characteristics of Taiji strategies are as follows:

a. to stay calm is to control,
b. to stall is to act, and
c. to borrow is to overcome.

Application of these strategies depends on the condition and initiatives of the opponent and adjusting one's action or reaction accordingly. In practice, Taiji strategies are basically a form of reactionary mechanism; that is to say, one reacts only upon receiving certain signals from the opponent via our senses such as sight, sound and touch. It is an anticipatory action and not a pre-planned action. A simple illustration of the *Reactionary System* is as follows:

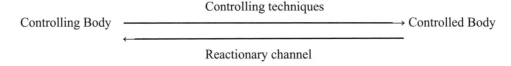

This Reactionary System is made up of three main components: the Controlling Body, the Controlled Body, and the Reactionary Channel. The Controlling Body is one that is well conditioned in terms of Taiji Readiness; the Controlled Body is the opponent; and the Reactionary Channel is the sensory system including sight, sound and senses within the confine of "Effective Scope of Mind Control" whereby the action or inaction of the opponent may be detected.

The operation of the Reactionary System is as follows:

a. When the Controlled Body remains outside our Scope of *Qi Shi*, our mind can send out signals to detect the action or inaction of the Controlled Body, just like radar sending signals to its surroundings. At the same time, our Scope of *Qi Shi* will be very well tuned to be in an optimum state of Taiji Readiness.

b. When the Controlled Body enters into our Effective Scope of *Qi Shi*, we can strike immediately with *cold jing*.

c. If the Controlled Body comes into close contact with our body, we can immediately 'wrap' up the opponent with our Scope of *Qi Shi*, detect his movements, and apply our internal energy to dissolve, borrow, and re-direct the opponent's energy onto his own person.

In practice, confrontation is a contest in technique, strength and mind. Different martial art disciplines have their special techniques and styles; and such techniques and styles change constantly in the heat of confrontation. Taiji strategies therefore are applied to adapt to various situations. For instance, the first strategy to *remain calm is to control* can be used under different scenarios. Master Luo Ji Hong explains as follows: *To remain calm in order to control can be viewed as a manufacturing factory which is you under an optimum state of Taiji Readiness. The opponent becomes a supplier of parts to be manufactured by your factory. When the supplier comes, you will welcome him with your fully charged Scope of Qi Shi. If the opponent moves fast, you act faster; if the opponent moves slowly, you act slowly. If the opponent exerts force on you, you absorb and re-direct the force back on him.*

On the other hand, if the opponent hesitates to come to you, you will move your Scope of *Qi Shi* to him, just like moving your mobile manufacturing factory or mobile rocket centre, to the supplier. You take the initiative to approach your opponent such that your opponent will be compelled to react, thereby breaking his state of calm. At this point, you will act like a cat catching a mouse: be alert to all the movements of the opponent, send out your signals to detect his movements, and assess his intention of action or inaction. Your reaction is not pre-determined, but rather anticipatory, exploratory and investigative. You do not pre-plan what your action will be, where do you apply your energy, or the direction of your movement. You simply wait, see, act or react.

When the opponent finally reacts to your investigative initiatives, he will be reacting in one of the three following ways:

a.   he will exert his force against you in which case you will react in the way described above;

b.   he will attempt to escape from your Effective Scope of *Qi Shi*, in which case, you will pursue and strike; or

c.   he will struggle to remain his state of calm, in which case, he has, in fact, already fallen prey to your investigative attempts and subject himself to your mind control. Master Luo Ji Hong describes this last scenario as *forcing the opponent (supplier) to offer his materials and parts to be manufactured by your factory.*

If, however, the opponent is equally prepared and well conditioned, you may adjust your energy output to the minimum such that the opponent might be led into a false sense of security, believing that you are losing ground in defence. When the opponent proceeds under this misguided conception, you will resume the power output, wrap the opponent within the confine of Scope of *Qi*, and destroy him totally. Or, if the opponent applies and maintains pressure on you at the point of contact, you may suddenly change the point of contact such that the opponent's energy becomes misapplied. Master Luo Ji Hong describes this scenario as *an attempt on your part to lure and induce the opponent to offer up his parts and materials to be manufactured by your factory.*

In short, in the process of control, one needs to be in the optimum state of Taiji Readiness such that all the techniques and strategies may be fully utilized to detect the movements of the opponent, to seek and take advantages of his weaknesses, and to re-apply one's energy on him when opportunity presents itself. The more critical point to note however is that in every movement, to stick is to recede, and to recede is to stick, as in the ideal state of Taiji where *Yin* and *Yang* co-exist and become inseparable.

SECTION 3: *The Characteristics of Taiji Psychological Readiness*

Psychological readiness, undoubtedly, has a decisive impact in confrontational competitions. Hence, training in psychological readiness has become an essential aspect of Taiji training in order to achieve the ideal State of Taiji Readiness.

The objective of training in Taiji psychological readiness is that through it, one's mind will become alert and calm, balanced and focused, capable of adjusting one's actions in terms of the movements of the opponent, and ready to detect, investigate and explore the intention of the opponent to the end that the opponent will be overcome.

The basic training in Taiji psychological readiness is gradual and progressive. *yi* or the mind is the basic training tool in the development of psychological readiness. Through the operation of *yi* on the body, the internal energy or *qi* will be collected in an orderly fashion to do work. Hence, the saying: *when yi applies, qi will be formed; when qi applies, jing will be formed.* All the basic training concepts in Taijiquan, such as heavy and light, fast and slow, are conducted under the direction of the mind. The classical Taiji treatise, *The Thirteen Moves and the Mind* explains as follows: "The outward appearance is relaxed and leisurely; the inward preparation is always focused". Taiji Master Li Yi Yu lists "Calmness of the Mind" as the first requirement in his writing *The Five Basic Essentials of Taiji*; and further emphasizes that *the heart (mind) needs to be calm in order to be focused.*

In actual confrontation, both sides will react very fast; opportunities will come and go in a split second. Those practitioners who are emotional and easily excitable will tend to overreact to the moves of the opponent, hence, acting to their own misfortune. Others who are slow and unresponsive will have their personalities reflected in their reactions to an opponent. Both types of personalities can impede progress to a desirable State of Taiji Readiness.

In order to maintain psychological balance, one's mind needs to be neutral and central, that is, neither overly aggressive (*Yang*), or overly passive (*Yin*). It is only when the mind remains neutral that one's energy can find full expression. Master Luo Ji Hong explains this condition in terms of a weigh scale. That is to say, the mind needs to be set at point zero on the scale first before energy can be expressed positively or negatively.

To conclude, the formation of Taiji Readiness, training in self-control and control of others, utilization of techniques and strategies in confrontation, are all conducted under the direction of the mind. Balance in psychological readiness is the critical factor in this process. Hence, traditional Taiji studies place *yi* or the mind as the most important factor in the overall training of Taijiquan.

The Ji Hong Taiji System

EVOLUTIONARY THEORY   APPLICATION   METHODOLOGY

TRAINING
AND
EXERCISES

Master Luo in Chen Style "Rotate Body and Back Strike" Posture (1998)

CHAPTER 7

The Training of Self-Control in Taijiquan

The training of self-control in Taijiquan includes the formation of Taiji's *Readiness State*, various athletic exercises and the practice of the different styles of Taijiquan's empty handed and weapon forms. It is through this training of *control of self* that a practitioner will improve the quality and substance of his/her athletic movements and develop an understanding of the athletic fundamentals required for Taijiquan. Training to control one's self will form a strong foundation for the next level – the training for self-defence with Taijiquan.

The authors have included illustrations of Taijiquan forms to enhance the reader's learning experience. These photographs are included for illustration purpose only, and are not intended as a teaching guide.

TOPIC 1: <u>Taiji's *Readiness State* and Training of Athletic Movements</u>

The training of Taiji's *Readiness State* begins with *mind directing the body*. The objective of *mind directing the body* is to adjust the body structure according to pre-determined requirements and guidelines, such as the *Five Bows Module*, which require the body to be stretched longitudinally and latitudinally. This stage is like building the frame of Air Bag-Like Elasticity (ABLE).

Body directing qi is the second stage in the formation of the ABLE Module. After the necessary body adjustments are made in the first stage, the mind will now direct the flow and distribution of *qi* in an orderly fashion within the body, such as *qi sinking to the dan tian*, *qi flowing around the body* and *Effective Scope of Qi Shi*, etc. This second stage is like pumping up air to pressurize the ABLE.

The third stage *qi directing the body* is constructed on the foundation of the first two stages. This stage involves the expansion and contraction of internal *qi* in the *dan tian* to create a ripple effect, and to increase the strength of the force field thus generating a powerful *spiral force*.

SECTION 1*:* *Training of "mind directing body"*

The training of *mind directing body* is to adjust the body structure under pre-determined guidelines and requirements, such as the *Five Bows Module* (Illustration.7-1-1) that requires stretching of the body longitudinally and latitudinally. This forms the ideal base structure to build upon. The correct body posture is the most important and fundamental step to enter the doorway of Taijiquan and one cannot claim to know Taijiquan without first comprehending this important step.

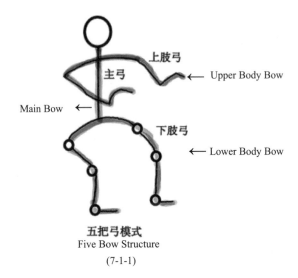

上肢弓 ← Upper Body Bow

主弓

Main Bow ←

下肢弓 ← Lower Body Bow

五把弓模式
Five Bow Structure
(7-1-1)

(a)   **Requirements for the *Main Bow***

The main bow (body trunk) is the central hub that connects all other parts of the body. The key for creating a good body posture is based on how well the main bow can be structured to comply with the required adjustments, and how this influences the movement of the other four bows (four limbs).

Required actions: the two main bow adjustments consist of, stretching along the spine latitudinally and stretching of the body's trunk longitudinally. As can be seen from (Illustration.7-1-2), the human spine has the three natural curves: neck, chest and lower back. First, focus your mind on the *ming men* and pull the *ming men* slowly back. This will reduce the curvature in the lower back and act as the central point from which all internal energy emanates. Allow the force to travel upward to pull up the top of the head (*bai hui*), which in turn reduces the curvature of the chest and the neck (Illustration.7-1-3). Also, allow the force to travel downward and to pull down the tailbone (*chang qiang* [長強]) (Illustration.7-1-4). Pulling back the *ming men* and reducing the curvature of neck, chest and lower back will result in the ideal configuration of a main bow that is filled with elastic power (Illustration.7-1-5).

The degree/intensity of these main bow adjustments depend on the style of Taijiquan. In Wu/Hao style Taijiquan, the requirement to pull the *bai hui* upward and the *chang qiang* downward must be extended beyond the physical body. The tailbone should be curved forward as if to create a platform for the *dan tian*. This creates a force that forms an invisible line that is connected in front of the body. In Chen style Taijiquan, the tailbone needs to be adjusted to point straight down to the ground, even slightly backward, but not to the extent of tilting the hip. In other words, the degree of the latitudinal adjustment of the main bow (spine) should change with different technical characteristics. However, these adjustments must follow one principle, namely to maintain the overall elasticity and power of the main bow.

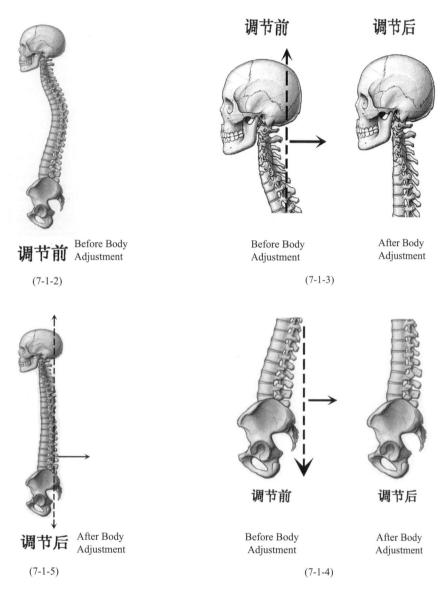

调节前　调节后

Before Body Adjustment　After Body Adjustment

(7-1-3)

调节前　Before Body Adjustment

(7-1-2)

调节后　After Body Adjustment

(7-1-5)

调节前　调节后

Before Body Adjustment　After Body Adjustment

(7-1-4)

The longitudinal adjustment of the main bow is also centered on the pulling back of the *ming men*. The force generated from pulling back the *ming men* not only travels vertically through the main bow as described above, but also horizontally. The spine forms a center line from where the force will travel to the right and left of the body. The horizontal center point between the right and left shoulder is an acupressure point called the *dai zhui*. The *dai zhui* is the key connection between the main bow and the upper-body/arm bows. The adjustment of the *dai zhui* is done by pulling back in same way and at the same time as in pulling back of the *ming men*. The force created from pulling back the *dai zhui* works together with the horizontal force that extends the two shoulders. This combined force will create the posture of *drawing in the chest and lifting the back* (Illustration.7-1-6).

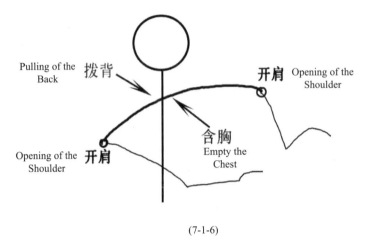

(7-1-6)

Moreover, the force resulting from pulling back the *ming men* travels horizontally to both ends of the hip joints thus creating an *open and rounded hip* (Illustration.7-1-7). The hip joints are also the key links between the main bow and the lower-body (leg) bows. Master Luo Ji Hong used as an analogy the engineering principle for constructing a bridge to explain the structure of latitudinal and longitudinal forces (Illustration.7-1-8). Such a unique structure creates not only an ideal elastic form but it can also absorb pressure from any direction.

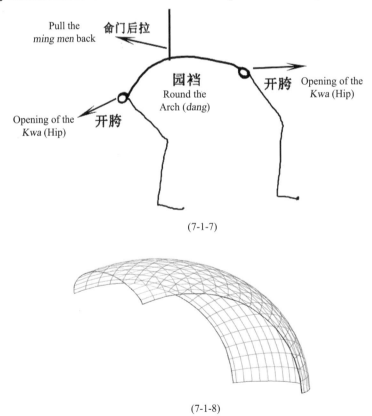

(7-1-7)

(7-1-8)

Exercise 1: <u>First Latitudinal Adjustment for the Main Bow</u>

Assume a shoulder width stance with one hand on the *ming men* (Illustration.7-1-9). Focus your mind to pull back the *ming men*, which will press against the hand at your back. Feel the energy traveling up and down from the *ming men* to create the posture of *lifting the head and hanging the hips*. It is important that this postural adjustment is created by the latitudinal adjustment of the body through the internal force.

(7-1-9)

Control check: Standing normally, have someone push at your *ming men* to create a penetrating force on the lower back; this force pushes your main bow at the contact point forward toward the belly button thus destabilizing the main bow (Illustration.7-1-10). After adjusting the body by pulling back the *ming men*, have someone again push with the same amount of force. Notice that the penetrating force is re-directed up- and downward thus strengthening the whole back and eliminating the natural curve in the lower back (Illustration.7-1-11). This control check can also be used to test the other natural curvatures, such as neck, chest and spine. The key is to check whether the whole spinal column forms <u>one</u> elastic body.

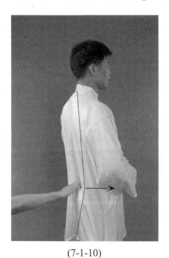

(7-1-10)

(7-1-11)

(7-1-12)

Exercise 2: <u>Second Latitudinal Adjustment for the Main Bow</u>

Assume again a shoulder width stance and let a partner hold a stick with both hands along your spine. The upper hand's knuckles should touch the occipital curve of the skull and the lower hand's knuckles should touch the *ming men* (Illustration.7-1-12). Adjust your main bow first by pulling back the *ming men* to touch your partner's lower hand; then allow the force to travel upward along the spine so that your upper back touches the stick and also reduces the curvature of your chest. Finally, when the force pulls your head up your occipital bone will touch your partner's upper hand. The force travels from the *ming men* also downward and straightens the tailbone thus creating the fourth point of contact with the stick. Although the adjustments to the main bow create a very strong readiness force, its detection is difficult because the movements are internal and very small. The use of a stick is very helpful and the four points of contact can guide you in achieving the proper body posture. For the exercise itself, the stick needs to be maintained vertically pointing to the ground; the amount of pressure on all four contact points should be the same. At first, practice in a static position. Later, up and down, left and right, forward, backward and turning movements can be added.

Control check: The above exercise is the best way to check the latitudinal force of the main bow. If you can maintain the four contact points while the stick is pointed straight down to the ground, you are fulfilling the requirements of *keeping the body straight and center* and *having a strong spine*. The key for a good body structure is a good foundation. An old Chinese proverb states *you cannot expect to achieve greatness if your head is always down and your back is always bent*. If you don't have a strong and straight spine your advancement in Taiji will be severely handicapped. It is essential that both the teacher and the student recognize the importance of this concept.

Exercise 3: <u>Longitudinal Adjustment for the Main Bow</u>

Once you understand the above described exercises for the latitudinal adjustment, the expanding force created by pulling the *ming men* also needs to travel along the spine to both sides of the body. When the longitudinal force expands from the *dai zhui* to both shoulders and continues to the other parts of the upper-body, the correct posture of *drawing in of the chest and lifting of the back* is created.

Technically speaking, the posture of *drawing in of the chest and lifting of the back* should be the end result of the main bow's longitudinal adjustment, but not by adjusting the physical structure. In other words the adjustment should occur from within and not by forcing the shoulders to curve using muscle power. Many practitioners misunderstood this concept which resulted in taking the wrong approach.

The force which is generated from pulling back the *ming men* also needs to travel downward through the spine to both hip joints and to continue to both legs. This longitudinal adjustment will create the posture of *open and rounded hip*.

In addition to directing the mind to achieve the above requirements, other tools, such as a rubber band, rope and cloth, can be used to practice the longitudinal adjustments of the main bow (Illustrations.7-1-13 and 7-1-14). These tools will help you to feel the force created by the longitudinal adjustment.

(7-1-13)

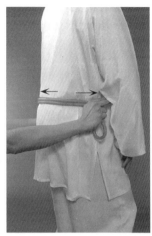

(7-1-14)

Control Check: While performing the longitudinal adjustments on the main bow your partner should push on your body at two locations, especially on the shoulders and hip joints. It is very important to do the latitudinal and longitudinal adjustments to the main bow by concentrating your mind and relaxing your muscles. The back of the main bow should feel like it is filled with *qi* and the front of the main bow, especially the chest and the front of the hip, should be relaxed and drawn in. It is important to create the right conditions for the next stage of exercises *qi sinking into dan tian*. All these adjustments are very subtle and must be maintained at all times. This is the required framework to create the Taiji Readiness State. It is because of the static nature of these adjustments that many practitioners have overlooked this very important step.

(b) Connection between the Main Bow and the Four Limb Bows

The Five Bows Module is not only used to achieve the proper body posture. We can also consider the *ming men* as the handle, the body's trunk as the main body and the four limbs as the tip of a whip. The tip is an extension of the handle and the body. The energy and substance created by the handle (*ming men*) and body (trunk) must be extended to the tip (four limbs) in a continuous and fluid fashion. In this way our arms, legs and body trunk are so well connected that they become one.

Exercise 1: Upper Body Bows and Main Bow Connection

Upon completion of the above described main bow adjustments, focus the mind on extending the horizontal pulling force from the *dai zhui*, through the shoulder joints to the elbows and to the fingertips. This will create a strong connection between the main bow and the upper body bows.

(a) Forward and Backward/Open and Close Exercise

Readiness position: Stand with your feet separated to shoulder width with the toes pointing forward. Focus your mind on pulling back the *ming men* and perform the latitudinal and longitudinal adjustments to the main bow. Bend your knees slightly and relax the arms so that they are lightly touching the thighs (Illustration.7-1-15).

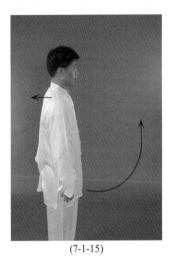
(7-1-15)

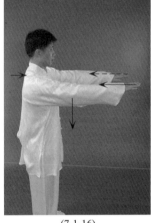
(7-1-16)

First movement: Extend the force, resulting from the main bow adjustment, to both hands. At the same time, raise both arms slowly to shoulder height, with both palms facing the ground and the tips of both hands pulling from the *dai zhui* (Illustration.7-1-16). In this way the *dai zhui* (not the shoulder) and the fingertips will form the two ends of the upper body bow. This will connect the upper body bow with the main bow into a system.

Second movement: Under the condition of the fingertips pulling from the *dai zhui*, turn both arms so that the palms face each other. Bring both hands towards the chest like holding a ball. Concentrate your mind and imagine that the *dai zhui* and the hands are pressing against each other, thus resulting in dropping the elbows and shoulders, thus to achieve the requirements of *sinking the shoulder and dropping the elbow* (Illustration.7-1-17). When both ends of the bow (*dai zhui* and fingertips) press against each other, the arm bows will bend and increase the bow's curvature. By compressing the spring-like force that has been created by this action the pressure of the bow will increase and a state of *open within a closed system* is achieved.

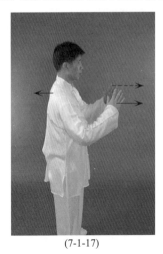
(7-1-17)

(7-1-18)

Third movement: Push both hands slowly forward and rotate them so that both palms are facing away from you. Pull the *dai zhui* in the opposite direction of the arms. Although the *dai zhui* can only be pulled back slightly, it is important to balance the amount of the opposite force (Illustration.7-1-18).

Repeat the second and third movements a few more times. The hands can also push upward diagonally when extending out and then come back or push downward diagonally when extending out and then come back. The key is that the *dai zhui* must be pulled in the opposite direction of the hand's movement in order to create tension. The above exercises can also be performed in a seated position. Repeated practice of the exercises will help to connect the upper body bow with the main bow and eventually become automatic. An even better result can be achieved when performing this exercise by putting a rubber band around the *dai zhui*, hands and elbows (Illustrations.7-1-19, 7-1-20 and 7-1-21).

| (7-1-19) | (7-1-20) | (7-1-21) |

Control check: The use of a rubber band as a training tool can provide a good test for this exercise. It shows clearly how the springy force can be created and maintained when both ends of the bow, A and B, press or pull against each other to bend or straighten the elbow joint (C). Another method is to have someone put the same amount of external pressure on the *dai zhui* and hands (Illustration.7-1-22), to check whether or not force is created in alignment and equal, but in an opposite direction, when the *dai zhui* pulls against the fingertips (Illustration.7-1-23). You can also check whether the force gets stronger and more elastic when the *dai zhui* presses against your partner's hand (Illustration.7-1-24).

Exercise 2: <u>Lower Body Bows and Main Bow Connection</u>

The force created by pulling back the *ming men* needs to flow downward from the main bow to the knees and feet. The *ming men* and the foot become two ends of the lower body bow with the knee being the handle of the bow. The author would like to point out that the *ming men* is the handle of the main bow as well as the end of the lower body bow. This relationship creates a very close and direct connection between the main bow and the lower body bow. The movements between two bows are inter-related, just like the relationship between the main bow and the upper body bow. The main difference is the adjustment between the main bow and lower body bow, which is usually done with both feet on the ground, creates a closed system. The feet are relatively still as the adjustments are usually between the *ming men*, hip and knees. The *opening of the hips and the formation of the arch*, will be created when pulling back the *ming men* and allow the hip to pull against the knees (Illustration.7-1-25). This condition must be maintained when performing any of the movements and exercises.

(7-1-22)

(7-1-23)

(7-1-24)

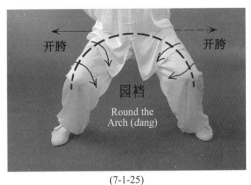

Open the
Kwa (Hip)

开胯

园裆

Round the
Arch (*dang*)

开胯

Open the
Kwa (Hip)

(7-1-25)

(a)   Up and Down Exercise

Readiness position: Stand with your feet slightly wider than shoulder width with your hands placed on the waist. Pull back the *ming men* slowly, with the knees slightly bent. Both legs spiral slightly inward to form the *opening of hips and the arch* position. (Illustration.7-1-26)

First movement: Slowly increase the pulling force between the *ming men* and the knees and continue to spiral the legs inward. Allow the body to assume a sitting position by sinking the hip and bending the knees. Maintain the upper body straight in a vertical position. The *ming men* is now pulling against the handle of the lower body bow (knee joint) at the same time compressing against the other end (feet) of the bow. This will create a very powerful and elastic force in the handle (knee joint) which is called *storing jing in the knee*. (Illustration.7-1-27)

Second movement: With the *ming men* and the knee joints pulling against each other in opposite directions, the *ming men* is also pulling against the feet. Both legs spiral slightly outward (do not lock the knees). (Illustration.7-1-28)

(7-1-26)   (7-1-27)   (7-1-28)

Repeat the first and second movements a few times. It is important to maintain the *opening of hips and the arch* position when performing this exercise and pay special attention to maintaining the balance between the *ming men* and both knees. If the pulling force from the *ming men* is stronger than the pulling force from the knees, the body will lean forward and the hip will be sticking out. (Illustration.7-1-29) If the pulling force from the knees is stronger, the body will lean backward and the hip joints will be locked. (Illustration.7-1-30)

The use of a rubber band is an excellent tool for this exercise. The rubber band helps not only to aid in the proper adjustment of the bows, but its resistance will also strengthen your lower body. Use a heavier gauge rubber band with one end fixed at the *ming men*, then wrapped around the hip down to the front of the knees and finally through the legs to be fixed at the bottom of the feet (Illustration.7-1-31). Follow the above requirements to perform the first and second movement repeatedly. (Illustrations.7-1-32 and 7-1-33)

113

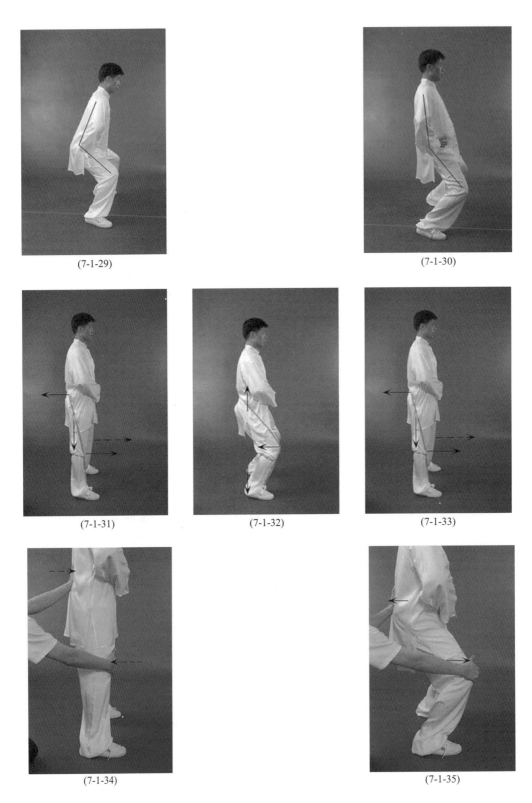

(7-1-29)

(7-1-30)

(7-1-31)

(7-1-32)

(7-1-33)

(7-1-34)

(7-1-35)

Control check: In addition to using the rubber band to determine how well one can maintain this elastic force when doing the up and down exercise, a partner can place one hand on your *ming men*, the other hand on your knee and apply equal pressure with both hands to prevent your *ming men* from pulling back and your knee from bending forward. (Illustration.7-1-34) If you simply try to sit down or bend your knee, the force from your partner will not allow you to do that. If you first allow your *ming men* to pull against your knees, then you can resist the external force from your. (Illustration.7-1-35)

(b)   Left and Right Exercise

Readiness position: The *ming men* and the knees pull against each other to create the *opening of hips and the arch* position in a horse stance. (Illustration.7-1-36)

First movement: Shift your weight to the left side and slowly compress the bottom of the left foot against the *ming men*. The left knee will bend with increased jing being created and stored there. At the same time, the bottom of the right foot will be pulling in the opposite directions from the *ming men* with the knee slightly bent. This will result in the left side being compressed and right side being pulled at the same time. (Illustration.7-1-37)

Second movement: Shift your weight and the *ming men* to the right and slowly compress the bottom of right foot. The right knee will bend with the increased jing being created and stored there. At the same time, the bottom of the left foot will be pulling in the opposite directions from the *ming men*, with the knee slightly bent. This action will result in the right side being compressed and the left side being pulled at the same time. (Illustration.7-1-38)

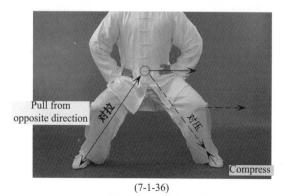

(7-1-36)

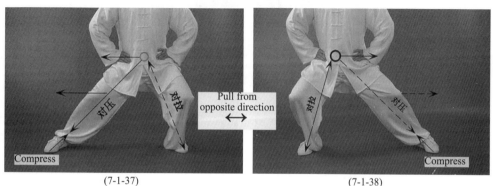

(7-1-37)   (7-1-38)

Repeat the first and second movements a few times. When performing this exercise pay attention to the relationship of the counteracting forces of pulling and compression between the *ming men* and both feet. These pulling and compression forces are constantly present and must be balanced. Use a rubber band to do the exercise (Illustrations.7-1-39, 7-1-40 and 7-1-41)

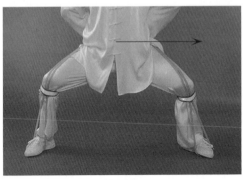

(7-1-39)

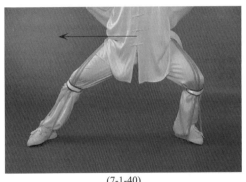

(7-1-40)

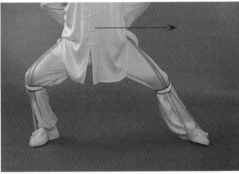

(7-1-41)

Control check: When doing the exercise of moving to the left, get someone to press against your outside left knee and another person to pull your right knee from the inside. (Illustration.7-1-42) When shifting the weight to the right side the opposite applies (Illustration.7-1-43) This kind of exercise is often used for higher intensity training to increase the strength of the lower bow.

(7-1-42)

(7-1-43)

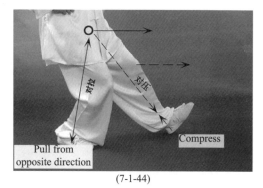

(7-1-44)

(c)   Forward and Backward Exercise

Readiness position: Place your left foot ahead of the right foot. The *ming men* pulls against both knees to create the *opening of the hips and the arch* position. Then sit down into a left empty step. (Illustration.7-1-44)

First movement: Shift your weight to the front foot and slowly compress the bottom of the front foot with the *ming men*. The left knee will bend because of the increased jing being created and stored there. At the same time, the bottom of the rear foot will be pulling the *ming men* in opposite directions to straighten the back leg, with the knee slightly bent. This action will result in a compression of the front foot and pulling of the rear foot at the same time. (Illustration.7-1-45)

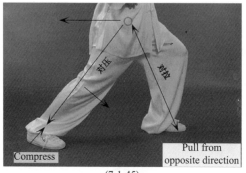

(7-1-45)

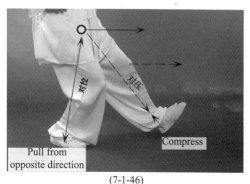

(7-1-46)

Second movement: Move your weight to the rear foot and slowly compress the bottom of the rear foot with the *ming men*. The right knee will bend due to the increase of jing being created and stored there. At the same time, the bottom of the front foot will be pulling against the *ming men* in a straight line, with the knee slightly bent as in the previous readiness position. (Illustration.7-1-46)

Repeat the first and second movements a few times and then change feet. You can also use a rubber band to intensify the exercise. (Illustrations.7-1-47, 7-1-48 and 7-1-49)

117

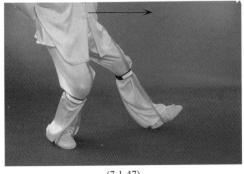

(7-1-47)

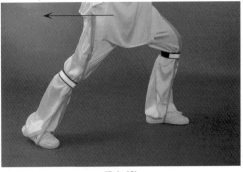

(7-1-48)

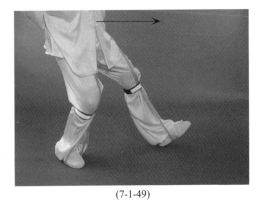

(7-1-49)

Control check: When moving your weight forward a partner can press the front of both knees. By this method you can check whether or not you can maintain the elastic force when bending your front knee and straighten your back knee. (Illustration.7-1-50) When moving your weight backward a partner can press the back of your front knee and press the front of your back knee at the same time. This helps to check whether you can maintain the elastic force when pulling your front knee and bending your back knee. (Illustration.7-1-51)

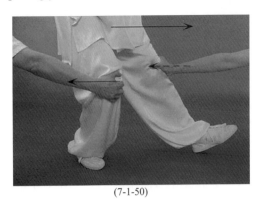

(7-1-50)

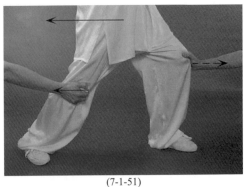

(7-1-51)

(d)   Spiral Turning Exercise

Readiness position: The *ming men* pulls against both knees to create the *opening of hips and the arch* position in a horse stance. (Illustration.7-1-52)

First movement: Under the direction of your main bow, turn your body slowly to the left. The *ming men* compresses in a spiral against the bottom of the right foot. This will bend your right knee to allow the build up of *jing* and to create an inward spiral in your right leg. At the same time, the *ming men* pulls spirally against the bottom of the left foot. Bend your left knee slightly and create an outward spiral in your left leg. (Illustration.7-1-53)

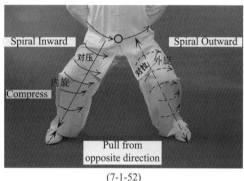   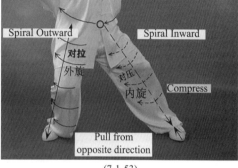

(7-1-52)   (7-1-53)

Second movement: Under the direction of your main bow, turn your body slowly to the right. The *ming men* compresses in a spiral against the bottom of the left foot. Bend your left knee to build up *jing* and to create an inward spiral in your left leg. At the same time, the *ming men* pulls spirally against the bottom of the right foot and creates an outward spiral in your right leg. (Illustration.7-1-54)

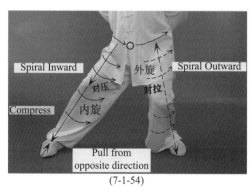

(7-1-54)

Repeat the first and second movements a few times. You can also use a rubber band to do the exercises (Illustrations.7-1-55, 7-1-56 and 7-1-57).

Control check: When performing the first movement get a partner to press your left knee and to pull your right knee to see how strong a force you can create. (Illustration.7-1-58) When doing the second movement get a partner to press your right knee and to pull your left knee. (Illustration.7-1-59)

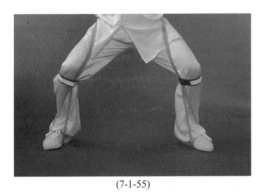

(7-1-55)

(7-1-56)

(7-1-57)

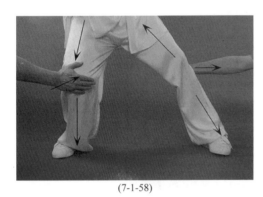

(7-1-58)

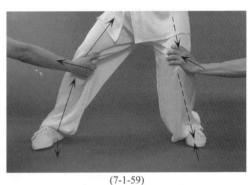

(7-1-59)

(c)   Coordination of the *Five Bows* into One System

This stage of exercises discusses the coordination of the upper, middle and lower parts of the body, and should only be attempted after understanding the exercises focusing on the individual body parts. However, it is through this coordination exercise that one is able to check on the individual body parts and the overall body posture and to understand what requires correction. It is quite common to improve certain parts and may expose weaknesses on others. Through such adjustments, different levels of continuous improvements can be reached.

It is easy to understand the importance of the main bow as expressed by the saying *waist is the number one master*. The main bow plays a major role in the overall coordination of

120

the body, as it connects to the other four bows. Previously, we have explained what adjustments the *ming men*, as the *handle of the main bow*, requires. When performing the exercises we must always pay attention to the waist. The *ming men* can be viewed as a hub that connects all five bows. The stretching force, which is created by pulling back the *ming men*, must extend to the main bow and the four limb bows to form one unified elastic body. This elastic force, which is created by all five bows working in a coordinated fashion, must be maintained throughout the practice of Taijiquan. All movements including open and close, bending and stretching, up and down and spiral turns, must be performed under this condition.

Exercise 1: <u>Forming of Three Spheres in a Stationary Posture</u>

Readiness position: Stand at a slightly wider stance than shoulder width with the toes pointing forward. Slightly pull back the *ming men* to get the main bow ready and in the *opening of hips and the arch* position. Both knees bend slightly and pull against the *ming men*. Perform *drawing in of the chest and lifting of the back* to bring both arms up from the side. Both palms face forward and pull against the *ming men* (although the *dai zhui* is the mid-point between the *ming men* and the hands, for now imagine that the hands are directly connected to the *ming men*). Your eyes should look straight ahead. (Illustration.7-1-60)

(7-1-60)   (7-1-61)

Movement: The *ming men* continues to pull against both knees to create the *opening of hips and the arch* position and sitting in a horse stance. The pulling forces will allow *jing* to be built up in the knees. At the same time, the *ming men* is also pulling against both arms to allow *jing* to be built up in the elbows, as you bring your arms closer to the chest with the fingers open and the palms facing each other like holding a ball in between them. Imagine another ball is being held by both arms and the third ball is being held between the legs from the *opening of hips and the arch* position. This is the *three spheres in a stationary position* exercise. (Illustration.7-1-61) The purpose of this exercise is to connect all five bows into one unified, elastic and well coordinated body, and to learn how to maintain this structure. The height of your stance and the length of time to remain in this position can be adjusted according to your endurance and strength. The key is to follow the requirements and progress at your own rate.

Exercise 2: <u>Empty step in a Stationary Posture</u>

Readiness position: The same as in the above exercise. (Illustration.7-1-62)

Movement: Shift your weight to the right leg and bend the right knee to sit on the right foot. Bring your left foot to the front with the heel lightly touching the ground. The left knee will bend slightly to form an empty step. At the same time, bring both arms closer together with both palms facing each other. The left elbow should be just below the shoulder height and slightly bent with the fingers at eye level. The right hand should be close to the left elbow. This position is the same as in Yang Style Taijiquan's *Playing the Pipa[1]*. (Illustration.7-1-63) Ensure that the *ming men* is pulling against the four limb bows and maintain a straight body. You can switch the front and back foot of this exercise. (Illustration.7-1-64)

| (7-1-62) | (7-1-63) | (7-1-64) |

Control check: Ask your partner to press on different parts of your body to check whether or not you are able to maintain the connection and elasticity of the five bows.

Exercise in a stationary position (*zhan zhuang[2]* [站樁]) is one of the traditional ways of training in Taijiquan. You can use any one of the movements in the form for this type of exercise. You will better understand the coordination required for the movement and feel the flow of the internal energy easier. Gradually you will maintain the stance for a longer period of time and can even achieve an automatic state of *stationary energy*. In addition, *zhan zhuang* exercises are a very effective way to build strength in your waist and legs. It is therefore essential to include Zhan Zhuang exercises in your training.

Exercise 3: <u>Motion Exercises in a Stationary Posture</u>

Motion exercises repeat a set of movements without stepping. This type of exercise requires the practitioner to maintain a good posture and connection while doing simple and repetitive movements. The simplicity of the movements helps the practitioner to concentrate and feel the flow of internal energy easier.

---

[1] *Playing the Pipa*: Sometimes translated as Strumming the Lute
[2] *zhan zhuang*: Standing like a Pole or Tree

122

(a) Up and Down, Open and Close Exercise

Readiness position: Stand slightly wider than shoulder width with the toes pointing forward. Pull back the *ming men* slightly to get the main bow ready and in the *opening of hips and the arch* position. Both knees bend slightly and pull against the *ming men*. Perform d*rawing in of the chest and lifting of the back* to bring both arms up from the sides. Both palms face forward and pull against the *ming men*. Two arms form a big curve like holding a big pole in front of you. (Illustration.7-1-65)

First movement: The *ming men* pulls against both knees and presses against both feet to evolve into a sitting position with *opening of hips and the arch*. The main bow must be maintained in a straight and vertical position. The hands pull against the *ming men* and bring them close to your chest with two middle fingers slightly touching each other to form a closed system, like holding a ball. Both legs are now bent and both arms are close. (Illustration.7-1-66)

Second movement: The *ming men* pulls against both feet causing the body to rise. At the same time, both arms open to the side. Both hands pull against the *ming men* in a straight line to go back to the readiness position. (Illustration.7-1-67)

(7-1-65)   (7-1-66)   (7-1-67)

Use of a Rubber Band for the exercise.

Get a stick that is as long as your body trunk. Tie one rubber band at the position of the *ming men* and one at the position of *dai zhui*. (Illustration.7-1-68) Place the stick on your back along the spine. Channel the rubber band at the *ming men* position around your hips down to and affixed to the front of the knees and then to underneath your feet. The rubber band at the *dai zhui* position is pulled around your shoulders and from there affixed to the elbows and then held by the hands. (Illustration.7-1-69) Repeat the first and second movements described above. (Illustrations.7-1-70 and 7-1-71)

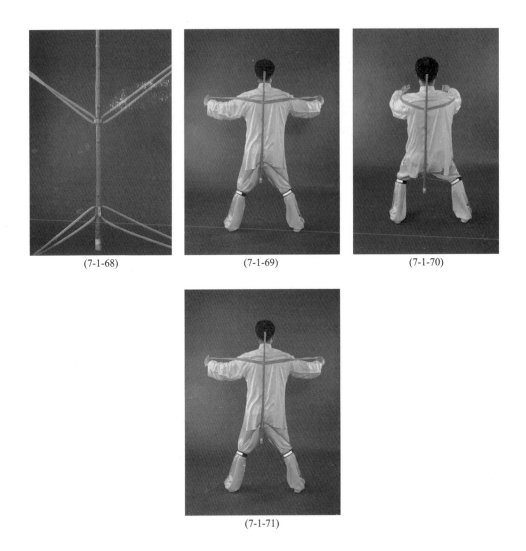

(7-1-68)   (7-1-69)   (7-1-70)

(7-1-71)

(b)   Forward and Backward, Open and Close Exercise

First movement: Turn your right toes 45 degrees outward and shift your weight on the right leg. The *ming men* presses against the bottom of the right foot. In the o*pening of hips and the arch* position, sink your hip and bend your knee. Bring your left foot up and move one step forward. The left heel lightly touches the ground and pulls against the *ming men*. At the same time bring both arms up, palms facing your chest and the two middle fingers slightly touching each other to form a holding the ball position. (Illustration.7-1-72)

Second movement: The *ming men* slowly compresses against the bottom of the front foot causing your weight to move forward. Bend the front knee to build up *jing*. At the same time, the *ming men* pulls against the bottom of the rear foot in a straight line. Bend the back knee slightly to form a bow stance. At the same time, the *dai zhui* and the *ming men* are pulling against each other to open and move both hands forward. (Illustration.7-1-73)

Third movement: Move your weight back via the *ming men* slowly pressing against the bottom of rear foot. Bend the rear knee to build up *jing*. At the same time, the *ming men* pulls against the bottom of front foot in a straight line. Lift the front toes to create an empty step. At the same time, sink and bend both elbows to bring both arms inwards. The two middle fingers touch slightly like holding a ball in front of your chest. (Illustration.7-1-74)

| (7-1-72) | (7-1-73) | (7-1-74) |

You can use a rubber band for the exercises. (Illustrations. 7-1-75, 7-1-76, 7-1-77)

| (7-1-75) | (7-1-76) | (7-1-77) |

(c) Spiral Turn Exercise

Readiness position: Stand at a slightly wider than shoulder width stance with both toes pointing forward. Pull back the *ming men* to connect the five bows. Allow the energy to travel downward through *opening of hips and the arch* and bend both knees into a horse stance. Also allow the energy to travel upward through *drawing in of the chest and lifting of the back* and *sinking the shoulders and lowering the elbows*. Lift both arms from the sides with elbows just above the waist with the right palm facing down and the left palm facing up. (Illustration.7-1-78)

First movement: Turn your main bow left which causes your right leg to spiral inward. The *ming men* presses spirally against the bottom of the right foot. The right knee will also make a spiral turn and bend. The left leg will turn spirally outward. The *ming men* pulls spirally against the bottom of the left foot. The right arm will follow the turning of the main bow to turn outward and forward to shoulder height with the right palm facing up. At the same time, the left arm will spiral inward and backward, so the hand is beside the waist with the left palm facing down. (Illustration. 7-1-79)

Second movement: Turn your main bow right which spirals your left leg inward. The *ming men* pulls spirally against the bottom of the right foot. At the same time, the left arm will follow the turning of the main bow to spiral outward and forward to the shoulder height, with the left palm facing up. The right arm spirals inward and backward, so the hand is at waist height with the right palm facing the down. (Illustration.7-1-80)

| (7-1-78) | (7-1-79) | (7-1-80) |

Repeat the first and second movements. You can use a rubber band to perform this exercise (Illustrations.7-1-81, 7-1-82 and 7-1-83)

| (7-1-81) | (7-1-82) | (7-1-83) |

Control check: Previously, we discussed the adjustments required for each bow as well as the different control methods when performing the various exercises. The key for the exercise of combining all five bows into one is coordination. You can get someone to press on the upper and lower bows at the same time. When moving, it can be checked whether you can maintain the elastic connectivity between the main bow and four limb bows.

SECTION 2:   *The Training of "Body directing Qi"*

As a result of the adjustments of the *mind* and *qi*, as explained in the process of *mind directing body*, the *qi sinking into dan tian* will turn the *dan tian* into a pressurized center. When the body is well adjusted, the *qi* in the *dan tian* will fill up the inner space of the body. By the enclosure of the limbs, an air column is created (the air space under the hip area defined by the enclosed legs and the upper air space defined by the enclosed arms) which will produce a powerful force field, called *Taiji Qi Shi* or *Presence of Qi*. This is the ideal model for the Air Bag-Like Elasticity *(ABLE)*.

The exercises of the *body directing qi* must be built on the foundation of the *mind directing body*. In the training of *mind directing body*, the *ming men* acts as a centre point controlling the five bows as a structure. From the *ming men* curved lines are stretched over the whole body, extending and stretching longitudinally and latitudinally. These curved lines form an ideal elastic container, just like installing pipes inside a structure or creating a radial tire with a steel belt or producing an elastic air bag system. This method creates the basic condition for the internal energy to be stored and ready for action.

The process of *body directing qi* is achieved through various adjustments (like opening and closing) in an area centering on the *ming men* in order to create and change the pressures inside the body. This is similar to the function of an accordion. By pushing and pulling of the accordion's bellows positive and negative pressures are created inside the air bag ready to produce sounds. In Taijiquan, *body directing qi* is the second stage in the formation of the Module *Air Bag-Like Elasticity*. As a result of the adjustments to the body parts during the process of *mind directing body*, the mind will direct the flow and distribution of *qi* in an orderly fashion and create, in conjunction with the movements of the body parts, the ideal *State of Taiji Readiness*. In the process of *body directing qi*, the body is the active part, and *qi* in comparison is relatively passive, which is important if we want to achieve the ideal form of *Taiji Readiness* or what we call *internal jing*.

(a) *Emptying Chest and Solidifying Abdomen* **and Q***i Sinking into Dan Tian* **Exercises**

The adjustments for *emptying chest and solidifying abdomen* and q*i sinking into dan tian* are strongly connected with the adjustments of the main bow. The stretching force created by pulling back the *ming men* extends the main bow latitudinally and connects the upper and lower parts of the body. This creates a clear path between the chest and abdomen. When the main bow makes longitudinal adjustments by *drawing in of the chest and lifting of the back*, the muscle groups around the shoulders, chest and back will be totally relaxed, directing the flow of qi from the chest cavity into the pelvic cavity. This is the phenomenon of *emptying chest and solidifying abdomen* and *qi sinking into the dan tian*. Master Hao Shao Ru explained the process of *qi sinking into the dan tian* as being similar to a melting of an icicle. The muscles relax and internal *qi* is melted ice that drips down to the *dan tian*. When performing *lifting the head and hanging the hips* the spine is like a wooden stick that always stands straight. Your spirit must be lifted up and your *qi* sinking down.

Exercise 1: <u>Sectional Relaxation</u>

Readiness position: You can be in different standing positions (Illustrations.7-1-84 and 7-1-85) or sitting positions. (Illustrations.7-1-86 and 7-1-87) Place one hand on top of the other, lightly tugged under the stomach. Pull back the *ming men* slightly and adjust the main bow latitudinally and longitudinally. Relax and close your eyes with the tongue lightly touching the roof of the mouth. Relax the all your muscles to get into a meditation state. Focus your mind to imagine your body is a big water-filled bag with three compartments: head and neck, chest cavity and abdominal cavity. (Illustration.7-1-88)

| (7-1-84) | (7-1-85) | (7-1-86) |
| (7-1-87) | (7-1-88) | (7-1-89) |

First movement: Focus your mind on the *bai hui* acupuncture point, exhale with a slow and deep breath. Relax the head and neck compartment to allow the *water level* drop to just underneath the neck. This will empty out the head and neck compartment completely. (Illustration.7-1-89)

128

Second movement: Focus your mind again on the second exhalation (you only need to concentrate on exhaling) to relax the area from beneath the neck to the chest cavity (include shoulders, chest and back). The *water level* will now drop below the second compartment. At this time, your head, neck and chest cavity should be totally relaxed and emptied. (Illustration.7-1-90)

Third movement: Focus your mind again on the third exhalation to relax the abdominal cavity. The *water level* is now dropped to the lower stomach (hip cavity), or in other words the *dan tian*. You have now created the conditions of *solidifying abdomen* and *qi sinking into dan tian*. (Illustration.7-1-91)

(7-1-90)   (7-1-91)

This exercise should be practiced regularly to clarify the feeling of sinking and relaxing and to make the process more natural. After doing the exercise for a long period of time, you will be able to sink your *qi* to wherever you want it.

Exercise 2: Adjustments of the *Main Bow* and *Emptying Chest and Solidifying Abdomen*

The Sectional Relaxation Exercise uses the technique of separation and compartmentalization in order to experience how the state of relaxation and sinking should feel. In the next step through *mind directing body*, the main bow is adjusted to create the basic energy force and combined with the adjustments of the mind and *qi* the requirements of *emptying chest and solidifying abdomen* and *qi sinking into dan tian* will be completed.

Readiness position: Same as Exercise 1.

Requirements of movements: Pull back the *ming men* slowly and adjust the stretching force longitudinally and latitudinally along the main bow. At the same time, focus your mind, starting at the top of the head's *bai hui* to complete all three-sectional relaxation adjustments, from top to bottom and coordinated with the breathing. The adjustment of the main bow should be in synchronization with the adjustments of *emptying chest and solidifying abdomen*. In other words, adjustments of the main bow centering on the *ming men*, direct the adjustments of *qi sinking into the dan tian*, thus fully demonstrating the key aspects of *body directing qi*.

The adjustments of the main bow and *qi sinking into the dan tian* in Taiji are considered *internal movements* and cannot be noticed from the outside. However, they constitute the key link to the internal power and practitioners must treat them with the importance that they deserve.

Control check 1: Place one hand in front of the chest and the other just below the stomach (Illustration.7-1-92) When performing the adjustment for *emptying chest and solidifying abdomen*, you can feel the internal adjustment inside the body. The whole upper body, chest, shoulders, back, etc, except for the spine, should feel like melting and dripping. The hand in front of the chest can feel the adjustments of *drawing in of the chest* and *emptying the chest*. At the same time the hand touching the stomach will feel how the abdomen gets fuller.

Control check 2: Through the adjustments of *emptying chest and solidifying abdomen* and *qi sinking into the dan tian*, an energy force is gathering in and filling up the *dan tian*. An external force can be applied to check how well the *dan tian* can maintain this energy force (Illustration.7-1-93). The requirement is to allow the *dan tian* to face any amount of pressure while breathing normally with the whole body relaxed.

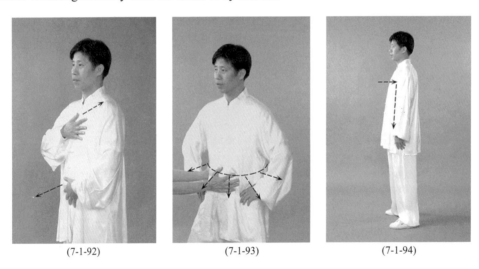

(7-1-92)   (7-1-93)   (7-1-94)

Exercise 3: <u>Adjustments of *Five Bows Combine into One* and *Dantian to the Four Limbs*</u>

After performing the adjustments for *emptying chest and solidifying abdomen* and *qi sinking into the dan tian* and achieving a highly tuned main bow, we need to use the internal energy force gathered in the *dan tian* to connect the main bow with the four limb bows. This process will enable your body, mind and *qi* to work together and reach the state of *internal and external combined into one*.

Readiness position: Stand at shoulder width. (Illustration.7-1-94)

First movement: Adjust the main bow for the *emptying chest and solidifying abdomen* and *qi sinking into the dan tian* requirements as explained above. (Illustration.7-1-95)

Second movement: Expand the stretching force from the center of the main bow, i.e., *ming men*, to the rest of the main bow and the four limb bows. At the same time, focus your mind to let the internal *qi* gather in the *dan tian*, then to flow to the four limbs and raise your arms to

130

shoulder height. Also, slightly bend hips and knees to spiral the *jing*. (Illustration.7-1-96) The spring-like elastic force which is created through the adjustments between the *ming men* and the *five bows*, as well as the pressurized system originating from the *dan tian* will turn the body into a *qi*-filled Air Bag-Like Elastic unit.

Third movement: Slowly drop your arms and focus your mind on leading the internal *qi* from the four limbs back to the *dan tian*. (Illustration.7-1-97)

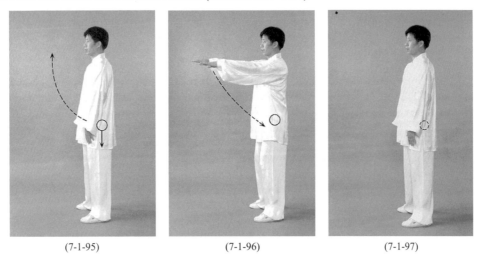

| (7-1-95) | (7-1-96) | (7-1-97) |

Repeat movements one, two and three. The key point of this exercise is to understand the adjustments required for *five bows into one* and the relationships between the *dan tian* and the four limbs.

Control check: Person 'A' (right) stands in a shoulder width posture, relaxing the whole body. Person 'B' places one hand on 'A's hip and another on 'A's arm. (Illustration.7-1-98) First, Person 'A' will perform the main bow adjustments and *qi sinking into the dan tian*. Person 'B' should feel how 'A's body stretches with increasing pressure, however, 'A's four limbs will still remain the same. (Illustration.7-1-99) Second, Person 'A' expands the adjustment between the main bow and the *dan tian* slowly to the four limbs and raises both arms to shoulder height. Person 'B' should now feel how 'A's whole body becomes fuller and more energized. (Illustration.7-1-100)

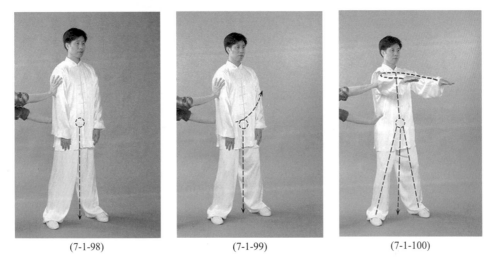

| (7-1-98) | (7-1-99) | (7-1-100) |

Exercise 4: *Hip and Arch Jing*

Body directing qi not only enables the body to form an *Air Bag-Like Elasticity* through predefined body adjustments, it also creates force fields outside of the body. This is known as *Taiji Qi Shi*, or *Presence of Qi*. Hip and arch jing is formed by the force field between the two legs below the hip. To achieve this, the *ming men* needs to be pulled back and the hip cavity to be opened up, in such a way that a well-rounded concave structure will be formed. A force field will be created, when the inside wall of the arch exerts the pressure towards the center of the arch.

(a)   First Exercise

Readiness position: Assume a slightly wider than shoulder-width stance. Put two hands on the side of the waist. Complete the necessary adjustments for *five bows into one* and *dan tian to the four limbs.* (Illustration.7-1-101)

First movement: First, imagine a large airbag on the ground between your legs. Slowly lower your body and imagine the inside wall of the arch, formed by your legs and waist, with many points which are all pushing inward. This posture will create a combined force field inside your legs and the reactionary force on the imaginary air bag will make the force field even stronger. (Illustration.7-1-102)

Second movement: Return to the readiness position. (Illustration.7-1-103)

Repeat the first and second movements.

(7-1-101)   (7-1-102)   (7-1-103)

(b)   Second Exercise

Place a large gymnastic ball between the two legs. Perform the necessary adjustments for *five bows into one* and *dan tian to the four limbs.* (Illustration.7-1-104)

First movement: Slowly lower your body to sit on the ball. At the same time, all points on the inner walls of both legs push inward to squeeze the ball to increase the pressure inside the ball. This action will create a strong *hip and arch jing.* (Illustration.7-1-105)

132

Second movement: Return to the readiness position. (Illustration.7-1-106)

Repeat the first and second movements. This exercise helps to apply an abstract concept to a concrete application; by applying pressure on the gymnastic ball, the reactionary force returning from the ball can be felt and thus can help to get the proper feeling of the *hip and arch jing*. Once you experience this feeling, do the exercise without the gymnastic ball.

(7-1-104)   (7-1-105)   (7-1-106)

Control check: Person 'A' assumes a horse stance position forming an arch with both legs. Person 'B' puts one hand on Person 'A's hip and the other on the upper leg (top part of the arch). (Illustration.7-1-107) 'B' slowly applies pressure on 'A's arch. If 'A' is able to relax, sink the hips and perform the corresponding adjustments, the external force together with the internal adjustment force will be directed through the inside of the arch towards its center. This will create a force field between the ground and the inside of the arch. 'B's external force will be slowly absorbed and turned into a force that strengthens 'A's *hip and arch jing*. (Illustration.7-1-108)

(7-1-107)   (7-1-108)   (7-1-109)

If 'B' applies pressure to 'A's arch and 'A' tightens up the leg muscles to form an arch (like a 'concrete' structure), the external force will be transferred through the legs to the bottom of the feet and connect with the ground. In this instance only hip and leg *jing* is created and not hip and arch *jing* (Illustration.7-1-109)

Exercise 5: <u>Embrace *the Qi Column*</u>

(a) First Exercise

Readinessposition:Assumeastanceslightlywiderthanshoulderwidth.(Illustration.7-1-110)

First movement: Fill the whole body with *qi*. Open up both arms to the side and raise them to shoulder height. (Illustration.7-1-111)

Second movement: Slowly sink down while bring the arms forward as if encircling a *qi column*. All adjustments must be centered on the core of the *qi column*. Similar to squeezing an accordion, the body and arms are squeezing toward the core of the *qi column* to create a positive pressure. (Illustration.7-1-112)

| (7-1-110) | (7-1-111) | (7-1-112) |

Second movement: Open the body and arms to pull away from the core of the *qi column*, similar to pulling the accordion, to create a negative pressure. (Illustration.7-1-113)

(b) Second Exercise

Readiness position: Hold a gymnastic ball in your arms and against your body. (Illustration.7-1-114)

First movement: Relax the body and arms to squeeze the ball from all angles. This will increase the pressure inside the ball. (Illustration.7-1-115)

Second movement: Slowly allow body and arms to reverse this action to change back the pressure inside the ball to its initial state. (Illustration.7-1-116)

(7-1-113)

(7-1-114)

(7-1-115)

(7-1-116)

Repeat the first and second movements. Although the movements are small and limited, this exercise helps to experience how the pressure inside the *qi column* changes when performing centrifugal and centripetal movements.

Control check: 'A' creates the position of hugging the *qi column*. 'B' places one hand on the inside wall and one hand on the outside wall of the *qi column*. (Illustration.7-1-117)

First movement: 'A' uses body and arms to squeeze the *qi column* to make it smaller and more compact. 'B' should feel the inside wall of the *qi column* compress inward while the outside wall is still relaxed. (Illustration.7-1-118)

Second movement: 'A' allows the body and arms to slowly open up from the core of the *qi column*. 'B' should feel the outside wall of the *qi column* expanding while the inside wall is relaxed. (Illustration.7-1-119)

(7-1-117)   (7-1-118)   (7-1-119)

(b) Taiji *Qi Shi* or *Presence of Qi*

The adjustments of *body directing qi* follow three stages. First, through the adjustment of the main bow, *qi sinking into the dan tian* is created. Second, follow the adjustments required for *five bows into one* to connect *dan tian and the four limbs.* Finally the *hip and arch jing* and the *qi column* are formed. With the help of these three stages, an ideal pressurized system or Air Bag-Like Elasticity (ABLE) is created, which is the formulation of the *Scope of Qi Shi*. This is a key component of creating the *State of Taiji Readiness*. Taiji *Qi Shi* serves also as the yardstick to judge how well a practitioner has learned Taiji's empty hand forms, weapons, and self-defence. This is why it is so important to maintain an effective scope of *Qi Shi* at all times.

Exercise 1

Readiness position: Assume a slightly wider than shoulder-width stance, relax the whole body with both arms dropped naturally. (Illustration.7-1-120)

First movement: Slowly pull back the *ming men* to direct the adjustments of *five bows into one*. At the same time, apply *qi sinking into the dan tian* to connect the *dan tian* with the four limbs. Lift both arms up from the side with the palms facing inward, like embracing a big *qi column*. (Illustration.7-1-121)

Second movement: Lower your body to a sitting position with the knees bent. Adjust the waist and legs to create a centripetal force to create a positive pressurized zone within the arch between the two legs. At the same time, the body and arms squeeze toward the center of the *qi column*, which creates a compressed and positive pressure. (Illustration.7-1-122)

Third movement: Raise the body back up slowly and expand the waist and legs to create a centrifugal force to develop a negative pressure. At the same time, expand the body and the arms to create a negative pressure in the center of the *qi column*. (Illustration.7-1-123)

Repeat the second and third movements.

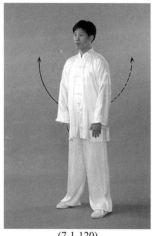

(7-1-120)

(7-1-121)

(7-1-122)

(7-1-123)

Exercise 2

Readiness position: place one gymnastic ball between the legs and one between both arms. Use *qi sinking into the dan tian* adjustments to create a high pressure zone in the *dan tian* thus constructing a structure of three balls into one with the *dan tian* being the (invisible) center ball. (Illustration.7-1-124)

First movement: Change to a sitting position with the knees bent. The waist and legs compress towards the *dan tian* creating a centripetal force for the ball between the legs and the ball between both arms, which results in an increase of the pressure in all three balls. (Illustration.7-1-125)

Second movement: Slowly raise the body by opening the hip joints and expanding the *dan tian*. The legs, body and arms are all moving away from the center, which allow all three balls to return to the same pressure as before. (Illustration.7-1-126)

Repeat the first and second movements.

| (7-1-124) | (7-1-125) | (7-1-126) |

Control check: 'A' connects all three balls into one with the *dan tian* being the center. 'B' puts one hand on the inside of 'A's thigh and the other hand on the inside of 'A's arm. (Illustration.7-1-127)

'A' creates a centripetal force with three balls. 'B' should be able to feel this force with both hands. (Illustration.7-1-128)

'B' puts one hand on the outside of 'A's thigh and the other hand on the outside of 'A's arm. 'A' creates a centrifugal force with the three balls. 'B' should feel this force with both hands. (Illustration.7-1-129)

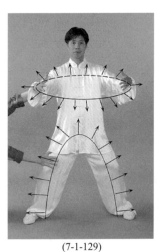

| (7-1-127) | (7-1-128) | (7-1-129) |

SECTION 3: *The Training of "Qi directing the Body"*

Qi directing body requires the formulation of the *Scope of Taiji Qi Shi* in the form of an Air Bag-Like Elasticity. First, focus your mind to gather and spread the internal *qi* to create the

138

state of *emptying the chest and solidifying the abdomen* and *soft outside but hard inside*. Then start the *dan tian* engine to expand the *internal qi* slowly to create a ripple effect throughout the whole *Qi Shi*. Movements of the *mind* lead to movements of *qi*, and finally result in movements of the *body. Wherever the mind goes, qi will follow.* It is *jing* initiated from the *dan tian* that moves in a wave from inside to the outside thus forming a unique model of Taijiquan's *moving force.*

(a) Distribution of Mass in Taiji *Qi Shi* and Training Enhancement Exercises

The requirements of *emptying the chest and solidifying the abdomen* and *soft outside but hard inside* clearly illustrate how mass needs to be distributed in the Taiji *Qi Shi*. These requirements will create pressure and force differences between internal and external and as well as between the upper and lower parts of the body. These are the fundamental basics of creating and storing *jing* as well as an important part of the *State of Taiji Readiness*.

Exercise 1: Emptying the Chest and Solidifying the Abdomen

(a) First Exercise

Readiness Position: Stand at a stance slightly wider than shoulder width, with the knees bent in a half sitting position and the arms open like embracing a *qi column*. Let the internal *qi* flow to every part of the body to energize the whole body. Imagine that the column of *Qi Shi* has three levels. The first level will be above the chest, the middle level is between the chest and pelvis and the third level is below the pelvis. (Illustration.7-1-130)

First movement: Relax and, from a meditative state, focus your mind to direct the *qi* in the first level to flow down to the second level. (Illustration.7-1-131)

Second movement: Continuing with the above, allow the *qi* to gather in the second level and to flow down to the third level, thus creating the state of *emptying the chest and solidifying the abdomen*. (Illustration. 7-1-132)

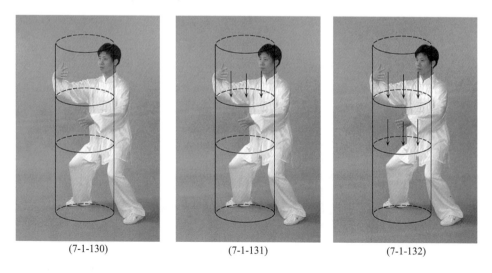

(7-1-130)   (7-1-131)   (7-1-132)

This exercise can be done from any stationary position.

(b) Second Exercise

Readiness position: Stand with your feet at shoulder width apart and complete the requirements of *five bows into one* and *dan tian connects with four limbs.* (Illustration.7-1-133)

First movement: Use your mind to direct the *qi* to sink from top to bottom. Raise both arms to shoulder height. Use the *dan tian* to move into a sitting position with the knees bent, increasing the pressure of the *hip and arch jing*. The raising of the arms, sitting down and sinking of *qi* should all be done at the same time. (Illustration.7-1-134)

Second movement: Slowly change back to the readiness position. (Illustration.7-1-135)

(7-1-133)   (7-1-134)   (7-1-135)

Perform the first and second movements repeatedly. Try to understand the *master and servant* relationship between the sinking of *qi* and the raising of the arms.

(c) Third Exercise

Readiness position: Stand with legs parallel and hands placed on the waist. (Illustration.7-1-136)

First movement: Use your mind to direct the *qi* to sink down and use this sinking force to push your right foot to step forward. (Illustration.7-1-137)

Second movement: Maintain the state of *emptying of the chest and solidifying the abdomen* to shift your weight to the right foot. (Illustration.7-1-138)

Third movement: Use your mind again to direct the *qi* to sink and push your left foot to step forward. (Illustration.7-1-139)

Repeat the first, second and third movements to form a walking exercise. One martial arts book mentioned that *punching is easy but stepping is difficult.* Extensive training is required to cultivate the ability to maintain the *Taiji Readiness State* at all times. When moving around or changing steps keep the *qi* and *jing* in the *dan tian.*

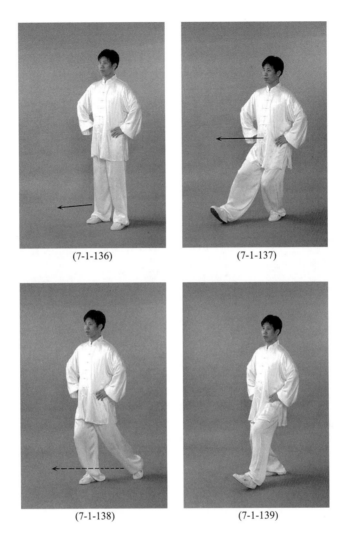

(7-1-136) (7-1-137)

(7-1-138) (7-1-139)

(d)   Fourth Exercise

Readiness position: Stand with legs parallel, the body slightly dropped and the two arms slightly bent. Place both hands on each side of the hip with the palms facing down. The whole *Qi Shi* should be full, relaxed and in a readiness state. (Illustration.7-1-140)

First movement: Use your mind to lower the *qi* inside the *Qi Shi* and use this sinking force to push your right foot one small step forward and to the right. At the same time push both arms up with right hand at the mouth level and left hand at the chest level. All movements must be done with the whole *Qi Shi* completely filled with *qi* (Illustration.7-1-141)

Second movement: Maintain the sinking of the *qi* and move your weight to the right foot at the same time lowering both arms down to the side of the hips. (Illustration.7-1-142)

Third movement: Continuing with sinking the *qi* to push your left foot forward one small step toward the left side. At the same time push both arms up, the left hand to mouth level and right hand to chest level. (Illustration.7-1-143)

Perform left and right movements repeatedly. This exercise is helpful to learn how to use the sinking force to move your arms and legs.

Control Check: 'A' on the right stands at shoulder width, both arms at the sides. 'B' puts one hand on 'A's hip and one hand on 'A's arm. (Illustration.7-1-144)

'B' increases the pressure on both hands. 'A' sinks down his *qi* to raise his arms. When 'B' feels that 'A' can first, relax, sink his hip down and, then raise his arms, 'A' has made the adjustments correctly. (Illustration.7-1-145)

(7-1-140)   (7-1-141)   (7-1-142)

(7-1-143)   (7-1-144)   (7-1-145)

Exercise 2: Training *Soft on the Outside and Hard on the Inside* in Taiji *Qi Shi*

Readiness position: Relax and from a meditative state form the *three-sphere* stationary position. Ensure the *Qi Shi* is always in a condition of fullness. (Illustration.7-1-146)

First movement: Focus your mind to relax all muscles in the whole body, so they feel heavy, similar to a piece of wet cotton. At the same time, direct the *qi* to gather inside the bone along the *bone line*[3]. The *bone line* is like a string in a musical instrument that is strong and flexible. (Illustration.7-1-147)

Second movement: Continuing with the adjustments started in the first movement, the mind and *qi* through the *bone line* increase the centripetal force in the *Qi Shi*. This will create a strong focussed force field in the core of the *Qi Shi*. (Illustration.7-1-148)

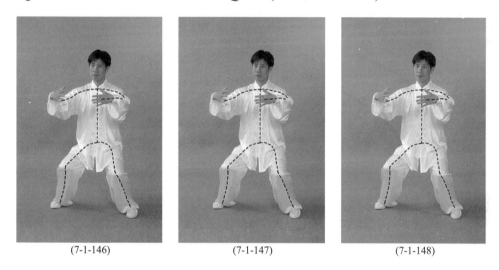

(7-1-146)	(7-1-147)	(7-1-148)

First Control Check: Readiness position: 'B' pushes 'A' from behind. (Illustration.7-1-149)

First movement: 'A' focuses his mind to relax all the muscles in the body and gather his *qi* along the spine's bone line. It should feel to 'B' like pushing a sack of wet cotton with nothing solid to grasp. (Illustration.7-1-150)

Second movement: In continuation of the adjustments from the first movement, 'A' uses the *dan tian* to move the *qi* along the spine's bone line, like a fully extended string with strong tension, to redirect and repel 'B's pressure. 'B' will feel the effect of *Steel Inside of Cotton.* (Illustration.7-1-151)

Second Control Check: Readiness position: 'B' grabs tightly the arms of 'A'. 'A' tightens his arm muscles to resist. (Illustration. 7-1-152)

First movement: 'A' focuses his mind to relax the muscles in the whole body and allows *qi* to immerse in the bone line of the whole body. The muscles become like the rubber coating of

---

[3] Bone line: classical Taiji theory holds that *qi* is held and travels through the marrow and along the tendons of the bones.

a wire and the bone line is the metal core. The mass and substance between inside and outside will be significantly different. 'B' can only grab the soft rubber or wet cotton but cannot touch the metal-like bone line. This is what some people referred to as *separation of bone from muscle*. (Illustration.7-1-153)

Second movement: 'A' uses his *dan tian* as the engine to create the *internal movement* with all the bone lines in the body. 'B' can only grab onto the "rubber coating" because the bones have been separated from the muscles. 'B' cannot get to or influence the movement of the bone line. However, the small force created by the very strong bone line can cut through the contact point of 'B' and break his structure and balance. Many people have reported a sensation akin to being cut by a knife or poked by a needle when they fight with a master of Taijiquan. (Illustration.7-1-154)

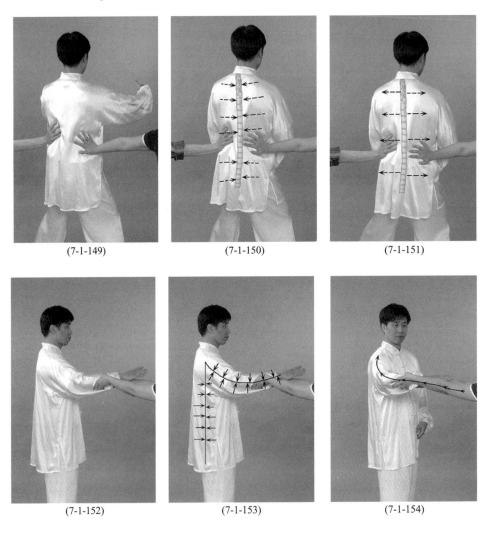

(7-1-149)   (7-1-150)   (7-1-151)

(7-1-152)   (7-1-153)   (7-1-154)

Third Control Check: Readiness position: 'A' stands in the *three-sphere* stationary position. 'B' puts one hand on 'A's thigh and the other hand on 'A's arm. (Illustration.7-1-155)

First movement: 'B' increases the pressure on the contact points. 'A' performs the adjustments of *immersing qi inside the bone* and at the same time creates a centripetal force toward the *Core of Qi Shi*, which creates a strong and highly pressurized zone. The whole body is *immersing inward* and in the state of *soft outside and strong inside*. (Illustration.7-1-156)

Second movement: In continuation with above adjustments, 'A' uses his *dan tian* to move the strong and highly pressurized *Qi Shi* towards 'B'. 'B' should feel strong pressure coming from the *Qi Shi* and the contact point will feel like being cut by a knife. (Illustration.7-1-157)

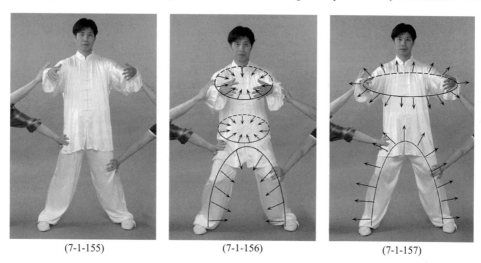

(7-1-155)   (7-1-156)   (7-1-157)

SECTION 4: *Training of Movements in the "Core of Taiji Qi Shi"*

Focus the mind on the *dan tian* to cause the *qi* to concentrate inside the *dan tian*. Second, expand the *qi* to the rest of the body. Third, extend the focus to the Taiji *Qi Shi*. Finally, use the movements and adjustments from the Taiji *Qi Shi* to target anything that gets in the *Qi Shi Effective Zone*. This is the training methodology using Taijiquan's model of *qi directing the body*.

1) Training of Internal Movements in the *Dan Tian*

Exercise 1

Readiness position: Stand with your feet shoulder width apart with both hands on the waist (outside wall of the *dan tian*). Adjust the body according to the requirements of *Taiji Readiness State* and maintain a full and filled *Qi Shi*. Pay special attention to the requirements of *sinking qi into the dan tian* to ensure the *dan tian* is filled and solidified. (Illustration.7-1-158)

First movement: Use your mind to move the internal *qi* to the right side of the *dan tian*. This will make the right half of the *dan tian* ball filled with positive pressure or *yang jing*, and the left half of the *dan tian* ball with negative pressure or *yin jing*. (Illustration.7-1-159)

Second movement: Concentrate your mind to move the *qi* to the left side of the *dan tian* thus creating a left *yang* and right *yin* situation. (Illustration.7-1-160)

(7-1-158)	(7-1-159)	(7-1-160)

Repeat first and second movements to move the *qi* in the *dan tian* doing right and left overlapping and bouncing movements. It is very important to do this exercise inside of the highly pressurized *dan tian* ball and never allow the *internal jing* get to the outside wall.

Exercise 2

Readiness position: Same as above exercise. (Illustration.7-1-161)

First movement: Use your mind to sink the *qi* to the lower part of the *dan tian* to create an upper *yin* and lower *yang* situation. (Illustration.7-1-162)

Second movement: Concentrate your mind to move the *qi* upward to the upper part of the *dan tian* to create an upper *yang* and lower *yin* situation. (Illustration.7-1-163)

Repeat the first and second movements to move the *qi* in the *dan tian* doing up and down overlapping and bouncing movements.

(7-1-161)	(7-1-162)	(7-1-163)

146

Exercise 3

Readiness position: Assume a shoulder width stance with one hand in the front of *dan tian* and the other hand at the back of *dan tian*. (Illustration.7-1-164)

First movement: Concentrate on moving the *qi* in the *dan tian* forward with the effect that the front part of the *dan tian* becomes full and the back part of the *dan tian* empty. (Illustration.7-1-165)

Second movement: Focus your mind to move the *qi* in the *dan tian* back so the back part of the *dan tian* is full and the front is empty. (Illustration.7-1-166)

Repeat the first and second movements to make the *qi* in the *dan tian* doing front and back overlapping and bouncing movements.

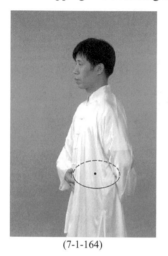 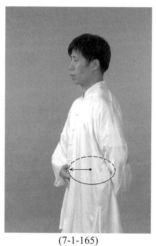 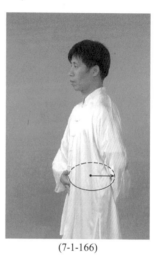

(7-1-164)   (7-1-165)   (7-1-166)

Exercise 4

Readiness position: Same as above exercise. (Illustration.7-1-167)

First movement: Use your mind to move the *qi* in the *dan tian* in small vertical, *clockwise*, and circular movements. With each turn the circle will become bigger. (Illustration.7-1-168)

Second movement: Concentrate your mind to describe with the *qi* in the *dan tian* a vertical, circular and *counter clockwise* movement. With each turn the circle will become smaller. (Illustration.7-1-169)

Third movement: Concentrate to produce with the *qi* in the *dan tian* small *horizontal*, circular and clockwise movements. With each turn the circle will get bigger. (Illustration.7-1-170)

Fourth movement: Use your mind to move the *qi* in the *dan tian* in horizontal, circular and *counter clockwise* movements. With each turn the circle will get smaller. (Illustration.7-1-171)

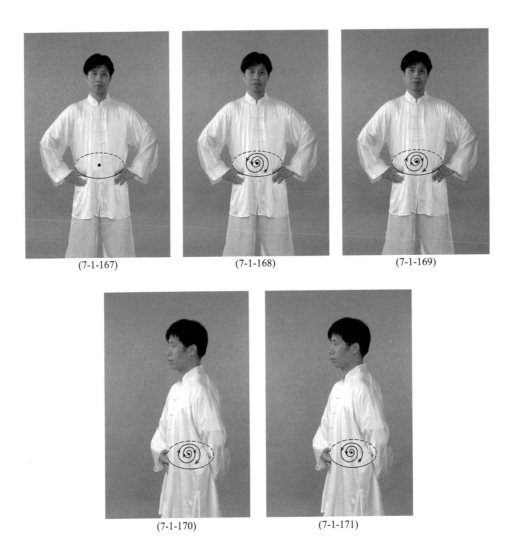

(7-1-167)   (7-1-168)   (7-1-169)

(7-1-170)   (7-1-171)

These exercises are important steps to start the *engine of internal qi* in the *dan tian*. The bouncing force and spiral force from *qi directing the body* must be started from this engine of internal *qi* in the *dan tian*. There is no set limit on how many circles to make.

2) *Gu Dang Jing*[鼓蕩勁] and Spiral Force Exercises

Gu dang jing[4] is formed by using the mind to move the internal *qi* in the *dan tian* back and forth or expand and contract it in an overlapping fashion to create and increase the pressure inside of the body. This force will start from within the *dan tian* and move outward in a ripple or wave motion to the inside of the Taiji *Qi Shi* (*qi* column) to create a bouncing force.

The *spiral* jing is formed by focusing the mind to turn the internal *qi* in spiral movements inside the *dan tian*. The turning movements will then be extended with the *qi* to the other *bows*.

---

[4]Gu dang jing: Wave Motion Force; analogous to the motion of liquid inside a pressurized container.

All turnings need to be done in a spiral form following the axis of each bow. The end result has this spiral force working like a washing machine agitator which causes the entire *internal qi* within the Taiji *Qi Shi* to spin in order to create the *spiral jing*.

Bouncing *jing* and spiral *jing* normally co-exist in all Taiji physical movements. Therefore, we can use different types of circular exercises to help us grasp the key concepts of bouncing force and spiral force.

Exercise 1: <u>Back and Forth Horizontal Circle Exercise</u>

Readiness position: Stand with one foot in front of the other. Relax the muscles in the whole body to make them feel heavy. Concentrate on the *dan tian* to increase the pressure of the *waist and arch jing*. Rest the left hand on the waist and lift the right hand in front of the chest. Maintain the whole Taiji *Qi Shi* in a full and pressurized condition. (Illustration.7-1-172)

First movement: Move the *qi* in the *dan tian* forward to create a *yang* force, which will move forward and expand the *Qi Shi*. Push the right hand forward. (Illustration.7-1-173)

Second movement: Turn the *Qi Shi* left by turning the *dan tian* left. Move the right hand toward the left side, as well as turning clockwise so the palm faces up. (Illustration.7-1-174)

| (7-1-172) | (7-1-173) | (7-1-174) |

Third movement: Move the *Qi Shi* back by moving the *dan tian* backward. This will pull the right arm back so the upper arm is touching the body. (Illustration.7-1-175)

Fourth movement: Turn the *Qi Shi* right by turning the *dan tian* right. Move the right hand toward right side as well as rotating it counter clockwise. (Illustration.7-1-176)

A large horizontal circle will be drawn when completing the above movements. The key is to understand how the bouncing force and spiral force are created in the Taiji *Qi Shi* by the movements of internal *qi* in the *dan tian*.

Repeat the exercise from both left and right sides.

(7-1-175)   (7-1-176)

Exercise 2: <u>Up and Down Vertical Circle Exercise</u>

Readiness position: Same as above exercise. (Illustration.7-1-177)

First movement: Turn the *Qi Shi* left by turning the internal *qi* in the *dan tian* left. At the same time, the right-hand moves toward the left side and turns clockwise. (Illustration.7-1-178)

Second movement: Continuing from the above movement, the internal *qi* in the *dan tian* moves downward to bring the *Qi Shi* down. At the same time the right-hand will push downward. (Illustration.7-1-179)

Third movement: In continuation from the above movement, turn the *Qi Shi* right by turning the *qi* in the *dan tian* right. Move the right hand toward the right side at the same time rotating it counter clockwise. (Illustration.7-1-180)

(7-1-177)   (7-1-178)   (7-1-179)

150

(7-1-180)   (7-1-181)

Fourth movement: From the above movement, bring the *Qi Shi* up by moving the *qi* in *dan tian* upward. However, you must also increase the downward pressure in the *waist and arch jing*. Also, bring the right-hand up. (Illustration.7-1-181)

A large up and down vertical circle will be drawn when completing the above movements. Repeat the exercises making circles clock- wise and counter clockwise.

Exercise 3: <u>Sideways Vertical Circle Exercise</u>

Readiness position: Sitting in a horse stance position with the left hand on the waist and the right hand up. The fingertips of the right hand should be at mouth level. (Illustration.7-1-182)

First movement: From the above position, turn the *Qi Shi* left by turning the internal *qi* in the *dan tian* to the left. Slightly shift to the right, rotating the right arm clockwise and bringing the right elbow toward the body with the right palm facing up. (Illustration.7-1-183)

Second movement: Sink the *Qi Shi* by sinking the internal *qi* in the *dan tian* while shifting back to a horse stance. The right hand presses down. (Illustration.7-1-184)

(7-1-182)   (7-1-183)   (7-1-184)

151

Third movement: Shift slightly to the right by moving the *Qi Shi* up and to the right using the internal *qi* in the *dan tian*. Push out the right hand. (Illustration.7-1-185)

Fourth movement: Continue from the above movement, turning the *Qi Shi* slightly to the left by turning the internal *qi*. Turn the right arm clockwise. (Illustration.7-1-186)

A large circle will be drawn counter clockwise by completing the above movements. (Illustration.7-1-187) The exercise can be repeated in clockwise and counter clockwise motions as well as left and right.

(7-1-185) (7-1-186) (7-1-187)

When drawing circles in the above exercises, it is very important to always keep in mind the *qi directing body* principles. Focus adjustments in the mind and *qi* by insuring all movements originate internally through *bouncing* and *spiral* force. After one has completely grasped the drawing of these circles in the fashion described above, different kinds of circles with any kind of free moving steps under the principles of *qi directing body* can be exercised. As a result, one will be able to use the internal movement of mind and *qi* to direct all physical movements.

The *mind directing body*, *body directing qi* and *qi directing body* are the basic requirements of all movement and the foundation of training in the *Taiji Readiness State*. They are also the keys to *control of self* in Taijiquan training. The substance of the *Taiji Readiness State* is an important gauge to judge how well one has trained in the *control of self* aspect of Taijiquan.

TOPIC 2: **Training of Chen Style Taijiquan**

A key component in Taijiquan training is form practice. The form is created from a set of technical movements and is to be performed in a specific order and under specific requirements. It is a key part of the self-control training in Taijiquan. The purpose of the form is to complete a set of very complicated and diversified movements, but still be able to create and maintain the *Taiji Readiness State*. This helps to move *Taiji Readiness* from a static to a dynamic state. Also, the movements in the form originated for the purpose of self-defence and fighting. It helps if one practices the form with an "imaginary enemy". This will assist in developing the skills that will enable the Taiji practitioner to utilize Taiji movements in a fighting situation.

Training in the form can be varied by adjusting the height of your stance, intensity of internal force and amount of pressure in your *qi* column. There are also different forms that provide their own uniqueness and different emphasis to make the Taiji learning experience more interesting.

There are two primary empty-hand Chen Style Taiji forms that are practiced today. We will introduce the first form in this book. Chen Style Taijiquan requires the co-existence of soft and hard. It contains fast as well as slow movements, winding/spiral actions and *fa jing* force. The emphasis on *chan si jing* is very important in Chen Style Taiji. With the *Qi Shi* in the fullness state, the turning of the *dan tian* will cause every part in the body to produce spiral turns around the axis of each bow. The whole body and the Taiji *Qi Shi* will be making spiral turns around the *Core of Qi Shi*. This combined *spiral force* will help produce a powerful *vibratory force (dou jing* [抖勁]*)* when executing specific movements in the form. It is very important to make sure sufficient winding is done before doing the *dou jing*. The trigger force must be done with crisp, sharp power. Avoid shaking the body to embellish the trigger force for the sake of showmanship.

Chen Style Taiji First Form Movements:

1.   Opening Form   (Illustrations 7-2-1 to 7-2-4)

(7-2-1)   (7-2-2)   (7-2-3)

(7-2-4)

2. Jin Gang Pounds Mortar (Illustrations 7-2-5 to 7-2-12)

(7-2-5)

(7-2-6)

(7-2-7)

(7-2-8)

(7-2-9)

(7-2-10)

(7-2-11)

(7-2-12)

3. Lazily Tying Coat   (Illustrations 7-2-13 to 7-2-19)

(7-2-13)

(7-2-14)

(7-2-15)

(7-2-16)

(7-2-17)

(7-2-18)

155

(7-2-19)

4. 60% Sealing and 40% Closing   (Illustrations 7-2-20 to 7-2-26)

(7-2-20)   (7-2-21)   (7-2-22)

(7-2-23)   (7-2-24)   (7-2-25)

(7-2-26)

5. Single Whip   (Illustrations 7-2-27 to 7-2-34)

(7-2-27)   (7-2-28)   (7-2-29)

(7-2-30)   (7-2-31)   (7-2-32)

(7-2-33) (7-2-34)

6. Jin Gang Pounds Mortar (Illustrations 7-2-35 to 7-2-42)

(7-2-35) (7-2-36) (7-2-37)

(7-2-38) (7-2-39) (7-2-40)

158

(7-2-41)

(7-2-42)

7. White Crane Spreads Its Wings   (Illustrations 7-2-43 to 7-2-47)

(7-2-43)

(7-2-44)

(7-2-44A)

(7-2-45)

(7-2-46)

(7-2-47)

8. Walk Obliquely & Twist Step (both sides)   (Illustrations 7-2-48 to 7-2-54)

(7-2-48)   (7-2-49)   (7-2-50)

(7-2-51)   (7-2-52)   (7-2-53)

(7-2-54)

9. First Closing   (Illustrations 7-2-55 to 7-2-58)

(7-2-55)   (7-2-56)   (7-2-57)

(7-2-58)

10. Wade Forward & Twist Step (both sides)   (Illustrations 7-2-59 to 7-2-63)

(7-2-59)   (7-2-60)   (7-2-61)

(7-2-62)　　　　　　　　　(7-2-63)

11. Walk Obliquely & Twist Step (both sides)   (Illustrations 7-2-64 to 7-2-70)

(7-2-64)　　　　　　　(7-2-65)　　　　　　　(7-2-66)

(7-2-67)　　　　　　　(7-2-68)　　　　　　　(7-2-69)

(7-2-70)

12. Second Closing (Illustrations 7-2-71 to 7-2-74)

(7-2-71)

(7-2-72)

(7-2-73)

(7-2-74)

13. Wade Forward & Twist Step (both sides)   Illustrations 7-2-75 to 7-2-79)

(7-2-75)   (7-2-76)   (7-2-77)

(7-2-78)   (7-2-79)

14. Hidden Hand Punch   (Illustrations 7-2-80 to 7-2-87)

(7-2-80)   (7-2-81)   (7-2-82)

164

(7-2-83)　　　　　　　(7-2-84)　　　　　　　(7-2-85)

(7-2-86)　　　　　　　(7-2-87)

15. Jin Gang Pounds Mortar   (Illustrations 7-2-88 to 7-2-94)

(7-2-88)　　　　　　　(7-2-89)　　　　　　　(7-2-90)

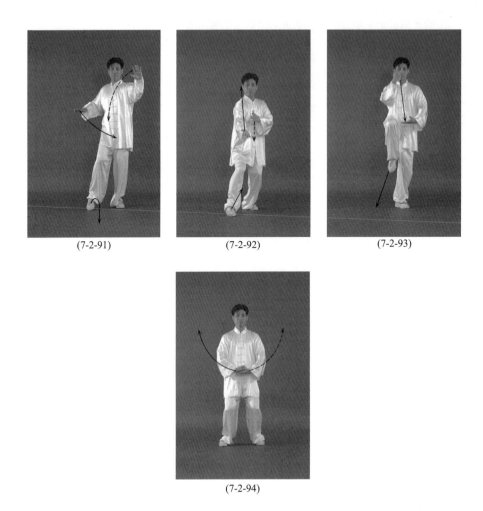

(7-2-91)   (7-2-92)   (7-2-93)

(7-2-94)

16. The Punch of Draping Over Body   (Illustrations 7-2-95 to 7-2-100)

(7-2-95)   (7-2-96)   (7-2-97)

(7-2-98)

(7-2-99)

(7-2-100)

17. Rotate Body and Back Strike   (Illustrations 7-2-101 to 7-2-105)

(7-2-101)

(7-2-102)

(7-2-103)

(7-2-104)

(7-2-105)

167

18. Green Dragon Emerges Out of Water (Illustrations 7-2-106 to 7-2-112)

(7-2-106)

(7-2-107)

(7-2-108)

(7-2-109)

(7-2-110)

(7-2-111)

(7-2-112)

19. Push With Both Hands　(Illustrations 7-2-113 to 7-2-117)

(7-2-113)　　　　　　(7-2-114)　　　　　　(7-2-115)

(7-2-116)　　　　　　(7-2-117)

20.　Three Changes of Palms　(Illustrations 7-2-118 to 7-2-120)

(7-2-118)　　　　　　(7-2-119)　　　　　　(7-2-120)

21. Fist Under Elbow   (Illustrations 7-2-121 to 7-2-123)

(7-2-121)

(7-2-122)

(7-2-123)

22. Slide Back and Whirl Arms (both sides)   (Illustrations 7-2-124 to 7-2-132)

(7-2-124)

(7-2-125)

(7-2-126)

(7-2-127)

(7-2-128)

(7-2-129)

170

(7-2-130)　　　　　(7-2-131)　　　　　(7-2-132)

23.　Step Back and Press Elbow　　　(Illustrations 7-2-133 to 7-2-137)

(7-2-133)　　　　　(7-2-134)　　　　　(7-2-135)

(7-2-135A)　　　　　(7-2-136)　　　　　(7-2-137)

171

24. Middle Winding (Illustrations 7-2-138 to 7-2-146)

(7-2-138)

(7-2-139)

(7-2-140)

(7-2-141)

(7-2-142)

(7-2-143)

(7-2-144)

(7-2-145)

(7-2-146)

25. White Crane Spreads Its Wings   (Illustrations 7-2-147 to 7-2-148)

(7-2-147)   (7-2-147A)   (7-2-148)

26. Walk Obliquely & Twist Step (both sides)   (Illustrations 7-2-149 to 7-2-155)

(7-2-149)   (7-2-150)   (7-2-151)

(7-2-152)   (7-2-153)   (7-2-154)

(7-2-155)

27. Lightning Fast Throw Through the Back   (Illustrations 7-2-156 to 7-2-165)

(7-2-156)   (7-2-157)   (7-2-158)

(7-2-158A)   (7-2-159)   (7-2-160)

(7-2-161)

(7-2-162)

(7-2-163)

(7-2-164)

(7-2-165)

28. Hidden Hand Punch (Illustrations 7-2-166 to 7-2-172)

(7-2-166)

(7-2-167)

(7-2-168)

(7-2-169)

(7-2-170)

(7-2-171)

(7-2-172)

29. 60% Sealing and 40% Closing (Illustrations 7-2-173 to 7-2-178)

(7-2-173)

(7-2-174)

(7-2-175)

(7-2-176)   (7-2-177)   (7-2-178)

30. Single Whip   (Illustrations 7-2-179 to 7-2-186)

(7-2-179)   (7-2-180)   (7-2-181)

(7-2-182)   (7-2-183)   (7-2-184)

(7-2-185)   (7-2-186)

31. Wave Hands Like Moving Clouds　(Illustrations 7-2-187 to 7-2-195)

(7-2-187)   (7-2-188)   (7-2-189)

(7-2-190)   (7-2-191)   (7-2-192)

(7-2-193)　　　　　　　(7-2-194)　　　　　　　(7-2-195)

32. High Pat on Horse　　　(Illustrations 7-2-196 to 7-2-200)

(7-2-196)　　　　　　　(7-2-197)　　　　　　　(7-2-198)

(7-2-199)　　　　　　　(7-2-200)　　　　　　　(7-2-200A)

33. Rub With Right Foot   (Illustrations 7-2-201 to 7-2-205)

(7-2-201)

(7-2-201A)

(7-2-202)

(7-2-203)

(7-2-204)

(7-2-205)

34. Rub With Left Foot   (Illustrations 7-2-206 to 7-2-207)

(7-2-206)

(7-2-207)

35. Side Kick With Left Heel (Illustrations 7-2-208 to 7-2-210)

(7-2-208)

(7-2-208A)

(7-2-209)

(7-2-209A)

(7-2-210)

36. Wade Forward & Twist Step (both sides) (Illustrations 7-2-211 to 7-2-215)

(7-2-211)

(7-2-212)

(7-2-213)

(7-2-214) (7-2-215)

37. The Punch of Hitting the Ground (Illustrations 7-2-216 to 7-2-221)

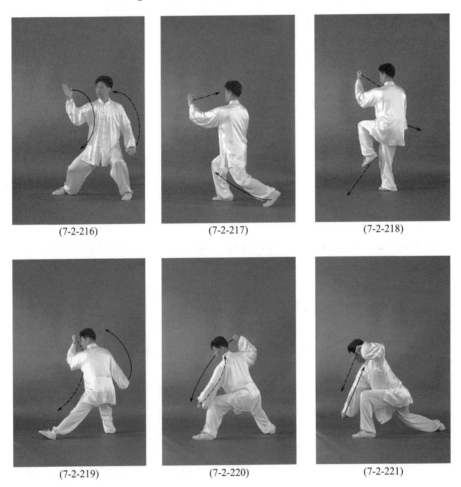

(7-2-216) (7-2-217) (7-2-218)

(7-2-219) (7-2-220) (7-2-221)

182

38. Turn Over Body, Jump and Kick Twice   (Illustrations 7-2-222 to 7-2-227)

(7-2-222)

(7-2-223)

(7-2-224)

(7-2-225)

(7-2-226)

(7-2-227)

39. Beast Head Pose   (Illustrations 7-2-228 to 7-2-236)

(7-2-228)

(7-2-228A)

(7-2-229)

(7-2-230)　　　　　　　(7-2-231)　　　　　　　(7-2-232)

(7-2-233)　　　　　　　(7-2-234)　　　　　　　(7-2-235)

(7-2-236)

40. Tornado Kick   (Illustrations 7-2-237 to 7-2-241)

(7-2-237)   (7-2-237A)   (7-2-238)

(7-2-239)   (7-2-240)   (7-2-241)

41. Side Kick With Right Heel   (Illustrations 7-2-242 to 7-2-244)

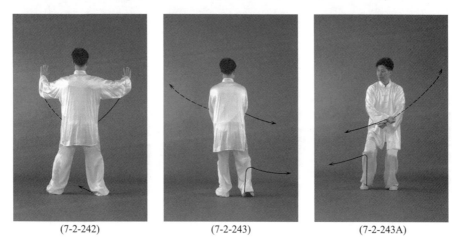

(7-2-242)   (7-2-243)   (7-2-243A)

(7-2-244)

42.　Hidden Hand Punch　　(Illustrations 7-2-245 to 7-2-253)

(7-2-245)　　　　　(7-2-246)　　　　　(7-2-247)

(7-2-248)　　　　　(7-2-249)　　　　　(7-2-250)

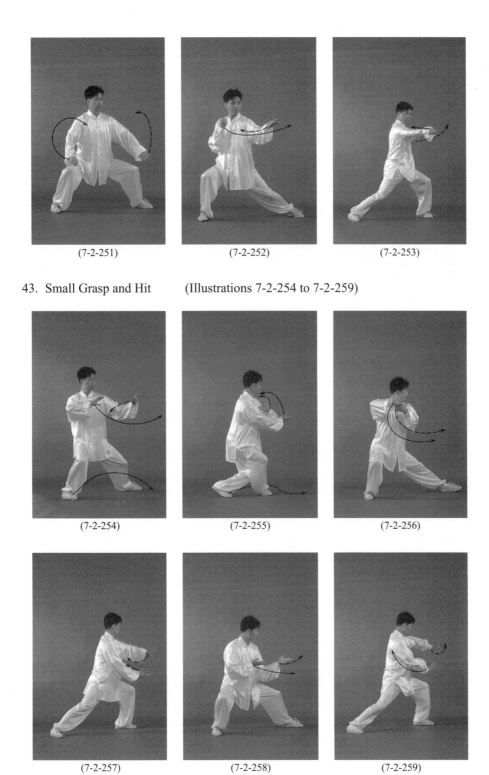

(7-2-251)　　　　　　　(7-2-252)　　　　　　　(7-2-253)

43. Small Grasp and Hit　　　(Illustrations 7-2-254 to 7-2-259)

(7-2-254)　　　　　　　(7-2-255)　　　　　　　(7-2-256)

(7-2-257)　　　　　　　(7-2-258)　　　　　　　(7-2-259)

44. Embrace Head and Push Mountain (Illustrations 7-2-260 to 7-2-266)

(7-2-260)

(7-2-261)

(7-2-262)

(7-2-263)

(7-2-264)

(7-2-265)

(7-2-266)

45. Three Changes of Palms   (Illustrations 7-2-267 to 7-2-269)

(7-2-267)   (7-2-268)   (7-2-269)

46. 60% Sealing and 40% Closing   (Illustrations 7-2-270 to 7-2-272)

(7-2-270)   (7-2-271)   (7-2-272)

47. Single Whip   (Illustrations 7-2-273 to 7-2-280)

(7-2-273)   (7-2-274)   (7-2-275)

(7-2-276)   (7-2-277)   (7-2-278)

(7-2-279)   (7-2-280)

48. Front Technique (Illustrations 7-2-281 to 7-2-282)

(7-2-281)   (7-2-282)

49. Back Technique (Illustrations 7-2-283 to 7-2-284)

(7-2-283) (7-2-284)

50. Part the Wild Horse's Mane (both sides)   (Illustrations 7-2-285 to 7-2-293)

(7-2-285) (7-2-286) (7-2-287)

(7-2-288) (7-2-289) (7-2-290)

(7-2-291)   (7-2-292)   (7-2-293)

51. 60% Sealing and 40% Closing   (Illustrations 7-2-294 to 7-2-302)

(7-2-294)   (7-2-295)   (7-2-296)

(7-2-296A)   (7-2-297)   (7-2-298)

(7-2-299) (7-2-300) (7-2-301)

(7-2-302)

52. Single Whip (Illustrations 7-2-303 to 7-2-311)

(7-2-303) (7-2-304) (7-2-305)

(7-2-306)

(7-2-307)

(7-2-308)

(7-2-309)

(7-2-310)

(7-2-311)

53. Stamp Both Feet   (Illustrations 7-2-312 to 7-2-316)

(7-2-312)

(7-2-313)

(7-2-314)

(7-2-315)

(7-2-316)

54. Fair Lady Works at Shuttle   (Illustrations 7-2-317 to 7-2-323)

(7-2-317)

(7-2-318)

(7-2-319)

(7-2-320)

(7-2-321)

(7-2-321A)

195

(7-2-322)   (7-2-323)

55. Lazily Tying Coat   (Illustrations 7-2-324 to 7-2-328)

(7-2-324)   (7-2-325)   (7-2-326)

(7-2-327)   (7-2-328)

56. 60% Sealing and 40% Closing　　(Illustrations 7-2-329 to 7-2-335)

(7-2-329)　　　　　　　　(7-2-330)　　　　　　　　(7-2-331)

(7-2-332)　　　　　　　　(7-2-333)　　　　　　　　(7-2-334)

(7-2-335)

57. Single Whip   (Illustrations 7-2-336 to 7-2-344)

(7-2-336)   (7-2-337)   (7-2-338)

(7-2-339)   (7-2-340)   (7-2-341)

(7-2-342)   (7-2-343)   (7-2-344)

58. Wave Hands Like Moving Clouds   (Illustrations 7-2-345 to 7-2-353)

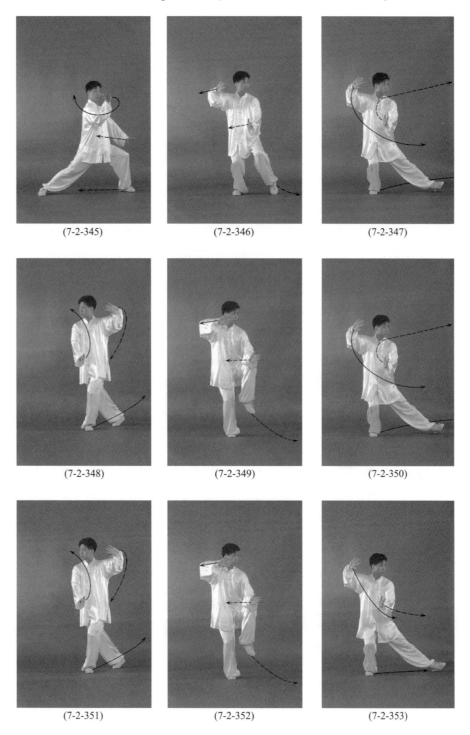

(7-2-345)   (7-2-346)   (7-2-347)

(7-2-348)   (7-2-349)   (7-2-350)

(7-2-351)   (7-2-352)   (7-2-353)

59. Sweep Kick and Stretch Down   (Illustrations 7-2-354 to 7-2-362)

(7-2-354)   (7-2-355)   (7-2-356)

(7-2-357)   (7-2-358)   (7-2-359)

(7-2-360)   (7-2-361)   (7-2-362)

60. Golden Pheasant Stands on One Leg   (Illustrations 7-2-363 to 7-2-374)

(7-2-363)

(7-2-364)

(7-2-365)

(7-2-366)

(7-2-367)

(7-2-368)

(7-2-369)

(7-2-370)

(7-2-371)

(7-2-372)

(7-2-373)

(7-2-374)

61. Slide Back and Whirl Arms (both sides)   (Illustrations 7-2-375 to 7-2-382)

(7-2-375)

(7-2-376)

(7-2-377)

(7-2-378)

(7-2-379)

(7-2-380)

(7-2-381)

(7-2-382)

62. Step Back and Press Elbow   (Illustrations 7-2-383 to 7-2-387)

(7-2-383)

(7-2-384)

(7-2-385)

(7-2-385A)

(7-2-386)

(7-2-387)

63. Middle Winding (Illustrations 7-2-388 to 7-2-396)

(7-2-388)	(7-2-389)	(7-2-390)
(7-2-391)	(7-2-392)	(7-2-393)
(7-2-394)	(7-2-395)	(7-2-396)

64. White Crane Spreads Its Wings (Illustrations 7-2-397 to 7-2-398)

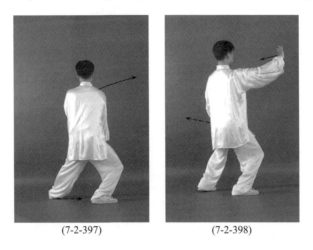

(7-2-397)   (7-2-398)

65. Walk Obliquely & Twist Step (both sides) (Illustrations 7-2-399 to 7-2-405)

(7-2-399)   (7-2-400)   (7-2-401)

(7-2-402)   (7-2-403)   (7-2-404)

(7-2-405)

66. Lightning Fast Throw Through the Back   (Illustrations 7-2-406 to 7-2-415)

(7-2-406)   (7-2-407)   (7-2-408)

(7-2-408A)   (7-2-409)   (7-2-410)

(7-2-411)

(7-2-412)

(7-2-413)

(7-2-414)

(7-2-415)

67. Hidden Hand Punch   (Illustrations 7-2-416 to 7-2-422)

(7-2-416)

(7-2-417)

(7-2-418)

(7-2-419) (7-2-420) (7-2-421)

(7-2-422)

68. 60% Sealing and 40% Closing   (Illustrations 7-2-423 to 7-2-428)

(7-2-423) (7-2-424) (7-2-425)

(7-2-426) (7-2-427) (7-2-428)

69. Single Whip   (Illustrations 7-2-429 to 7-2-436)

(7-2-429) (7-2-430) (7-2-431)

(7-2-432) (7-2-433) (7-2-434)

(7-2-435)　　　　　　　　(7-2-436)

70. Wave Hands Like Moving Clouds　(Illustrations 7-2-437 to 7-2-445)

(7-2-437)　　　　　　(7-2-438)　　　　　　(7-2-439)

(7-2-440)　　　　　　(7-2-441)　　　　　　(7-2-442)

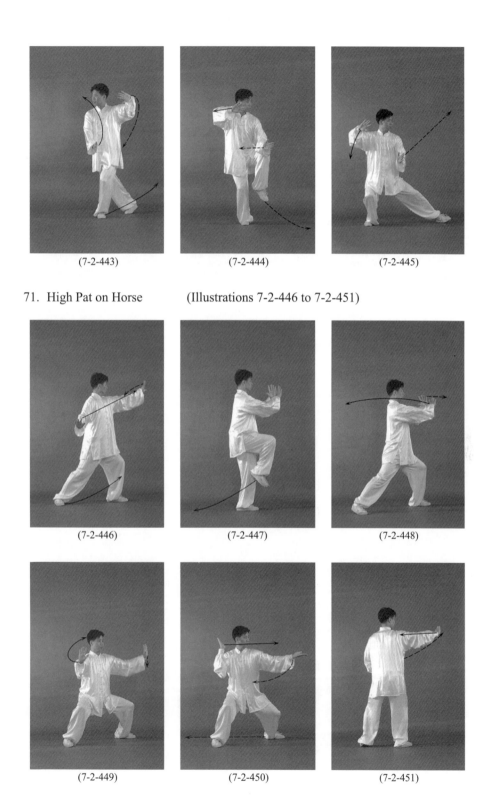

(7-2-443)　　　　　(7-2-444)　　　　　(7-2-445)

71. High Pat on Horse　　　(Illustrations 7-2-446 to 7-2-451)

(7-2-446)　　　　　(7-2-447)　　　　　(7-2-448)

(7-2-449)　　　　　(7-2-450)　　　　　(7-2-451)

72. Cross Hands & Sweep Kick With One Leg   (Illustrations 7-2-452 to 7-2-459)

(7-2-452)

(7-2-453)

(7-2-454)

(7-2-455)

(7-2-456)

(7-2-457)

(7-2-458)

(7-2-459)

73. The Punch of Hitting the Crotch   (Illustrations 7-2-460 to 7-2-468)

(7-2-460)

(7-2-461)

(7-2-462)

(7-2-463)

(7-2-464)

(7-2-465)

(7-2-465A)

(7-2-466)

(7-2-467)

(7-2-467A)   (7-2-468)

74. White Ape Presents Fruit   (Illustrations 7-2-469 to 7-2-471)

(7-2-469)   (7-2-470)   (7-2-471)

75. 60% Sealing and 40% Closing   (Illustrations 7-2-472 to 7-2-474)

(7-2-472)   (7-2-473)   (7-2-474)

214

76. Single Whip   (Illustrations 7-2-475 to 7-2-482)

(7-2-475)

(7-2-476)

(7-2-477)

(7-2-478)

(7-2-479)

(7-2-480)

(7-2-481)

(7-2-482)

77. The Dragon on the Ground   (Illustrations 7-2-483 to 7-2-485)

(7-2-483)   (7-2-484)   (7-2-485)

78. Step Up to Form Seven Stars   (Illustrations 7-2-486 to 7-2-487)

(7-2-486)   (7-2-487)

79. Step Back to Mount Tiger   (Illustrations 7-2-488 to 7-2-491)

(7-2-488)   (7-2-489)   (7-2-490)

216

(7-2-491)

80. Turn Around and Sweep With One Leg (Illustrations 7-2-492 to 7-2-497)

(7-2-492)

(7-2-493)

(7-2-494)

(7-2-495)

(7-2-496)

(7-2-497)

81. The Cannon of Confronting the Opponent   (Illustrations 7-2-498 to 7-2-502)

(7-2-498)   (7-2-499)   (7-2-500)

(7-2-501)   (7-2-502)

82. Jin Gang Pounds Mortar   (Illustrations 7-2-503 to 7-2-508)

(7-2-503)   (7-2-504)   (7-2-505)

(7-2-506)

(7-2-507)

(7-2-508)

83. Closing Form   (Illustration 7-2-509)

(7-2-509)

TOPIC 3: **Training of Yang Style Taijiquan**

The Yang Style of Taijiquan consists mainly of *opening and closing* movements to be done under a very large *Qi Shi* with grace. These opening and closing movements, which centre on the *Core of Qi Shi,* will start from internal and expand outward in a rippling wave to create the *bouncing force*. Traditionally, all Yang Style Taijiquan movements must be done with spiral action. There is no *fa jing* in any part of the form. You can, however, enhance the level of training by using trigger force intermittently throughout the form. This is a good way to check the level and intensity of the *Taiji Readiness State* when practicing the form.

Yang Style Taiji First Form Movements:

   1.   Pre-Opening Stance   (Illustration 7-3-1)

(7-3-1)

   2.   Opening Form   (Illustrations 7-3-2 to 7-3-3)

         (7-3-2)   (7-3-3)

3. Grasp Peacock's Tail (Illustrations 7-3-4 to 7-3-18)

(7-3-4)

(7-3-5)

(7-3-6)

(7-3-7)

(7-3-8)

(7-3-9)

(7-3-10)

(7-3-11)

(7-3-12)

(7-3-13)   (7-3-14)   (7-3-15)

(7-3-16)   (7-3-17)   (7-3-18)

4.   Single Whip   (Illustrations 7-3-19 to 7-3-23)

(7-3-19)   (7-3-20)   (7-3-21)

(7-3-22)

(7-3-23)

5. Raise Hands   (Illustrations 7-3-24 to 7-3-27)

(7-3-24)

(7-3-25)

(7-3-26)

(7-3-27)

6.   White Crane Spreads Its Wings   (Illustrations 7-3-28 to 7-3-30)

(7-3-28)   (7-3-29)   (7-3-30)

7.   Brush Knee & Twist Step (left)   (Illustrations 7-3-31 to 7-3-35)

(7-3-31)   (7-3-32)   (7-3-33)

(7-3-34)   (7-3-35)

8. Play the Pipa   (Illustrations 7-3-36 to 7-3-38)

(7-3-36)   (7-3-37)   (7-3-38)

9. Brush Knee & Twist Step (L-R-L)   (Illustrations 7-3-39 to 7-3-52)

(7-3-39)   (7-3-40)   (7-3-41)

(7-3-42)   (7-3-43)   (7-3-44)

(7-3-45)　　　　　　　(7-3-46)　　　　　　　(7-3-47)

(7-3-48)　　　　　　　(7-3-49)　　　　　　　(7-3-50)

(7-3-51)　　　　　　　(7-3-52)

10. Play the Pipa   (Illustrations 7-3-53 to 7-3-55)

(7-3-53)   (7-3-54)   (7-3-55)

11. Brush Knee & Twist Step (left)   (Illustrations 7-3-56 to 7-3-59)

(7-3-56)   (7-3-57)   (7-3-58)

(7-3-59)

12. Step Up, Parry and Punch (Illustrations 7-3-60 to 7-3-66)

(7-3-60)

(7-3-61)

(7-3-62)

(7-3-63)

(7-3-64)

(7-3-65)

(7-3-66)

13. Apparent Closing   (Illustrations 7-3-67 to 7-3-69)

(7-3-67)

(7-3-68)

(7-3-69)

14. Cross Hands   (Illustrations 7-3-70 to 7-3-71)

(7-3-70)

(7-3-71)

15. Embrace Tiger, Return to Mountain   (Illustrations 7-3-72 to 7-3-82)

(7-3-72)

(7-3-73)

(7-3-74)

229

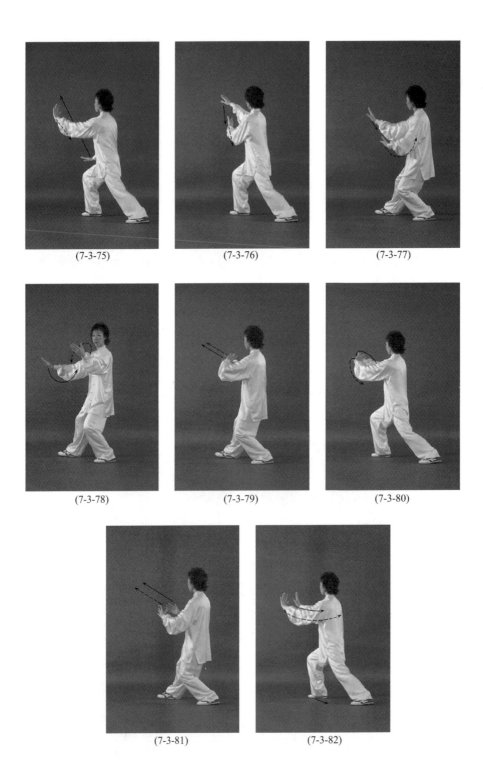

(7-3-75)　　　　　　　　(7-3-76)　　　　　　　　(7-3-77)

(7-3-78)　　　　　　　　(7-3-79)　　　　　　　　(7-3-80)

(7-3-81)　　　　　　　　(7-3-82)

16. Fist Under Elbow (Illustrations 7-3-83 to 7-3-88)

(7-3-83)

(7-3-84)

(7-3-85)

(7-3-86)

(7-3-87)

(7-3-88)

17. Step Back & Repulse Monkey (L-R-L) (Illustrations 7-3-89 to 7-3-100)

(7-3-89)

(7-3-90)

(7-3-91)

(7-3-92)　　　　　　　(7-3-93)　　　　　　　(7-3-94)

(7-3-95)　　　　　　　(7-3-96)　　　　　　　(7-3-97)

(7-3-98)　　　　　　　(7-3-99)　　　　　　　(7-3-100)

18. Diagonal Flying

(Illustrations 7-3-101 to 7-3-104)

(7-3-101)

(7-3-102)

(7-3-103)

(7-3-104)

19. Raise Hands

(Illustrations 7-3-105 to 7-3-107)

(7-3-105)

(7-3-106)

(7-3-107)

20. White Crane Spreads Its Wings   (Illustrations 7-3-108 to 7-3-110)

(7-3-108)   (7-3-109)   (7-3-110)

21. Brush Knee & Twist Step (left)   (Illustrations 7-3-111 to 7-3-115)

(7-3-111)   (7-3-112)   (7-3-113)

(7-3-114)   (7-3-115)

22. Needle at the Sea Bottom (Illustrations 7-3-116 to 7-3-119)

(7-3-116) (7-3-117) (7-3-118)

(7-3-119)

23. Flash Arms   (Illustrations 7-3-120 to 7-3-122)

(7-3-120) (7-3-121) (7-3-122)

24. Turn and Chop With Fist   (Illustrations 7-3-123 to 7-3-127)

(7-3-123)   (7-3-124)   (7-3-125)

(7-3-126)   (7-3-127)

25. Step Up, Parry and Punch   (Illustrations 7-3-128 to 7-3-133)

(7-3-128)   (7-3-129)   (7-3-130)

(7-3-131)　　　　　　(7-3-132)　　　　　　(7-3-133)

26. Step Up and Grasp Peacock's Tail　　　(Illustrations 7-3-134 to 7-3-144)

(7-3-134)　　　　　　(7-3-135)　　　　　　(7-3-136)

(7-3-137)　　　　　　(7-3-138)　　　　　　(7-3-139)

(7-3-140)   (7-3-141)   (7-3-142)

(7-3-143)   (7-3-144)

27. Single Whip   (Illustrations 7-3-145 to 7-3-150)

(7-3-145)   (7-3-146)   (7-3-147)

(7-3-148)　　　　　　　　(7-3-149)　　　　　　　　(7-3-150)

28. Wave Hands Like Moving Clouds   (Illustrations 7-3-151 to 7-3-163)

(7-3-151)　　　　　　　　(7-3-152)　　　　　　　　(7-3-153)

(7-3-154)　　　　　　　　(7-3-155)　　　　　　　　(7-3-156)

(7-3-157)　　　　　　　(7-3-158)　　　　　　　(7-3-159)

(7-3-160)　　　　　　　(7-3-161)　　　　　　　(7-3-162)

(7-3-163)

29. Single Whip   (Illustrations 7-3-164 to 7-3-168)

(7-3-164)

(7-3-165)

(7-3-166)

(7-3-167)

(7-3-168)

30. High Pat on Horse   (Illustrations 7-3-169 to 7-3-170)

(7-3-169)

(7-3-170)

31. Kick With Toe (right & left)   (Illustrations 7-3-171 to 7-3-184)

(7-3-171)   (7-3-172)   (7-3-173)

(7-3-174)   (7-3-175)   (7-3-176)

(7-3-177)   (7-3-178)   (7-3-179)

242

(7-3-180)   (7-3-181)   (7-3-182)

(7-3-183)   (7-3-184)

32. Turn and Kick With Left Heel   (Illustrations 7-3-185 to 7-3-187)

(7-3-185)   (7-3-186)   (7-3-187)

33. Brush Knee & Twist Step (left-right)   (Illustrations 7-3-188 to 7-3-196)

(7-3-188)   (7-3-189)   (7-3-190)

(7-3-191)   (7-3-192)   (7-3-193)

(7-3-194)   (7-3-195)   (7-3-196)

34. Brush Knee, Punch Down   (Illustrations 7-3-197 to 7-3-200)

(7-3-197)   (7-3-198)   (7-3-199)

(7-3-200)

35. Turn and Chop With Fist   (Illustrations 7-3-201 to 7-3-205)

(7-3-201)   (7-3-202)   (7-3-203)

(7-3-204)

(7-3-205)

36. Step Up, Parry and Punch   (Illustrations 7-3-206 to 7-3-211)

(7-3-206)

(7-3-207)

(7-3-208)

(7-3-209)

(7-3-210)

(7-3-211)

246

37. Kick With Right Heel   (Illustrations 7-3-212 to 7-3-214)

(7-3-212)

(7-3-213)

(7-3-214)

38. Tame the Tiger (left)   (Illustrations 7-3-215 to 7-3-218)

(7-3-215)

(7-3-216)

(7-3-217)

(7-3-218)

39. Tame the Tiger (right)   (Illustrations 7-3-219 to 7-3-220)

(7-3-219)   (7-3-220)

40. Turn Back and Kick With Right Heel   (Illustrations 7-3-221 to 7-3-223)

(7-3-221)   (7-3-222)   (7-3-223)

41. Strike Opponent's Ears With Both Fists   (Illustrations 7-3-224 to 7-3-226)

(7-3-224)   (7-3-225)   (7-3-226)

42. Kick With Left Heel   (Illustrations 7-3-227 to 7-3-229)

(7-3-227)

(7-3-228)

(7-3-229)

43. Turn and Kick With Right Heel   (Illustrations 7-3-230 to 7-3-232)

(7-3-230)

(7-3-231)

(7-3-232)

44. Step Up, Parry and Punch   (Illustrations 7-3-233 to 7-3-238)

(7-3-233)

(7-3-234)

(7-3-235)

(7-3-236) (7-3-237) (7-3-238)

45. Apparent Closing (Illustrations 7-3-239 to 7-3-240)

(7-3-239) (7-3-240)

46. Cross Hands (Illustrations 7-3-241 to 7-3-242)

(7-3-241) (7-3-242)

47. Embrace Tiger, Return to Mountain (Illustrations 7-3-243 to 7-3-253)

(7-3-243)	(7-3-244)	(7-3-245)
(7-3-246)	(7-3-247)	(7-3-248)
(7-3-249)	(7-3-250)	(7-3-251)

(7-3-252)

(7-3-253)

48. Side-Step, Single Whip   (Illustrations 7-3-254 to 7-3-258)

(7-3-254)

(7-3-255)

(7-3-256)

(7-3-257)

(7-3-258)

49. Part the Wild Horse's Mane (R-L-R)   (Illustrations 7-3-259 to 7-3-270)

(7-3-259)   (7-3-260)   (7-3-261)

(7-3-262)   (7-3-263)   (7-3-264)

(7-3-265)   (7-3-266)   (7-3-267)

(7-3-268)   (7-3-269)   (7-3-270)

50. Step Up and Grasp Peacock's Tail　(Illustrations 7-3-271 to 7-3-285)

(7-3-271)   (7-3-272)   (7-3-273)

(7-3-274)   (7-3-275)   (7-3-276)

(7-3-277)　　　　　　(7-3-278)　　　　　　(7-3-279)

(7-3-280)　　　　　　(7-3-281)　　　　　　(7-3-282)

(7-3-283)　　　　　　(7-3-284)　　　　　　(7-3-285)

51. Single Whip   (Illustrations 7-3-286 to 7-3-291)

(7-3-286)   (7-3-287)   (7-3-288)

(7-3-289)   (7-3-290)   (7-3-291)

52. Fair Lady Works at Shuttles (Four Corners) (Illustrations 7-3-292 to 7-3-312)

(7-3-292)   (7-3-293)   (7-3-294)

(7-3-295)   (7-3-296)   (7-3-297)

(7-3-298)   (7-3-299)   (7-3-300)

(7-3-301)   (7-3-302)   (7-3-303)

(7-3-304)   (7-3-305)   (7-3-306)

(7-3-307)   (7-3-308)   (7-3-309)

(7-3-310)   (7-3-311)   (7-3-312)

53. Step Up and Grasp Peacock's Tail (Illustrations 7-3-313 to 7-3-327)

(7-3-313)

(7-3-314)

(7-3-315)

(7-3-316)

(7-3-317)

(7-3-318)

(7-3-319)

(7-3-320)

(7-3-321)

(7-3-322)　　　　　　(7-3-323)　　　　　　(7-3-324)

(7-3-325)　　　　　　(7-3-326)　　　　　　(7-3-327)

54. Single Whip　　(Illustrations 7-3-328 to 7-3-332)

(7-3-328)　　　　　　(7-3-329)　　　　　　(7-3-330)

(7-3-331)   (7-3-332)

55. Wave Hands Like Moving Clouds   (Illustrations 7-3-333 to 7-3-345)

(7-3-333)   (7-3-334)   (7-3-335)

(7-3-336)   (7-3-337)   (7-3-338)

(7-3-339)

(7-3-340)

(7-3-341)

(7-3-342)

(7-3-343)

(7-3-344)

(7-3-345)

56. Single Whip　　(Illustrations 7-3-346 to 7-3-350)

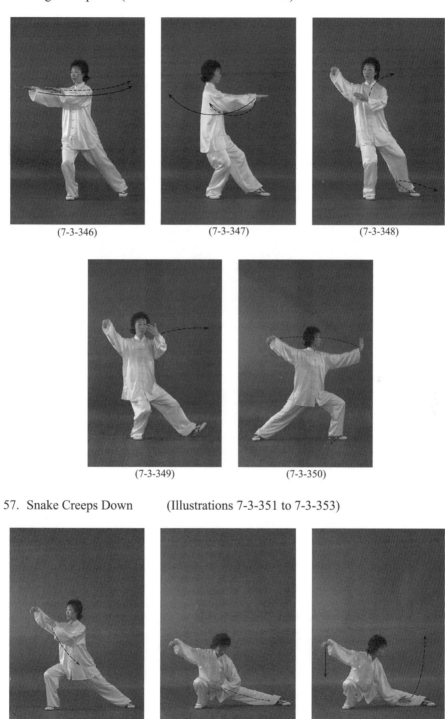

(7-3-346)　　　　　(7-3-347)　　　　　(7-3-348)

(7-3-349)　　　　　(7-3-350)

57. Snake Creeps Down　　(Illustrations 7-3-351 to 7-3-353)

(7-3-351)　　　　　(7-3-352)　　　　　(7-3-353)

58. Golden Rooster Stands on One Leg (L-R)   Illustrations 7-3-354 to 7-3-357)

(7-3-354)   (7-3-355)   (7-3-356)

(7-3-357)

59. Step Back & Repulse Monkey (L-R-L)   (Illustrations 7-3-358 to 7-3-368)

(7-3-358)   (7-3-359)   (7-3-360)

(7-3-361)　　　　　　　(7-3-362)　　　　　　　(7-3-363)

(7-3-364)　　　　　　　(7-3-365)　　　　　　　(7-3-366)

(7-3-367)　　　　　　　(7-3-368)

60. Diagonal Flying (Illustrations 7-3-369 to 7-3-372)

(7-3-369)

(7-3-370)

(7-3-371)

(7-3-372)

61. Raise Hands (Illustrations 7-3-373 to 7-3-375)

(7-3-373)

(7-3-374)

(7-3-375)

62. White Crane Spreads Its Wings   (Illustrations 7-3-376 to 7-3-378)

(7-3-376)   (7-3-377)   (7-3-378)

63. Brush Knee & Twist Step (left)   (Illustrations 7-3-379 to 7-3-383)

(7-3-379)   (7-3-380)   (7-3-381)

(7-3-382)   (7-3-383)

64. Needle at Sea Bottom　　(Illustrations 7-3-384 to 7-3-387)

(7-3-384)

(7-3-385)

(7-3-386)

(7-3-387)

65. Flash Arms　　(Illustrations 7-3-388 to 7-3-390)

(7-3-388)

(7-3-389)

(7-3-390)

268

66. White Snake Shows Its Tongue   (Illustrations 7-3-391 to 7-3-394)

(7-3-391)

(7-3-392)

(7-3-393)

(7-3-394)

67. Step Up, Parry and Punch   (Illustrations 7-3-395 to 7-3-400)

(7-3-395)

(7-3-396)

(7-3-397)

(7-3-398)　　　　　　(7-3-399)　　　　　　(7-3-400)

68. Step Up and Grasp Peacock's Tail　　　(Illustrations 7-3-401 to 7-3-411)

(7-3-401)　　　　　　(7-3-402)　　　　　　(7-3-403)

(7-3-404)　　　　　　(7-3-405)　　　　　　(7-3-406)

(7-3-407)   (7-3-408)   (7-3-409)

(7-3-410)   (7-3-411)

69. Single Whip   (Illustrations 7-3-412 to 7-3-417)

(7-3-412)   (7-3-413)   (7-3-414)

271

(7-3-415)　　　　　　(7-3-416)　　　　　　(7-3-417)

70. Wave Hands Like Moving Clouds　(Illustrations 7-3-418 to 7-3-430)

(7-3-418)　　　　　　(7-3-419)　　　　　　(7-3-420)

(7-3-421)　　　　　　(7-3-422)　　　　　　(7-3-423)

(7-3-424)　　　　　　　(7-3-425)　　　　　　　(7-3-426)

(7-3-427)　　　　　　　(7-3-428)　　　　　　　(7-3-429)

(7-3-430)

71. Single Whip   (Illustrations 7-3-431 to 7-3-434)

(7-3-431)   (7-3-432)   (7-3-433)

(7-3-434)

72. High Pat on Horse & Cross Palms   (Illustrations 7-3-435 to 7-3-439)

(7-3-435)   (7-3-436)   (7-3-437)

(7-3-438)

(7-3-439)

73. Turn and Front Kick With Right Heel   (Illustrations 7-3-440 to 7-3-442)

(7-3-440)

(7-3-441)

(7-3-442)

74. Brush Knee and Punch   (Illustrations 7-3-443 to 7-3-446)

(7-3-443)

(7-3-444)

(7-3-445)

275

(7-3-446)

75. Step Up and Grasp Peacock's Tail　　　　　(Illustrations 7-3-447 to 7-3-457)

(7-3-447)　　　　　(7-3-448)　　　　　(7-3-449)

(7-3-450)　　　　　(7-3-451)　　　　　(7-3-452)

(7-3-453) (7-3-454) (7-3-455)

(7-3-456) (7-3-457)

76. Single Whip (Illustrations 7-3-458 to 7-3-462)

(7-3-458) (7-3-459) (7-3-460)

(7-3-461)

(7-3-462)

77. Snake Creeps Down (Illustrations 7-3-463 to 7-3-465)

(7-3-463)

(7-3-464)

(7-3-465)

78. Step Up to Form Seven Stars (Illustrations 7-3-466 to 7-3-467)

(7-3-466)

(7-3-467)

79. Step Back to Ride Tiger　　　(Illustrations 7-3-468 to 7-3-471)

(7-3-468)

(7-3-469)

(7-3-470)

(7-3-471)

80. Spinning Lotus Kick　　　(Illustrations 7-3-472 to 7-3-478)

(7-3-472)

(7-3-473)

(7-3-474)

(7-3-475)

(7-3-476)

(7-3-477)

(7-3-478)

81. Draw Bow to Shoot Tiger   (Illustrations 7-3-479 to 7-3-481)

(7-3-479)

(7-3-480)

(7-3-481)

82. Step Up, Parry and Punch   (Illustrations 7-3-482 to 7-3-487)

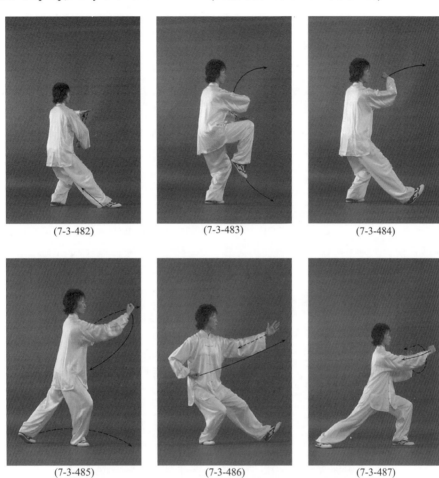

(7-3-482)   (7-3-483)   (7-3-484)

(7-3-485)   (7-3-486)   (7-3-487)

83. Apparent Closing   (Illustrations 7-3-488 to 7-3-489)

(7-3-488)   (7-3-489)

84. Cross Hands   (Illustrations 7-3-490 to 7-3-491)

(7-3-490)   (7-3-491)

85. Closing Form   (Illustrations 7-3-492 to 7-3-493)

(7-3-492)   (7-3-493)

Principle 4:   <u>Weapons Training</u>

Weapons' training is a very good way to build up internal strength and stamina. The additional weight and extension to the limbs adds a level of difficulty and increases the amount of internal strength required in Taijiquan. This type of training will also expand the *Effective Scope of Qi Shi* because of the demand for a higher level of coordination between *yi*, *qi* and *jing*.

SECTION 1*:   Lan* [攔] *(block), Na* [拿] *(grip) and Za* [扎] *(thrust) of the Spear*

Readiness position: Assume a horse stance holding the spear with both hands in front of the body pointing to your left. Complete the required adjustments of *Taiji Readiness State* to connect your *yi*, *qi* and *jing* with the spear. The spear now forms part of your body and the *Effective Scope of Qi Shi* has been expanded. Look in the same direction the spear is pointing. (Illustration.7-4-1)

(Illustration.7-4-1)

First movement: Use the *dan tian* to make a left turn and change into a left bow stance. The left hand turns in counter clockwise so that the palm faces up. At the same time, the *jing* stored in the body pushes the right hand to thrust *(Za)* the spear forward in the direction of left hand. The *jing* is projected all the way to the tip of the spear. (Illustration.7-4-2)

Second movement: Continuing from above, use the *dan tian* to make a quick right turn and revert back into a horse stance. The right hand turns counter-clockwise and quickly moves backward and up, so that the elbow points down and the palm faces away from you. At the same time, use the left hand as an anchor point to draw a half circle with the tip of spear in the *lan* position (the size of circle can be adjusted as required). (Illustration.7-4-3)

(Illustration.7-4-3)

Third movement: Continuing from above, use the *dan tian* to turn slightly left. At the same time, the right hand pushes downward to the waist area and the left hand turns clockwise with the palm facing down. The purpose of these movements from both hands is to make the spear turn in counter clockwise so the tip of the spear describes a half circle from left to the top. Slightly press the spear downward into the *na* position. (Illustration.7-4-4)

(Illustration.7-4-4)

Fourth movement: Repeat the first movement. (Illustration.7-4-5)

(Illustration.7-4-5)

All of the above movements, *lan, na* and *za* must be performed from internal to external and in continuous motion. The above exercise can be done alternating left and right sides.

SECTION 2: *Drawing Circles with the Spear*

Exercise 1: <u>Drawing a Big Circle with the Spear</u>

Readiness position: Hold the spear with both hands in front of the body in a horse stance with the spear pointing to your right. Complete the required adjustments of the *Taiji Readiness State* to connect your *yi, qi* and *jing* with the spear. Put two targets in front of you two meters distance from each other. (Illustration.7-4-6)

(Illustration.7-4-6)

First movement: Use the *dan tian* to turn right and move the body forward. Turn the right hand counter-clockwise and press down while turning the left hand and pulling up. The spear touches the body between chest and abdomen and the spear tip points at Target 1. (Illustration.7-4-7)

(Illustration.7-4-7)

Second movement: Continuing from above, the body turns left shifting the weight back. Turn the right hand clockwise and pull up. Bring the left hand up, causing the spear point to drop and touch Target 2. The spear haft touches the right chest and the tip of the spear makes a half circle between the two targets. (Illustration.7-4-8)

(Illustration.7-4-8)

The key of this exercise is that the body and the spear becoming one when performing all the movements. The movements are required to be practiced in a continuous and fluid motion. If you use *Buffalo Strength* to perform the above exercise, it will greatly increase your internal *jing*. If you do the movements at high speed it will be a very good aerobic exercise.

Exercise 2: <u>Drawing a Small Circle with the Spear</u>

Readiness position: All requirements are similar to the above exercise, except that the distance between the two targets will be reduced to one third. (Illustration.7-4-9)

(Illustration.7-4-9)

First movement: Perform the first movement in the above exercise so the tip of the spear is pointed toward Target 1. (Illustration.7-4-10) This exercise is the same as the above described Exercise 1, except for the shorter distance.

(Illustration.7-4-10)

Second movement: Perform the second movement in the above exercise so the tip of the spear is pointed toward Target 2. (Illustration.7-4-11)

(Illustration.7-4-11)

Repeat the first and second movements. You can alternate this exercise from left and right stances.

SECTION 3: *Drawing Continuous Circles with the Spear*

Readiness position: Same as above two exercises but using four targets. (Illustration.7-4-12)

(Illustration.7-4-12)

First movement: Same as above two exercises with the tip of the spear pointing toward Target 1. (Illustration.7-4-13)

(Illustration.7-4-13)

Second movement: Same as above two exercises with the tip of the spear pointing toward Target 4. (Illustration.7-4-14)

(Illustration.7-4-14)

Third movement: Same as the first movement of the above two exercises with the tip of spear describing a medium half circle, pointing to Target 2. (Illustration.7-4-15)

(Illustration.7-4-15)

Fourth movement: Same as the second movement of the above two exercises with the tip of the spear making a small half circle pointing to Target 3. (Illustration.7-4-16)

(Illustration.7-4-16)

Fifth movement: Same as the first movement of above two exercises with the tip of the spear making a medium half circle pointing to Target 1. (Illustration.7-4-17)

(Illustration.7-4-17)

This is an exercise to draw big, medium and small circles with the spear. You can also change it to different combinations of circles and change between left and right stances.

SECTION 4: *Long Pole Shaking Exercise*

Readiness position: Hold a long pole with both hands at chest height in a horse stance. Complete the required adjustments of the *Taiji Readiness State* to connect your *yi, qi* and *jing* with the staff. This will also expand your *Effective Scope of Qi Shi.* (Illustration.7-4-18)

(Illustration.7-4-18)

First movement: Make a sudden short turn of the *dan tian* to the left that causes your whole body and *Qi Shi* to *fa jing*. Bring your left hand slightly back and push your right hand slightly forward. This will thrust the tip of the staff in a left direction. (Illustration.7-4-19)

(Illustration.7-4-19)

Second movement: Create an overlapping force by moving your *dan tian* swiftly to the right before the pole tip has completed moving left. This will cause the whole body and *Qi Shi* to do a right *fa jing*. Push your left hand slightly forward and pull your right hand slightly back. This will thrust the tip of the staff to the right. (Illustration.7-4-20)

(Illustration.7-4-20)

This exercise must be done from internal to external using *spiral force*, *bouncing force* and *overlapping force*. The movements are small but swift and powerful. It is important that the external movements are caused by rotating the *dan tian* and not from using the arms.

Each overlapping movement will increase the bending of the staff, which will also require more strength to handle. This is an excellent exercise to help build up strength and stamina.

292

CHAPTER 8

Training Methods to Control the Opponent in Taijiquan

The control of an opponent in Taijiquan is based on *self-control*, use of the principle of the state of *Taiji Readiness* a person's abilities (like power, speed, reaction etc.) and the application of various martial art techniques and strategies to overcome an opponent.

Like other martial arts, Taijiquan also uses kicks, strikes, throws and joint locks (*qin na* [擒拿]) as fundamental fighting techniques. The difference, however, is that Taijiquan uses these combat techniques to not only physically defeat the opponent, but more so to manipulate and gain control over the opponent's *jing lu* with the ultimate goal to totally dominate an opponent.

Taiji's techniques to control an opponent comprise of many practice drills and training methods. For reference, the reader will be introduced below to some practical and simple examples.

SECTION 1:   Taijiquan Push-Hands - Methods and Illustrations

The previous generations of Taijiquan masters invented formalized Taijiquan push-hand exercises to practice techniques and training methods for the control of opponents more effectively. The reason behind establishing such Taiji practice methods are to raise the standard of self-control and to practice methods for the control of an opponent's *jing lu*. The practice of such drills is the foundation for achieving satisfying results when those controlling techniques are applied in a real situation.

(1) Push-Hands Exercises

Cooperative push-hands drills are exercises where two persons practice by facing each other in a proper stance with their hands in contact. They cooperate by maintaining contact through continuous body/hand movements. The goal is to deal with a partner's external force, maintain the *Taiji Readiness State* and use techniques to control the partner. Each of the various Taijiquan styles has their own push-hands theory and training methods. Below some of the more basic and practical exercise methods are introduced.

(a) Single-Handed, Horizontal Circle Exercise Method

Exercise 1: *demonstrated by Sifu Luo Hong Yuan (A) and Rex Lau (B)*

Getting Ready:
(A) at the right and (B) at the left face each other in a horse stance. Each partner rests the

left hand relaxed at the waist and the right hand extended forward to contact crosswise at the wrists (or lower forearm) area. Both maintain the *State of Taiji Readiness*. (Illustration.8-1-1)

(8-1-1)   (8-1-2)

Action 1:
Led by the *dan tian,* (A) moves and presses with his entire *Taiji Qi Shi* forward. (A)'s right hand slightly pushes forward to the right at an angle towards (B). (B) shifts his weight backwards and, at the same time, uses his right hand to lead and neutralize (A)'s force. (Illustration.8-1-2)

Action 2:
(B) initiates a right turn by spiralling the right arm slightly right while leading the force to the right. (A) responds by turning the torso left and with the right arm adhering to and following (B)'s lead to extend and spiral outward to the left. (Illustration.8-1-3)

(8-1-3)   (8-1-4)

Action 3:
(B) initiates by shifting his weight forward and extending his arm to push with his right hand. (A) shifts his weight backwards while his right hand absorbs (B)'s push. (Illustration.8-1-4)

294

Action 4:

(A) turns right, spiralling the right arm inward. (B) turns left with the right arm extended spiralling outward. (Illustration.8-1-5)

(8-1-5)

Exercise Requirements:

Both partners proscribe with their contact points a big horizontal circle. The drill can be practiced with either left or right foot lead. During practice, special attention has to be directed to maintain the *State of Taiji Readiness* (full pressure, relaxed with *qi* sunk down, and keeping the *yang* point on the inside of the arms). This drill concentrates on the *hip and arch jing*. Both partners sink their *qi* and *jing* down to their waist and *kwa* [胯] area (hip) to a create a strong *hip and arch jing*. All movements should start from the *dan tian*. Using *gu dang jing,* the pressure vibrates sequentially, section by section, outwards in a spiral fashion.

All the following exercises have these same requirements.

(b) Single Handed Vertical Circles

Getting Ready:

(A) and (B) face each other, assuming a horse stance with the right foot placed forward and both connecting their right hands crosswise at their wrists in an upward arc. The left hand rests relaxed at the waist. (Illustration.8-1-6)

(8-1-6)

(8-1-7)

Action 1:

(B) initiates the move by turning the torso to the right and simultaneously leads by spiralling the right arm inward. (A) adheres and follows (B) with a left turn of the torso aided by the right arm spiralling outward, then extending left. (Illustration.8-1-7)

Action 2:

(B) initiates by sinking down and pushing down with the right hand. (A) sticks to and follows (B)'s downward movement while (B)'s the right hand continues to lead down. (Illustration.8-1-8)

(8-1-8)

(8-1-9)

Action 3:

(A) initiates a right turn with his torso whereby the right arm spirals inward leading to the right. (B) responds by turning his torso left with the right arm spiralling outward and extending to the left. (Illustration.8-1-9)

(8-1-10)

Action 4:

(A) initiates by an upwards motion of the body, with the right hand pushing up. (B) adheres to and follows (A)'s upward motion. (Illustration.8-1-10)

Exercise Requirements:

Both partners' contact point moves in a big vertical circle in front of their bodies. The drill can be practiced with either a left or right foot lead. The key is to maintain the *hip and arch jing* during all upward, downward and turning motions.

(c) Double Handed, Push-Hands Exercises

Getting Ready:
Similar as before, except that both partners are in a higher stance with their weight shifted backwards, their right wrists in contact and adhering to each other. (Illustration.8-1-11)

(8-1-11)

(8-1-12)

Action 1:
(B), on the left, initiates by shifting his weight forward. All four hands are in contact and are intertwined to perform a pressing action (*ji* [挤]). The right hand is placed in front, with the palm facing inward, (B)'s left hand rests on (A)'s right lead arm with the palm facing downward. (A) remains in his back stance, with the weight resting on his rear left leg. (A)'s hands rest lightly on (B)'s left elbow and wrist area. (Illustration.8-1-12)

(8-1-13)

(8-1-14)

Action 2:
(B)'s right forearm follows (A)'s left forward and downward extended forearm with his palm facing down. (Illustration.8-1-13)

Action 3:

(A) initiates a forward motion by slowly pushing with both separated hands on (B)'s upper forearm/elbow joints. (B) transfers his weight to the rear foot and follows (A)'s push with his right hand placed at (A)'s left elbow joint area. (B)'s left hand remains in contact with (A)'s left wrist. (Illustration. 8-1-14)

Action 4:

(A) moves by shifting his center forward into a bow stance. Again, (A)'s two hands perform *ji* with the left hand in front, the palm facing inwards towards the center line. The right hand connects to the top of (B)'s left forearm, the palm facing downward. (B) follows by continuing to sit back on his left hind leg and his both hands remain lightly pushing at (A)'s right elbow and wrist. (Illustration.8-1-15)

(8-1-15)

(8-1-16)

Action 5:

(A)'s left forearm follows (B)'s right forearm which is extended forward and downward with the palm facing down. (Illustration.8-1-16)

(8-1-17)

(8-1-18)

Action 6:

(B)'s centre shifts forward, both hands perform a light forward push which is directed upwards at (A)'s right elbow and wrist. (A) adheres to this push and neutralizes the push by sitting back on the hind left leg while (A)'s left hand still adheres lightly to (B)'s right elbow. (Illustration.8-1-17)

Action 7:
(B) goes into a right bow stance with both hands in *ji* mode, while (A) sits back to neutralize and his hands press down (*an* [按]) at (B)'s forearm. (Illustration.8-1-18)

Exercise Requirements:
During the repeated circular movements of back and forth, pushing and squeezing between the two partners, special attention must be paid to being relaxed, continuously adjusting the balance between a solid and empty stance, and sinking the *jing* to the *dan tian*. Although some movements appear straight and square, keep the motion round during the continuous flowing movement. Once familiar with this exercise, one should try to get the feeling and overall concept of the *dan tian*-generated explosive and rippling effect of the *jing* (especially the *chan si jing*), which develops from Taijiquan's *Qi Shi* centre.

(d) Double Handed Push-hands Exercises (Ninety Degrees Stance)

Getting ready:
(A) leads with the right leg and sinks into a horse stance, with the right arm extended and the palm facing up. The left hand is placed in front of the right shoulder. (B) extends his left leg and steps to the outside of (A)'s right leg. (B)'s left knee contacts against (A)'s right knee. (B)'s right hand touches the wrist of (A)'s extended right arm. (B)'s left hand connects with (A)'s upper right arm. (Illustration.8-1-19)

(8-1-19)

(8-1-20)

Action 1:
(A) turns his torso right into a bow stance with the left arm performing a forward *ji*. [ ] (A)'s right hand follows (B)'s left extended arm, reaches downward with the palm facing downward. (B) follows (A)'s action with a slight turn to the left. (B)'s left wrist adheres to (A)'s left wrist in a cross-handed fashion. (B)'s right palm lightly pushes on (A)'s left elbow. (Illustration.8-1-20)

Action 2:

(A) turns left with his left hand lightly grabbing (B)'s left wrist and his right forearm adhering in a cutting fashion to the mid section of (B)'s left forearm. (A) then initiates a lead to the left. (B) follows this motion by turning the torso right which starts to carry his now extended left arm spiralling outward. (B)'s right hand is in front of his own left shoulder. (Illustration.8-1-21)

(8-1-21)

(8-1-22)

Action 3:

(A) continues turning left and to sink his torso at the same time both hands perform a downward pull (*lu* [履]) to the side. (B) continues to turn his torso to the left and to extend his left arm. (Illustration.8-1-22)

Action 4:

(B) turns left into a bow stance. The left forearm follows (A)'s extended right arm to reach downward with his palm facing down. Simultaneously, (B)'s bent right arm moves in front of his chest and performs *ji*. At the same moment, (A) turns his torso right places his hands at (B)'s right elbow and wrist. (Illustration.8-1-23)

(8-1-23)

(8-1-24)

Action 5:

(B)turnshistorsoright.Hisrighthandlightlygrabs(A)'srightwristandsimultaneouslyplaces his left hand on the mid-section of (A)'s right upper arm to initiate *lu*. (Illustration.8-1-24)

Action 6:

(B) continues his right turn and sinks into a horse stance. His right hand lightly grabs (A)'s right wrist and his left hand is lightly placed at the mid section of (A)'s upper right arm. (A) follows by turning his torso left and lowers his stance. (A) leads and pulls his right arm while placing his left hand in front of his right shoulder. (Illustration.8-1-25)

(8-1-25)

Exercise Requirements:

These movements require a more demanding level of *hip and arch jing* and a higher intensity and quality of exercising. While the upper body performs circling and *chan si jing* movements, the lower limbs are required to simultaneously adhere, yield and stabilize. These drills are the foundation training for future controlling of the opponent's legs and the development of throws and other take down techniques.

(2) *Question and Answer* Training Method

Question and Answer is a system of two-person exercises where one person constantly changes force, direction and speed and the other person has to interpret the signal through the contact point and react appropriately. In the *question and answer* exercises the person who sends out a signal is *questioning* and the one who responds with changes is *answering*. The person who actively sends out different signals challenges the person who is answering to respond appropriately to the signal and to try to avoid resistance. The answerer should follow and stick to the sender's body movement without separation and gradually master the ability of *fast action is met by fast response, slow action is met by slow response. If the opponent does not move, I do not move, and upon his slightest move, I have already started within.* The *question and answer* training method is the self-examination of one's *Taiji Readiness State* and the ability to adapt and change one's *jing lu* to ever-changing situations. The goal is to improve one's sensitivity by listening to the opponent and also to learn how to increase one's speed to react appropriately.

(a) Listening _Jing_ (_ting jing_) [聽勁])

Ting jing describes a kind of training method where the opponent gets a question through the hand's contact point to read a movement's direction, force and speed. Through the contact point one listens to an opponent's changes. By this kind of practice, skin sensitivity and the judgment of the brain is developed. Requirements for this practice are relaxation, full concentration, calmness, light touch and flowing movements. Another requirement is to develop _stillness in motion_ in order to gradually improve one's sensitivity. Finally one reaches a level of sensitivity that is so high that the right reaction is triggered when a feather or a fly lands on the contact point.

Through the practice of contact drills where the forearms are in constant touch, the _ting jing_ will develop eventually. _Ting jing_ will help to feel the extent of an opponent's _questioning jing_ that pertains to strength, weakness, speed, and direction. By using one's mind (_yi_), an opponent's movements can be sensed through the contact of the skin and one can direct one's _qi_ flow accordingly. These drills train agility and sensitivity. The use of brute or mechanical strength in one's movements must be avoided. Therefore, a relaxed, yet very mentally alert and focused mind is crucial. One's quiet response should follow as a logical result to an opponent's initiative, but although one's move is started later it accomplishes its purpose earlier and faster. One's overall sensitivity is so high that even _the landing of feather's weight on you_ cannot escape of being noticed.

(b) Proper Internal Adjustments and Response

The way of how to react appropriately after receiving a reaction from an opponent, forms the key part of the "Question and Answer" method for push hand exercises. Normal people get used to get a signal via the contact point and then they instantly react from the hand. However, in Taijiquan training a like response (in a saying it is referred to as "reaction from the branch") would result in a mistake and is therefore not permitted. How shall it be done properly? Master Luo Ji Hong said: _Jing must react and change from the inside of the body_. Such changes include the target, direction, root, speed, hardness and softness, light and heavy etc. In this way, _you can know yourself and know your opponent_, and the principle _my opponent does not know me, but I know everything_ will apply. This kind of _kung fu_ is also known as _understanding and knowing jing_. In the Taiji Classic _Song of the 13 Postures_, it advises the reader to pay attention to the _mind controlling the body_ and that change should start from the waist. If you continuously focus on your waist area, then you control your _dan tian_ with calmness and stillness but your _qi_ is like boiling water. Thus, body adjustments result from changes emanating from the _dan tian_. The _dan tian_ is the original starting center of _Qi Shi_. Through the contact point you receive a signal; through the signal you go through the _dan tian_ changing procedure, and then you adjust your whole body and _Qi Shi_. _Dan tian_ changes include movements in all directions and rotation. The intensity of the response depends on the opponent's signal. The _dan tian_ movement creates adjustments throughout the body. It is the basis of _Qi Shi_ vibration, spiral _jing_ and prepares for the storage of _jing_ (_chui jing_ [蓄勁]) and explosive _jing_ (_fa jing_). The _dan tian's_ internal changes require one to be very stable and to conceal them from the opponent. When the _dan tian_ is adjusting, the contact point with the opponent should maintain in stillness. Don't let the opponent feel the internal change. Somebody once described this kind of _ting jing kung fu_ as _the spirit of decision-making comes from knowing_. Applied internal adjustment can be described as _your strategy must stay hidden_.

302

Internal adjustments are practiced by first doing the simple repeating pattern, which was described above together with all the basic push-hands patterns. Upon advancing to a higher level of skill and when mastering one or two handed patterns you can combine them. The person doing the questioning can change the movement any time. Finally the drill can be done without any pattern, like a freestyle question and answer method. This level of training it is close to a real push-hands encounter.

In two-person exercises, one can do the questioning, the other the answering and then switch. During the exercises both partners should communicate, test each other's accuracy and give the partner feed-back right away.

In the context of push-hands, a vital question would be how to react appropriately after receiving questioning signals. Normally, an untrained person reacts using only the hands, which is contrary to Taiji principles. So what is the proper answer? Master Luo Ji Hong once said; *your jing should start from within you at the dan tian and move through sequential changes.*

(3) *Buffalo Strength* Training

Buffalo Strength training is an auxiliary exercise to develop special skills and *peng jing* (spring-like, elastic power).

The *Question and Answer* training is for developing a quick response trigger. *'If you rely only on the quick response in push-hands and lack internal power you are only doing passive without active, you have a light weapon without a heavy weapon and it is hard to move your opponent or do a clean fa jing. On the other hand you will be moved by the opponent easily'* (Gu Liu Xin's in his book '*Chen Style Taijiquan*', page 264). During the push-hands exercises one should practice *Buffalo Strength*, which is a heavy, elastic, tough, spring-like *jing*. It is often called *peng jing*. *Buffalo Strength* push-hands require both partners to build up their pressure and perform the training pattern, until their body reaches the state of *peng jing*. This method of push-hands exercise not only improves your level of neutralization but also increases your *jing* efficiently. This is a very important part of Taiji push-hands.

In general, *Buffalo Strength* push-hands exercises use the technique of *feeding jing* (*wei jing* [喂劲]). To establish the correct pressure level, the one with the greater internal strength (*jing*) of the two must use the method of feeding *jing*, whereby he should adjust his internal force level to his/her partner's *jing* level. If both partners possess an equal potential of *jing*, the push-hands training should be carried on by each fully loaded.

As in the *question and answer* push-hands practice, the *Buffalo Strength* push-hands method first trains different specific patterns. Once all these patterns are familiar, they should be combined and finally practiced as exercises which are not bound to any particular pattern. If the transfer of *jing* in this type of *Buffalo Strength* push-hands is steady, heavy and sinking, the Taiji *Readiness State* must be maintained. Depending on the opponent, one's responses must use the necessary amount of *jing* to achieve the desired effect.

In a real push-hands situation, *Buffalo Strength* is a very heavy, frightening weapon. It is also a good method to test the level of your partner's push-hands ability. Before touching hands, adjust the intensity of your internal pressure. If the opponent is unable to neutralize after receiving *jing*, or loses contact or is being controlled, use a clear technique to *fa jing*. According to the Taiji Classic's; *if I feel a loose contact (diu [丢]) I must hit (fa jing), and execute with a clean technique. If the opponent can still follow my change, I will react to the opponent's jing, adapt and keep trying.*

SECTION 2:   Control of the *Jing Lu* - Techniques and Illustrations

When sparring, one has to be able to adapt and change every technique instantly as a situation can change within a split second. Under such volatile sparring situations, what techniques can be used to achieve victory? All styles of martial arts must address this issue.

In Taijiquan, the answer lies, in part, through the control of an opponent's *jing lu* thus causing the opponent to lose control of self and the ability to move. Methods of controlling the *jing lu* are *chuan jing*, *na jing* and *fa jing*[1].

(1) *Chuan Jing* Training and Illustrations

Exercise 1: *demonstrated by Sifu Luo Hong Yuan (A) and Fan Zhang (B)*

Getting Ready:
(A) on the right and (B) on the left stand facing each other. (A) assumes the Taiji *Readiness State* and imposes his *yi* on the opponent (B). *Qi* accumulates at the *dan tian* and the internal pressure is up and ready for action. (Illustration.8-2-1)

(8-2-1)   (8-2-2)

Action 1:
(A) and (B) both step forward with the right foot and initiate contact. (B) extends his right hand while (A) lightly adheres to (B)'s extended hand at the wrist and elbow area. (A) initiates the *Qi Shi* from the *dan tian* and moves forward, while always keeping his *yi*

---

[1] see Chapter 6

on sinking the *qi* down and collecting at the *dan tian* for stability. The overall appearance is light on the top (*yin*) and heavy at the bottom (*yang*) while *qi* is directed along the *bone line*. This is the readiness state of stored *jing*. (Illustration.8-2-2)

Action 2:
Leading with fully elastic pressure that originates in the *dan tian*, (A) moves and presses forward to take advantage of (B) who is not ready to emit *jing*. (A) uses an upward *peng jing*, first aiming at the *dai zhui* acupuncture point between the shoulder blades to lock up (B)'s shoulder joint and then follows up the momentum with a downward *jing* directed at the *ming men* which causes (B)'s spine to lock up at the waist area. (Illustration.8-2-3)

(8-1-3)   (8-2-4)

Exercise 2:

Getting Ready:
Use the same preparatory process as mentioned in the previous exercise. (Illustration.8-2-4)

Action 1:
(A) and (B) initiate contact like in the previous exercise. (Illustration.8-2-5)

(8-2-5)   (8-2-6)

Action 2:

(B) initiates by directing a forward pressing action at (A). (A) responds by leading from his *dan tian*, turning right and sitting back slightly, first to lead (B)'s oncoming *jing* into emptiness. Then (A) aims at (B)'s *dai zhui* to take control of and lock (B)'s right arm/shoulder by pulling centrifugally. As a result this pull effect is extended to (B)'s *ming men* and thereby locks (B)'s spine at the *dan tian*. (Illustration.8-2-6)

Exercise 3:

Action 1:

(A) on the left and (B) on the right each use their right hand to *an* (push down) at each other's left upper arm. Each opponent uses his left hand attached to the opponent's right arm just above the elbow area. (Illustration.8-2-7)

(8-1-7)

(8-1-8)

Action 2:

(B) moves his right leg forward and positions it between (A)'s legs and simultaneously increases his right hand push. (Illustration.8-2-8)

Action 3:

(A) yields and advances by a combination of sinking his torso and turning his waist left. The left turn moves both of (A)'s arms along, whereby the right hand pushes (B)'s to the opposite direction. (A)'s left hand has a pull effect on (B)' right arm. (A)'s right hand pushes forward in a press-push manner to lock (B)'s left torso and simultaneously (A)'s left hand spirally pulls at (B)'s right hand to lock (B)'s right torso. This action is applied using two different *jings* at (B)'s body. (Illustration.8-2-9)

(8-2-9)

Exercise Requirements:

When applying the principles of *chuan jing*, use a well timed *qang jing* to connect to opponent's joints, just as the opponent's *jing lu* is about to take action. In the event that the opponent has already started to expand his/her *jing*, apply *lead and stretch jing* (*yin jing*) to lead an opponent into a controlled situation. While performing this action maintains the Taiji *Readiness State* at all times. This means your *qi* should be collected and focused, your *jing* preserved and stored up to lay down the foundations to apply *na jing* and *fa jing* later.

(2) *Na Jing* Training and Illustrations

Excercise 1: *demonstrated by Sifu Luo Hong Yuan (A) and Fan Zhang (B)*

Action 1:
(A) on the right and (B) assume their preparatory stance in their usual contact posture. (Illustration.8-2-10)

(8-2-10)

(8-2-11)

307

Action 2:

(A) moves his whole body forward and uses his right hand to immobilize (B)'s right wrist. (A)'s left hand adheres tightly to push (B)'s right upper arm. The idea is to lock (B)'s joint at the *dai zhui* and ultimately lead to locking of the *ming men*. (Illustration.8-2-11)

Action 3:

On following through with the above action, (A) turns slightly right, using his both hands to guide (B)'s right arm and upper torso. The action first connects to the *dai zhui* and then the *ming men* and then twists the *main bow* (spine) by a clockwise action leading to bend and control (B)'s *jing lu*. (Illustration.8-2-12)

(8-2-12)

Exercise 2: *demonstrated by Sifu Luo Hong Yuan (A) and Fan Zhang (B)*

Action 1:
(A) and (B) assume the preparatory pose as before. (Illustration.8-2-13)

(8-2-13)   (8-2-14)

Action 2:

(A) moves forward and pushes with both hands upwards at (B) thereby connecting to (B)'s *dai zhui* and *ming men*. (Illustration.8-2-14)

Action 3:

After (A) connected to (B)'s *jing lu*, (A) continues to turn right and thereby locks (B) causing (B)'s body to twist clockwise using the *dai zhui* as a pivot. When the *dai zhui* starts moving (A) moves down to use the *ming men* as a pivot to bend and control (B). (Illustration.8-2-15)

(8-2-15)

Exercise 3: *demonstrated by Sifu Luo Hong Yuan (A) and Richard Anderson Omura (B)*

Action 1:

(B) on the right moves forward with a right hand push. (A) uses his right hand to grab (B)'s right wrist and put his left hand on (B)'s elbow. (A) follows the momentum leading to a connection situation. (Illustration.8 -2-16)

(8-2-16)

(8-2-17)

Action 2: (A) moves his left foot forward to trap (B)'s right knee from behind and simultaneously uses *spiral jing* to twist (A)'s right wrist and elbow inward thus reversely locking up (A)'s joints and seizing his *jing lu*. (Illustration.8-2-17)

Action 3:
(B) struggles to escape from the joint locking action and counters with an outward right spiral turn, by simultaneously turning his right upper arm outward and sinking his elbow. (Illustration.8-2-18)

| (8-2-18) | (8-2-19) |

Action 4:
(A) turns his torso to the right taking advantage of (B)'s turning momentum. (A) grabs (B)'s right arm and extends (B)'s hand which is adhering to (A)'s chest. (A)'s left hand, in the meantime fills up with *jing* and will act like a knife cutting forward at (B)'s elbow, while his left knee continues to push (B)'s right calf down. (A) uses his whole body *jing* to totally lock (B)'s *jing lu* in the wrist, elbow, shoulder, waist and the knee. (Illustration.8-2-19)

Exercise 4: *demonstrated by Sifu Luo Hong Yuan (A) and Richard Anderson Omura (B)*

Action 1:
(A) advances his right leg to immediately immobilize (B)'s left leg, and uses his right hip to lock (B)'s waist. (A)'s right upper arm and left lower arm join together to lock (B)'s neck. (A) uses his left hand to tightly hold on to his own right hand, thus reinforcing the power of his arms. (A) now turns and pulls with his both arms downwards towards the ground, supported by his whole body which is directed downwards and using the momentum to create a tremendous clamping down force center directed at (B)'s heart. The resulting effect is the control of (B)'s main bow. (Illustration. 8-2-20)

Action 2:
As a follow through of the above move, (A) directs the *dan tian* to sink and turn left, thus creating a downward spiral *jing* that totally locks up (B) section by section. (Illustration. 8-2-21)

310

(8-2-20)   (8-2-21)

(3) *Fa Jing* Training and Illustrations

Using *chuan jing* and *na jing* to control opponent's *jing lu* should help to create a situation of "*I feel very comfortable and in control, but you are being controlled by me*". This situation can be used for a timely *fa jing* technique to completely and totally control an opponent's *jing lu* or push him away as a completion of the controlling of the *jing lu* procedure. United together, effectively and sequentially in a timely manner, *chuan jing, na jing* and *fa jing* are the keys to controlling an opponent in Taijiquan.

Exercise 1: *demonstrated by Sifu Luo Hong Yuan (A) and Fan Zhang (B)*

Action 1:
(A) on the left and (B) stand facing each other and connect with their right hands touching cross handed at the wrist area. (Illustration.8-2-22)

(8-2-22)   (8-2-23)

Action 2:
(B) on the right initiates a push forward and (A) on the left responds by moving and sitting backwards leading this push upward to neutralize this action. (A) uses *lead and stretch jing* (*yin jing*) to connect to and lock (B). (Illustration.8-2-23)

311

Action 3:

(A) sinks his torso down and turns right. His right hand pushes downward and utilizes *na jing*, which causes (B) to tilt and bend forward. (Illustration.8-2-24)

(8-2-24)

(8-2-25)

Action 4:

Following next, (A) takes advantage of having locked (B)'s *jing lu* and uses a sudden drop down of (B) by pulling him with his right hand down and at the same time pushing him with his left hand down (*cai jing*), which causes (B) to quickly fall down. (Illustration.8-2-25)

Exercise 2: *demonstrated by Sifu Luo Hong Yuan (A) and Fan Zhang (B)*

Action 1:

(A) at the left and (B) each use their right hand to grasp the others' left upper arm. The left hands adhere to the outside of the right arm. (Illustration.8-2-26)

(8-2-26)

(8-2-27)

Action 2:

(A) sinks his torso down and simultaneously turns left. Both hands open up whereby (A) uses a forward and upward *qang jing* to connect to and lock (B). Simultaneously his left hand recedes downward and uses *lead and stretch jing* (*yin jing*) to lock (B). (Illustration.8-2-27)

312

Action 3:

(A) moves his left leg a small half step forward, turns his torso right with his right hand smoothly resting on (B)'s left shoulder forming the shape of a hook and starts to pull (B) downward. Simultaneously (A)'s left hand stretches (B)'s right hand and extends it by pushing it left and upward. Both *jings* applied on (B), make his body twist and bend by using the *ming men* as supporting/pivot point. (Illustration. 8-2-28)

(8-2-28)

(8-2-29)

Action 4:

(A) uses (B)'s forward leaning position and momentum to quickly emit *fa jing* which causes (B) to fall down. (Illustration.8-2-29)

Exercise 3: *demonstrated by Sifu Luo Hong Yuan (A) and Fan Zhang (B)*

Action 1:

(A) at the right and (B) face each other with both arms in contact. (Illustration. 8-2-30)

(8-2-30)

(8-2-31)

Action 2:

(A) turns quickly to the left and steps with his right foot forward in between (B)'s legs (*dang*). (A)'s right hand is placed under (B)'s right armpit. (A)'s right arm moves forward and upward to achieve *chuan jing* and at the same time he pulls (B)'s right arm towards his stomach. (Illustration.8-2-31)

Action 3:
(A) now turns his torso to the right and sinks down. Both hands grab (B)'s right arm to apply *na jing* and thus cause (B) to bend forward by using his *ming men* as supporting/pivot point. (Illustration. 8-2-32)

(8-2-32)

(8-2-33)

Action 4:
(A) continues his right turning motion and suddenly emits *fa jing* clockwise, sending (B) away. (Illustration. 8-2-33)

Exercise 4: *demonstrated by Sifu Luo Hong Yuan (A) and Fan Zhang (B)*

Action 1:
Both (A) at the right and (B) face each other, both with their right hands in crosswise contact. (Illustration. 8-2-34)

(8-2-34)

(8-2-35)

Action 2:
(A) suddenly turns his torso left and at the same time executes shaking power (*dou jing*) while (A)'s right arm continues to extend forward and upward. (Illustration. 8-2-35)

314

Action 3:

(A) pushes with his whole body forward by taking a right forward step between (B)'s legs (*dang*) and hits (B)'s right inside thigh with his knee. (A) keeps his body moving forward, fills his arms with *jing* and forces (B)'s upper body to bend backwards resulting in *na jing*. (Illustration.8-2-36)

(8-2-36)   (8-2-37)

Action 4: Quickly following Action 3, (A)'s *dan tian* emits a *gu dang jing* which follows his hip and shoulder to emit an explosive strike (*kao jing [*靠劲*]*) as (B) is sent flying back. (Illustration.8-2-37)

SECTION 3: Techniques and Training Methods for Kicking, Hand Strikes and Throwing

Kicks and hand strikes are an important part of Taijiquan's control of the opponent. Unfortunately, recent Taiji generations paid more attention to the form and push-hands training and ignored the training of kicks and hand strikes. This seriously affected the inheritance of Taijiquan's art from one generation to the other. Taijiquan's kicking and hand strike techniques are based on Taiji's "Readiness State", use of the advantage of Taiji's internal power (*jing*) and speed. In a real situation the complete procedure of techniques, *chuan*, *na* and *fa jing* is applied at the first moment of contact with the opponent. Kicks and strikes are used to control the opponent. Once the opponent is under control, one's kicking and striking can be more effective. Kicking and striking, together with the control of the *jing lu* is a perfect combination and a Taijiquan specialty.

(1) Taiji's State of Readiness

Achieving the Taiji State of Readiness *before* contact with an opponent is crucial. From the ideal State of Readiness one is able to react instantly; effectively making use of one's techniques while preventing the opponent from using his.

Taiji readiness creates a strong internal pressure in form of stored energy. This *chui jing* creates stability within, is not visible to an outsider and expresses itself through calmness.

Externally, this State of Readiness gives one the demeanour of an eagle following the rabbit or a cat ready to catch a mouse. A strong State of Readiness creates an *effective scope of control*. Once an opponent enters this *effective scope of control,* he/she is covered or controlled by this spirit, *yi* and *qi*. In the process of creating the Taiji State of Readiness the *bows* are loaded (like a pulled back bow is ready to release the arrow). No further adjustments are necessary in order to strike. The following examples help illustrate the Taiji State of Readiness.

Demonstrated by Sifu Luo Hong Yuan (A) and Richard Anderson Omura (B)

Example 1
(A) on the right and (B) on the left face each other at a fixed distance. Invisibly, (A) adjusts internally into the State of Readiness that will put him into an upright posture, being totally ready to act and alert to all of his surroundings. His *Qi Shi* is fully pressurized, sunk and concentrated in the *dan tian*. (A) is now ready for motion and waiting to *fa jing*. (A) waits quietly for (B)'s initial move, while placing (B) under his *effective scope of control* to be able to effectively capture any signal sent out by (B). (Illustration.8-3-1)

(8-3-1)

(8-3-2)

Example 2
In a continuation of the scenario developed in Example 1, (A) maintains the state of *effective scope of control*. By applying Taiji's total focus and leading by the *dan tian*, (A) mobilizes his *Qi Shi* to press directly forward and overwhelm (B). This causes (B) to step back slower than (A)'s advance. (B) is now in (A)'s effective striking range and (A) can prepare to act. (Illustration.8-3-2)

Example 3
Further to Examples 1 and 2, (B) is now pressing forward. Led by the *dan tian*, (A) adjusts the center of his *effective scope of Qi Shi*, and shifts backwards, thus creating in front of (B) sort of a vacuum causing a negative drawing pressure. If (B) would continue to advance forward, he would be drawn in by this negative pressure and get a feeling of *the more one goes forward; the more steps are needed to reach the target*. (Illustration.8-3-3)

(8-3-3)

Summary:

The creation of Taiji's Readiness State and its subsequent adjustments is achieved by *qi directing the body*. The *jing* produces a vibrating and spiralling "internal movement" inside the body. It is created by a pressure differential which accumulates at the *dan tian*. As a first step, assume the basic Taiji readiness posture, which is continuously adjusted in accordance to the signals telegraphed by your opponent and consequently allows for following up with accurate and effective responses.

(2) Training and Illustrations for Kicking

Exercise 1: *demonstrated by Sifu Luo Hong Yuan (A) and Richard Anderson Omura (B)*

Action 1:

(A) at the right and (B) on the left stand to face each other. (A) has assumed Taiji's Readiness State, collected his *jing* and covers (B) with his *effective scope of control*. (Illustration.8-3-4)

(8-3-4)

(8-3-5)

Action 2:

Before (B) can react, (A) quickly emits *fa jing* with a sidekick that is directed to the outside area of (B)'s hip and connects all the way up to (B)'s *ming men*. This action causes (B)'s *jing lu* to be disrupted at the *ming men*. This type of kick uses *chuan jing* to connect to the *ming men*, *na jing* to lockup the hip joint, and *fa jing* to disrupt the *jing lu*. (Illustration.8-3-5)

317

Exercise 2: *demonstrated by Sifu Luo Hong Yuan (A) and Richard Anderson Omura (B)*

Action 1:
(A) at the left and (B) stand facing each other, both assuming a right-lead posture. (Illustration.8-3-6)

(8-3-6)

(8-3-7)

Action 2:
Using his *Qi Shi*, (A) initiates a right side kick to (B)'s right side chest and armpit area. Because (A)'s kick was directed by his *Qi Shi*, the impact is magnified and results in the disruption of (B)'s *jing lu* at the *ming men*. (Illustration.8-3-7)

Exercise 3: *demonstrated by Sifu Luo Hong Yuan (A) and Richard Anderson Omura (B)*

Action 1:
(A) on the left and (B) on the right face each other in a left forward stance. (Illustration.8-3-8)

(8-3-8)

(8-3-9)

Action 2:
(A) suddenly performs a left kick, striking and sealing (B)'s left knee from the side. This action would not only damage (B)'s the left knee joint but also disrupt (B)'s *jing lu* up to his *ming men*. (Illustration.8-3-9)

318

Exercise 4: *demonstrated by Sifu Luo Hong Yuan (A) and Richard Anderson Omura (B)*

Action 1:
(A) on the left and (B) on the right face each other in a left forward stance. (Illustration.8-3-10)

| (8-3-10) | (8-3-11) |

Action 2:
(A) takes advantage of (B) not having made any movement, and initiates a left thrust kick at (B)'s left knee. (Illustration.8-3-11)

Action 3:
If (B) tries to retreat, (A) immediately steps his left foot down and switches to kick with his right foot forward and upwards at (B)'s left upper arm/shoulder area. This action should lock up (B)'s joint at the arm and shoulder area, momentarily seizing his *jing lu*. (Illustration. 8-3-12)

(8-3-12)

Summary:
There are many kicking techniques and here we introduced only a few simple sidekick methods. Regardless of the techniques used, the key requirements are to connect (*chuan*), lock (*na*), and control of the opponent's *jing lu*.

319

(3) <u>Training and Illustrations for Hand Strikes</u>

Exercise 1: *demonstrated by Sifu Luo Hong Yuan (A) and Richard Anderson Omura (B)*

Action 1:
Basic movements for striking targets by hand: (B) on the left puts up both hands vertically with his palms facing forward and filled with *jing* (a boxing target can also be used). (A), on the right gets ready (Taiji Readiness State) to strike. (Illustration.8-3-13)

(8-3-13)   (8-3-14)

Action 2:
Led by his *dan tian*, (A) moves his *Qi Shi* forward and at the same time performs a right turn with his waist and throws a straight punch with *chan si jing* at (B)'s palm or target. Because this punch is carried out with *Qi Shi* to create the impact, although the fist has already hit the target, the body is still moving forward to increase the speed of the strike and the time on the target. At the same time, your mind guides the *jing* through the target all the way up to the *dai zhui* and then to the *ming men.* This force causes (B)'s main bow to get connected, locked, twisted left and bent. (Illustration.8-3-14)

Action 3:
(A) follows up with a sudden sharp turn to the left to perform a right hand punch at (B)'s left hand. By using his whole-body force (*jing*) (A) locks up and seizes (B)'s *jing lu*. (Illustration.8-3-15)

(8-3-15)

Exercise 2: *demonstrated by Sifu Luo Hong Yuan (A) and Richard Anderson Omura (B)*

Action 1:
(A) on the right and (B) face each other by standing at a distant range. (Illustration.8-3-16)

(8-3-16)

(8-3-17)

Action 2:
In a swift forward move (A) performs *fa jing* with his right hand to grasp (B)'s left hand and press down. Simultaneously (A) uses his left palm to strike at (B)'s left jaw/face. The momentum from this thrust against (B)'s head would move to the *dai zhui* and lock up (B)'s main bow (spine). (Illustration. 8-3-17)

Exercise 3: *demonstrated by Sifu Luo Hong Yuan (A) and Richard Anderson Omura (B)*

Action 1:
(A) on the left and (B) stand in a bow stance facing each other. (B) raises both hands with his palms directed forward and advances. (A) adjusts his *Qi Shi* backwards to lead (B) into emptiness. (Illustration. 8-3-18)

(8-3-18)

(8-3-19)

Action 2:
(B) takes a left step forward and continues to advance. (A) seizes the moment as (B) steps forward. He suddenly directs his *Qi Shi* forward to create an explosive shaking force (*dou jing*). (A) then uses his left hand to jab at (B)'s right palm, causing (B)'s torso to bend backwards. (A) seals (B)'s left hand by extending his whole body forward and

at the same time extending his left forearm. (Illustration.8-3-19)

Action 3:
Following up, (A) quickly turns left and throws a right punch, using his right arm to press downward and seal (B)'s upper left arm, while his right fist strikes at (B)'s face/neck causing a lock up and distortion to (B)'s main bow. (Illustration.8-3-20)

(8-3-20)

Summary:
There are countless ways to carry out various striking techniques. Very often, however, the simplest methods turn out to be the most effective and practical. In Taijiquan, regardless of what striking techniques are used, one is always required to utilize Taiji's *Qi Shi* to create a *jing* force all over your body. Therefore, in striking, there is *chuan* and *na*. Strikes and the control of an opponent's *jing lu* are coordinated to achieve a more effective control.

(4) Training Illustrations for Throwing Techniques

Exercise 1: *demonstrated by Sifu Luo Hong Yuan (A) and Richard Anderson Omura (B)*

Action 1:
(A) at the right, steps forward with his right foot and traps (B)'s left foot. (A) then uses his right hip to press against (B)'s left waist and hip area. Now (A) wraps his right arm around (B)'s neck, joins both hands to form a headlock. (A) now pulls his arms down to together with his body's pressing forward motion to connect and lock (B)'s spine. (Illustration.8-4-1)

Action 2:
(B) tries to resist and escape. (A) increases the downward pressure on (B)'s hip and continues to keep his two arms tightly wrapped around (B)'s neck. (A) then pull's (B)'s spinal column up but continues to press his hip on (B)'s hip to the effect that (B)'s main bow is stretched in opposite directions. (Illustration.8-4-2)

(8-4-1)

(8-4-2)

Action 3:

After *chuan* and *na* (B)'s body and *jing lu*, (A) now quickly spiral's his torso to the left and simultaneously sweeps at (B)'s right leg backwards and upwards, while (A)'s arms holding (B)'s neck spiral downwards. The result of these coupled actions is that (B) is being thrown down diagonally in a heel over head spin. (Illustration.8-4-3)

(8-4-3)

Exercise 2: *demonstrated by Sifu Luo Hong Yuan (A) and Richard Anderson Omura (B)*

Action 1:
(A) on the left and (B) face each other in a left forward stance. (Illustration.8-4-4)

Action 2:
(B) initiates a forward step and throws a left punch at (A). (A) shifts his weight backwards and his left hand follows (B)'s punch and thus stretches (B)'s left arm. (A)'s uses a quick lead *jing* (*yin jing*) to extend (B)'s punch into "emptiness". (Illustration.8-4-5)

(8-4-4)

(8-4-5)

Action 3:
(B) turns his torso left, withdraws his left hand and instead punches with his right. (A) sinks down, turns left while his left arm moves forward and upward to block and lead (B)'s right arm. (A) connects to and locks (B)'s spine. (Illustration.8-4-6)

(8-4-6)

(8-4-7)

Action 4:
Next, (A) steps forward and traps (B)'s left leg while (A)'s right hip sinks down and presses against (B)'s left hip. Simultaneously (A)'s left hand grabs and twists (B)'s right hand to stretch and wrap it against his chest. (A)'s right arm wraps around and squeezes (B)'s neck by using his whole body's *jing* to control (B)'s body and *jing lu*, causing it to twist, lock and bend. (Illustration.8-4-7)

Action 5:
(A) turns his body quickly left and his right leg sweeps (B)'s leg in a backward and upward motion. (A)'s right arm squeezes and locks (B)'s neck and quickly throws (B) forward and down. (Illustration.8-4-8)

324

(8-4-8)

Exercise 3: *demonstrated by Sifu Luo Hong Yuan (A) and Richard Anderson Omura (B)*

Action 1:
(A) on the left and (B) on the right face each other with their left hands leading. (Illustration.8-4-9)

(8-4-9)   (8-4-10)

Action 2:
(A) catches the signal of (B)'s intention to move and (A) quickly responds by advancing his step and striking with his left palm or fist at (B)'s head. (A) is able to *chuan* and *na* (B)'s *dai zhui* and main bow. (Illustration.8-4-10)

Action 3:
(A) catches the moment as (B)'s torso is tilted backwards. He sinks suddenly down while his left hand continues to push forward and grabs (B)'s left inner knee with his right hand to perform an upward push. (Illustration.8-4-11)

Action 4:
(A) now turns quickly left and places his left hand on (B)'s neck and presses downward. (A)'s right hand pulls and flips (B)'s right leg upward resulting in (B) falling spirally down with his head downward and feet upward. (Illustration.8-4-12)

(8-4-11)

(8-4-12)

Exercise 4: *demonstrated by Sifu Luo Hong Yuan (A) and Richard Anderson Omura (B)*

Action 1:
(A) on the right and (B) face each other each in a right leg forward stance. (Illustration.8-4-13)

(8-4-13)

(8-4-14)

Action 2:
Just before (B) starts his motion, (A) quickly dashes forward and pushes hard with both hands on (B)'s shoulders, connecting to and locking up (B)'s main bow and *jing lu*. This causes (B)'s torso to tilt backwards. (Illustration.8-4-14)

Action 3:
(A) uses (B)'s backward tilted posture to perform a quick forward and sudden drop in front of (B). At the same time (A) uses a shoulder strike directed at (B)'s waist, and grabs behind (B)'s knees. (Illustration.8-4-15)

Action 4:
In continuation from the above, (A) uses his right shoulder to strike forward and downward at (B)'s waist while both his hands pull (B)'s knees upward to cause (B)'s body to fall backwards. (Illustration.8-4-16)

326

(8-4-15)

(8-4-16)

Exercise 5: *demonstrated by Sifu Luo Hong Yuan (A) and Fan Zhang (B)*

Action 1:
(A) on the left and (B) face each other putting their right hands on each other's left upper arm and their left hands adhering at each other's elbow. (Illustration.8-4-17)

(8-4-17)

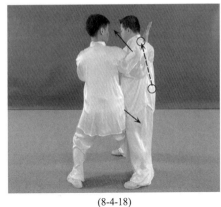

(8-4-18)

Action 2:
(A) suddenly turns left and steps with his right foot forward in between (B)'s legs. (A)'s right hip presses against (B)'s left hip. (A)'s right arm moves under (B)'s left armpit and his left hand pulls (B)'s right hand, stretching and wrapping it in front (A)'s chest (*yin jing*). (Illustration.8-4-18)

Action 3:
In the following action, (A) continues his left turn executing *fa jing* while his right leg sweeps back and upwards against (B)'s left leg. (A)'s foot sweeping action and hand hold causes (B) to be thrown down. (Illustration.8-4-19)

(8-4-19)

Exercise 6: *demonstrated by Sifu Luo Hong Yuan (A) and Fan Zhang (B)*

Action 1:
(A) on the left and (B) face each other with both hands in contact. (Illustration.8-4-20)

(8-4-20)

(8-4-21)

Action 2:
(A)'s steps forward with his right foot, connects to (B)'s collarbone and executes a short upward and forward *fa jing* to lock up (B)'s main bow. Simultaneously, (A) grabs (B)'s right arm and pulls it downward. (Illustration.8-4-21)

Action 3:
(A), using (B)'s reaction force momentum, suddenly turns right, placing his right hand like a hook on (B)'s shoulder to pull (B) to the right and downward, causing (B)'s body to bend forward and twist. At the same time (A) places his left hand on (B)'s right shoulder blade. (Illustration.8-4-22)

Action 4:
Following from the above action, (A) takes advantage of (B)'s *jing lu* being connected

328

to and locked up by continuing to turn right. (A) performs a *fa jing* where his right hand pulls down and his left hand pushes at the same time; resulting in (B) leaning forward and falling down. (Illustration.8-4-23)

(8-4-22)   (8-4-23)

Exercise 7: *demonstrated by Sifu Luo Hong Yuan (A) and Fan Zhang (B)*

Action 1:
(B) on the left steps forward with both hands pushing at (A)'s chest. (A) maintains his State of Readiness by sinking down absorbing and storing his *jing*. (Illustration.8-4-24)

(8-4-24)   (8-4-25)

Action 2:
(B) continues to push forward, but (A) suddenly takes a small step backwards with his left leg to open up his *Qi Shi*. This causes (B)'s force to lead into emptiness. (A) rounds and expands both arms to cover (B) with his *Qi Shi*. (Illustration.8-4-25)

Action 3:
Now (A) quickly sinks down, puts both hands on (B)'s shoulder blades to pull (B)'s torso down and cause (B) to lean forward. (Illustration.8-4-26)

Action 4:

(A) continues his downward motion executing a *fa jing* which causes (B) to fall to the floor. (Illustration.8-4-27)

(8-4-26)

(8-4-27)

Summary:

Throwing techniques are an important part of Taiji's system to control an opponent. *Fa jing* causes the opponent to lose balance and fall. It can only be applied after connecting and locking (*chuan* and *na*) an opponent's *jing lu*. If one can apply such throwing techniques in a real encounter it will demonstrate the real Taijiquan.

To master Taijiquan's *kung fu* to *Control the Opponent,* one must pay attention to the entire regimen of Taijiquan training. As a first step, one must create a good foundation for *self-control* before one can begin practicing control an opponent. The key to attaining a high level in Taijiquan is to follow the classical theories properly and with careful attention.

Through the complete mastering of all postures, comes the stage of gradually awakening the awareness of jing. Through gradual realization of the awareness of jing comes the stage of intuitive enlightenment. Without a long period of arduous and persistent effort one can never see the light.

Assiduously practicing *zhao fa* will enable one to develop *dong jing*. Practice and cultivation of *dong jing* will eventually lead to the attainment of *shen ming* [神明] where you are no longer restricted by the forms but become one with the Taiji. Conversely, if one does not conscientiously practice the forms nor analyze and incorporate the classical theories and principles, one can never attain *shen ming*.

GLOSSARY

an [按]:　　　　　　　　To press down.

bai hui [百會]:　　　　　An acupuncture point located at the crown of the head.

Ba Gua Zhang [八卦掌]: (Eight Trigram Palm). An internal style noted for its circle-walking
　　　　　　　　　　　　and extensive use of the palm for attack and defence.

Ba Ji Quan [八極拳]:　 (Eight Extremes Boxing). A traditional northern style noted for its
　　　　　　　　　　　　powerful short-range attacks.

Buffalo Strength:　　　 the intense, continuous internal pressure that appears similar to the
　　　　　　　　　　　　slow, methodical power of a buffalo when pulling a plough or
　　　　　　　　　　　　pushing a grindstone. *Buffalo Strength* is relentless, unwavering and
　　　　　　　　　　　　requires a high degree of endurance to maintain.

cai jing [采勁]:　　　　Pull down power.

Chan Si Jing [纏絲勁]:　Silk Reeling Energy (Force). So named because it resembles the
　　　　　　　　　　　　unraveling of a silkworm cocoon. The cocoon is constructed from
　　　　　　　　　　　　a single continuous thread. When unraveling, the thread comes off
　　　　　　　　　　　　in a spiral motion. The Ji Hong Taiji System (among many others)
　　　　　　　　　　　　holds that *chan si jing* (also known as spiral force) is common to all
　　　　　　　　　　　　styles of Taiji.

chang qiang [長強]:　　The tailbone or base of the spinal column.

Chang Quan [長拳]:　　Northern Fist. A style of modern wushu developed in northern China.

chui jing [蓄勁]:　　　　To compress and store *jing* just prior to its release.

Chou Si Jing [抽絲勁]:　(Pulling Silk Force) similar to *Chan Si Jing* but here the emphasis is
　　　　　　　　　　　　on a constant pressure and rate of *jing*.

cold power:　　　　　The ability to instantly emit a powerful force, seemingly from
　　　　　　　　　　　　nowhere.

dai mai [带脉]:　　　　(Girdle Vessel). A *qi* vessel that encircles the waist passing through
　　　　　　　　　　　　both the *dan tian* and the *ming men*.

dai zhui [大椎]:　　　　An acupuncture point located on the spinal column between the two
　　　　　　　　　　　　shoulder blades.

dan tian [丹田]:   A spherical space inside the abdominal cavity approximately three inches below the navel where *qi* is said to be collected and stored.

diu [丟]:   A break in a connection; a loose contact during push-hands.

dong jing [懂勁]:   The advanced ability to sense your opponent's energy, to "read" his intentions and consequently to be able to anticipate and control his movements while maintaining control of your energy flow.

double yang [雙重]:   Equal distribution of weight/*qi*/intent between left and right sides of the body, front and back, upper and lower sections of your frame. Double-weightedness. To be avoided according to classical Taiji teaching.

dou jing [抖勁]:   Vibratory force.

Enlightenment Teacher: The term usually given to the instructor who initiates a student into the wonders of Taiji.

fa [发]:   Release – Add to your opponent's incoming *jing*, and when you feel that you are in control, release the combined *jing* in a sudden, quick manner.

fa jing [發勁]:   Emission of "explosive" power or trigger force. Sudden, powerful and highly focussed, *fa jing* emanates from the *dan tian*.

fu [敷]:   Control (as in to control the actions of another).

gu dang jing [鼓蕩勁]:   (Wave Motion Force) analogous to the rippling or wave motion of liquid inside a pressurized container.

hua yin [化 引]:   Dissolve (neutralize) and lure – Lure your opponent into using his *jing* then neutralize his force to put him off balance.

ji [擠]:   To press forward.

jing [勁] :   Literally "swift power". Can be translated as force, energy, power or strength. *Jing* can be all of these and more. A good analogy is comparing iron and steel. Both are made from the same element, but one is refined and, consequently stronger and more pliable. If you think of muscular strength as iron, *jing* would be steel.

jing lu [劲路]:   Literally: Path of Energy. In this context, the principle means to control your opponent's total energy (in all its forms) while hiding the source of your own energy.

jiu jitsu: A Japanese martial art noted for its ground fighting and joint lock techniques.

Ke Jia [客家]: One of the nationalities from Central China who migrated to Southern China (and in particular, Guangdong Province) in the 18th century.

kwa [胯]: The hips (or more precisely, the hip bones)

lan [攔]: To block (with a spear).

lu [履]: To pull down.

Luan Huan Jue [亂環訣]: (Spontaneous Circular Technique). The ability to instantly determine which application will best counter your opponent's skills. One must cultivate *dong jing* and *zhao fa* in order to become proficient with *Luan Huan Jue*.

Ma Hua [麻花]: A deep-fried pastry where the batter is slowly piped into the hot oil using a spiral motion resulting in a "knot" shaped delicacy.

ming men [命門]: Literally "Gate of Life". It is an acupuncture point along the spine in the small of the back directly behind the navel.

na [拿]: Capture (or seize) -- Use one hand to seize, use both hands to capture. The point of capture is to lock the joints, terminate at the root, and break your opponent's posture.

peng jing [掤勁]: Expansion force, fending-off or warding-off power. Often used as an all-encompassing term for internal power. Taijiquan is often called Peng Quan because of its focus on the cultivation of internal power.

qi [氣]: The easiest definition is internal energy. The full meaning is very complex and extremely difficult to translate precisely. *Qi* cannot be seen but its effects can be felt. A combination of breathing, body alignment/dynamics and *yi* are said to accumulate, store and move *qi*.

Qigong: Exercises (moving and/or stationary) to develop and enhance the collection and storage of *qi* in the body.

qin na [擒拿]: To grip/seize and manipulate the joints of an opponent.

qing [擎]: To lift or hold up.

san shou [散手]: Free-style, full-contact combat developed in China. A number of Taiji stylists from within China and from the west have had success in International *san shou* competitions.

shen ming [神明]:   An epiphany or an attainment of enlightenment. In Taijiquan, it is the highest stage to which one can strive. It is said a master who has gained *shen ming* is so perfectly attuned to the principles of Taiji he no longer reacts through conscious thought. His movements are instinctive, subconscious and no longer bound by form.

ting jing [聽勁]:   Listening *jing*. An integral part of *dong jing*, it is the ability to pick up subtle clues from your opponent telegraphing his intentions.

tui shou [推手]:   Taiji push-hands. A two-person exercise/contest used to develop reflex, balance, internal power, sensitivity and understanding of the power and potential of Taijiquan.

wei jing [喂勁]:   Feeding *jing*. Releasing just enough *jing* to match your opponent while keeping the rest carefully hidden.

Xia Quan [俠拳]:   (Knight Boxing). A very old traditional northern style of Chinese martial art whose most famous form is patterned after the movements of a crane.

Xing Yi [形意]:   Mind-Form Boxing. Xing Yi is an internal style known for its linear movements and explosive power.

Yang Chun [詠春]:   (also known as Wing Chun). A southern style noted primarily for its fast, compact hand techniques.

yi [意]:   Can be translated as intent, mind or spirit.

Yi Jing [易經]:   (also written as I Ching). The *Yi Jing* or Book of Changes is an ancient Chinese divination manual and book of wisdom.

yin jing [引 勁]:   The ability to draw energy away from the centre of the opponent.

Yong Quan [湧泉]:   Literally: Bubbling Spring. An acupuncture point located in the centre of the sole of the foot.

za [扎]:   To thrust (with a spear).

zhan zhuang [站樁]:   Literally: Standing like a Pole or Tree. Often used as a form of meditation, it is an exceptional training method for learning to properly align the body and develop *qi* circulation.

zhao fa [着法]:   Movements, or more precisely, the practical applications of movements from the forms.